美国总统演讲系列

BARACK HUSSEIN OBAMA II

INTERRACIAL VOICE

奥巴马演说

跨越种族的声音

任宪宝◎编著

中国言实出版社

图书在版编目（CIP）数据

奥巴马演说：跨越种族的声音 / 任宪宝编．—北京：中国言实出版社，2014.5

ISBN 978-7-5171-0455-1

Ⅰ．①奥… Ⅱ．①任… Ⅲ．①奥巴马，B.—演讲—汇编 Ⅳ．①D771.209

中国版本图书馆 CIP 数据核字（2014）第 045230 号

责任编辑：陈昌财

出版发行 中国言实出版社
地 址：北京市朝阳区北苑路 180 号加利大厦 5 号楼 105 室
邮 编：100101
编辑部：北京市西城区百万庄路甲 16 号五层
邮 编：100037
电 话：64924853（总编室） 64924716（发行部）
网 址：www.zgyscbs.cn
E-mail：yanshicbs@126.com
经 销 新华书店
印 刷 北京市玖仁伟业印刷有限公司
版 次 2014 年 7 月第 1 版 2014 年 7 月第 1 次印刷
规 格 787 毫米 ×1092 毫米 1/16 印张 18.25
字 数 288 千字
定 价 35.00 元 ISBN 978-7-5171-0455-1

出版说明

自 1776 年《独立宣言》发表至今，美国建国已有两百三十多年。在这一历史阶段中，先后产生了四十四任总统。作为总统共和制国家的美国，其总统兼国家元首和政府首脑双重身份于一身，其在三权分立的国家政治架构中拥有极大的权力和影响力，在国家政治生活中拥有举足轻重的地位。正如美国第二十六任总统西奥多·罗斯福所说，美国总统是“国王和总理大臣的统一体”。

在美国，演讲是任何一个准备从政的人士必须具备的基本技能。无论地方议会议员、地方行政首脑还是美国联邦国会议员乃至美国总统，都是通过以演讲为基本形式的竞选活动产生的，这就决定了演讲这种活动在美国政治生活中的重大意义。而作为国家最高领导人的美国总统，他们的演讲往往在表明个人政治见解和基本立场、展露自身意志品质和性格特点的同时，在某种程度上还代表了美国的制度设计与价值观念、反映了美国的文化背景与社会演变。他们的演讲大都是针对当时美国所面临的国内外重大问题，讨论国家内政外交政策的优劣得失，表明解决问题的态度，指出今后的施政方向，激励和动员美国人民克服困难、奋力前行。从美国总统的演讲中，我们可以看到他们对时代潮流的认识、把握和对国家意志的充分表达，可以看到他们的政治才华和不同的人格魅力，还可以看到美国在其国家发展所经历的一个又一个时代转折点上，怎样面对困难、迎接挑战、坚韧不拔，一步步走向成功与成熟。

美国总统的演讲事先大多经过了精心的准备，语言精炼、用词规范、措辞讲究、逻辑严密，不但文采斐然、优美动人，而且有的放矢、言之有物。同时，每个总统的演讲都具有鲜明的个性特色。有的晓之以理，发人深省；有的动之以情，感人肺腑；有的则充满思辨，促使人们对人生、社会乃至世界进行更深层次的思考。

《美国总统演讲系列》丛书，重点选取了美国自成立以来几位重要总统的演讲，其中既有他们的就职演讲、卸任演讲，也有他们在重大事件发生时发表的演讲以及针对一些特定案例向公众发表的演讲等。选取这些演讲，并不代表我们认同其所包含的思想倾向或价值取向，只是想帮助广大读者从这些演讲中，加深对美国国情、美国社会的了解。相信广大读者在对这些演讲进行欣赏的同时，一定会对其反映出的世界观、价值观等做出正确的分析和判断。

编　者

2014 年 5 月

前言

奥巴马（全名：Barack Hussein Obama II，贝拉克·侯赛因·奥巴马二世，1961年8月4日），美国第四十四任总统，出生于美国夏威夷州火奴鲁鲁，他的父亲祖籍是肯尼亚（The Republic of Kenya）。奥巴马是首位拥有黑人血统，并且童年在亚洲（印度尼西亚）度过的美国总统，与不同地方、不同文化背景的人共同生活过。2008年11月5日，奥巴马当选美国第四十四任（第五十六届）总统，他也是美国首位混血“黑人”总统。2011年4月4日，奥巴马宣布竞选2012年美国总统。2012年11月6日晚（当地时间），奥巴马在美国大选中获得超过270张选举人票，连任美国总统。

奥巴马的童年和青少年时期分别在印尼和夏威夷度过，后以优等生的学业成绩从哈佛法学院毕业。1996年，当选伊利诺伊州参议员，2004年11月当选为美国联邦参议员，是美国历史上第五位有非裔血统的联邦参议员。2007年2月10日，他以承诺结束伊拉克战争及实施全民医疗保险制为竞选纲领，正式宣布参加2008年美国总统选举，并于2008年11月5日正式当选。

就任总统后，他全面实施恢复美国经济的经济复兴计划，对能源、移民、公民医疗保健、教育、税政等领域进行变革；军事上主张从阿富汗和伊拉克撤军，并向伊斯兰世界表示友善而非以武力相威胁，还和核武大国俄罗斯签署削减核武器的《布拉格条约》。

老奥巴马出生在肯尼亚西部一个贫穷的小村庄，但是他的家庭在当地仍然属于较富有的家庭。奥巴马的祖父在城市做过小办事员、家庭厨师等各种杂役，回到家乡后以精明的头脑经营一个不错的小农庄。老奥巴马在学校时成绩优异，性格顽皮，后因经常违反学校的纪律而遭到开除，引起父亲的暴怒。后来在两名热心的美国教师的联系和帮助下，获得了去海外读书的机会和奖学金。老奥巴马将在家乡的妻子柯齐亚和孩子留给母亲照顾，先去夏威夷，后到达美国，在读书期间与邓纳姆相遇，生下奥巴马。奥巴马的祖母和许多亲戚如今仍住在那个小村庄，老奥巴马 1982 年因车祸去世后也埋在村内。

奥巴马两岁时，父母分居，随后离婚。他的父亲前往哈佛大学攻读博士学位，最终返回肯尼亚。而他的母亲则嫁给了一位印度尼西亚籍的学生 Lolo Soetoro，并诞下一个女儿。奥巴马六岁时，与母亲一家迁居到印度尼西亚首都雅加达。四年后，奥巴马回到夏威夷，与外祖父母住在一起。从五年级起，奥巴马就读于位于檀香山的大型私立学校 Punahou 学校，且在当地读到十二年级，于 1979 年毕业。后来母亲与继父离婚，他便随母迁居美国本土。

到达美国本土后，奥巴马首先在加利福尼亚州的洛杉矶西方学院求学两年，期间在该校《宴会》杂志发表了诗歌《老爹》，后被《纽约客》杂志转载并广为流传。西方学院的学业结束后，他转至纽约市的哥伦比亚大学哥伦比亚学院，在那里主修政治学及国际关系。1983 年，奥巴马毕业于哥伦比亚大学，毕业后在国际商务公司工作了一年。1985 年到芝加哥工作，主持了一个非营利计划，以协助当地教堂为穷困的居民组织好职业培训。

他于 1988 年进入哈佛大学法学院，主修法律。1990 年 2 月，由于被选为《哈佛法学评论》的首位非洲裔美国人主席，他首次获得了全国性的认可。奥巴马 1991 年毕业于哈佛大学的法学院，获得了“极优等”法学博士的学位。回到芝加哥后，奥巴马主持了一次选民登记活动，且为民权律师事务所 Miner, Barnhill & Galland 工作。后来，自 1993 年至 2004 年当选联邦参议员前的十一年中，奥巴马一直在芝加哥大学法学院任职宪法讲师。

1992 年，奥巴马与同校的米歇尔·鲁滨逊结婚，两人供职于芝加哥的同一家律师事务所。

1996 年，奥巴马在芝加哥当选为伊利诺伊州国会参议员，并在之后的三年中连任；2000 年，他挑战已担任了四年联邦众议员的波比·拉什（前黑豹党成员和社区活动家），竞选联邦众议员一席。选举结果为拉什获得 61% 的选票，他以 30% 的选票最终失败，此后也将主要精力投入到伊利诺伊州的参议工作中，编撰了要求对可能判死刑罪犯的审问必须录像的法律。

2002 年，他竞选连任伊利诺伊州参议员。2003 年 1 月，民主党重新取得议会的控制权，他被提名为州卫生与公众服务委员会主席。在他的立法提案中，他帮助编撰了《工作所得抵税法》，为低收入家庭提供援助，还致力于为一些无法承担健康保险的居民起草相关立法项目，协助通过了增加对艾滋病预防和病人照料的项目预算。

2004 年 7 月，美国民主党召开全国代表大会，奥巴马被指定在第二天做“基调演讲”。（所谓“基调演讲”，就是民主党人阐述本党的纲领和政策宣言，通常由本党极有前途的政治新星来发表，1988 年做“基调演讲”的人就是时任阿肯色州州长的克林顿。）奥巴马不负众望，他亲自撰写演讲稿，并发表了题为“无畏的希望”（The Audacity of Hope）的慷慨激昂的演讲。在演说中他提出消除党派分歧和种族分歧，实现“一个美国”的梦想。该演讲后，奥巴马成为全美知名的政界人物。同年 11 月，奥巴马以高达 70% 的选票顺利当选，成为美国历史上第五位非洲裔联邦参议员。

2007 年 2 月 10 日，奥巴马在伊利诺伊州斯普林菲尔德市正式宣布参加 2008 年美国总统大选，并提出了重点在“结束伊拉克战争以及实施全民医疗保险制度”的竞选纲领。

2008 年 1 月 4 日，在俄亥俄州民主党初选大会上，奥巴马赢得了 38% 的支持率，领先于知名度高于自己的约翰·爱德华兹以及希拉里·克林顿，在民主党诸位候选人中领跑。

2008 年 6 月 3 日，奥巴马因其票数领先于希拉里·克林顿，被定为民主党总统候选人；同年 8 月 23 日，在民主党全国代表大会上奥巴马被正式提名，从而成为了美国历史上首个非洲裔总统大选候选人。

2008 年 11 月 5 日，奥巴马击败共和党候选人约翰·麦凯恩，正式当选为美国第四十四任总统。当晚他在芝加哥发表当选演说，并以支持他的一位百岁选民为例，以数个“Yes we can”（是的，我们可以做到）来阐述美国人民非凡的创造力、美国社会的不断进步以及美国实力的强大，这次演说非常有震撼力，并富于强烈的感情色彩，有些黑人倾听时不禁流下了眼泪，“是的，我们可以（或：我们能够做到）”也成了他的名言。

2011 年 4 月 4 日，奥巴马宣布将参加 2012 年总统竞选。民调显示，2009 年奥巴马的支持率最高达到 59%，而后开始滑落。2011 年 1 月降至 48% 的水平，而由于经济手段改革与医疗体制改革受挫，奥巴马的支持率持续走低。到 3 月末降到最低的 38%，后因击毙拉登而上升。4 月又由于前述原因轻微下降。他的支持率平均在四五成之间，属于中等水平。

2011 年 11 月，福布斯 2011 权力人物榜奥巴马排名第一。尽管在处理高失业率和经济衰退问题上的措施不足，导致奥巴马在国内支持率下降，但他在世界舞台上的表现完全不同。随着“基地”组织领导人本·拉登和利比亚前领导人卡扎菲相继被击毙，奥巴马的影响力迅速上升。

2012 年 5 月 5 日，在美国弗吉尼亚州里士满的弗吉尼亚州联邦大学，奥巴马参加竞选集会，正式启动其争取连任的竞选之路，并先后在俄亥俄州和弗吉尼亚州两个重要的“摇摆州”举行了两场竞选集会。

2012 年 10 月 28 日，一场来势凶猛的飓风“桑迪”冲击美国东海岸，搅乱了本已进入倒计时的美国总统大选，飓风过后，奥巴马和共和党总统候选人罗姆尼的支持率开始出现变化。根据盖洛普民调显示，多数美国人看好奥巴马出任下一届美国总统。10 月 31 日盖洛普发布的民调结果显示，有 54% 的人认为奥巴马能够打败罗姆尼，获得总统连任，只有 34% 的人选择支持罗姆尼。这与 8 月份奥巴马最高支持率 58%、罗姆尼 36% 的支持率的差距基本一致。

2012 年 11 月 1 日，奥巴马和罗姆尼开始了最后一轮造势拉票工作。奥巴马大范围走访摇摆州，还邀请前总统克林顿为其助威；而罗姆尼则带领搭档瑞安等人展开跨越十一个州的“闪电战”。根据全国广播公司和《华尔街日报》11 月 4 日公布的民调数据，奥巴马在有投票意愿的美国选民中支持率为 48%，而罗姆尼支持率为 47%，两人不相上下。

美国总统大选的选民投票于当地时间 2012 年 11 月 6 日举行，由于投票日当天并非法定节假日，因此越来越多的选民愿意选择提前投票。从提前投票的情况看，奥巴马较罗姆尼更胜一筹，但优势并不如四年前。奥巴马夫妇也鼓励选民提前投票，这也是历史上首次美国总统候选人夫妇不在选举日投票。

2012 年 11 月 6 日，奥巴马在总统大选中获得超过 270 张选举人票，连任总统。 11 月 10 日，佛罗里达州官方确认，奥巴马在 2012 年总统大选中赢得了该州的 29 张选举人票。奥巴马最后赢得 332 张选举人票，罗姆尼获得 206 张选举人票。

奥巴马于 2013 年 1 月 20 日在总统就职典礼上宣誓就职，美国总统选举宣告最终结束。

奥巴马就任总统后，美国正处于由房地产次贷危机引发的金融危机的蔓延期，全国经济异常萧条。为消除危机的负面影响，他对前任政府的某些政策做了比较大胆的改革，如制定耗资巨大的经济复兴计划、医疗改革、移民政策调整、能源战略修订、税收政策调整、教育体制改革等。

他通过对低收入家庭和企业就业岗位的减税，同时增加政府支出，来加大政府对财政、经济的刺激力度。他还将布什政府用于救市的 7000 亿美元中的余额（约 3500 亿美元）用于房屋业主和小企业的贷款供应，目的是要稳定房产市场和小企业的就业状况。

在环境与能源问题方面，他强调利用风能、太阳能和地热驱动车辆，为工厂提供能源。对于新能源的研究和开发，他实行加强支持力度和增加政府支出的举措。

关于美国的国际贸易政策，他主张以“公平”原则对贸易伙伴实行保护主义，并提出了修订北美自由贸易协定的构想。他还就中国的人民币汇率和对华贸易逆差问题，提出希望与中国方面进行谈判。

在货币政策上，他十分关注利率大幅度波动给经济带来的不利影响，主张加大对金融市场的监管力度。

为应对美国失业率上升的严峻形势，2011 年 6 月，奥巴马在视察北卡罗来纳州时抛出“一揽子刺激就业措施”，希望在 2012 年扭转就业低迷的困境。

2008 年 11 月 16 日，在美国国会会议上，当选总统后的奥巴马与候任新财政部长蒂莫西·盖纳及新白宫首席经济顾问劳伦斯·萨默斯探讨了经济复兴计划，26 日提名联邦储备委员会前主席保罗·沃尔克为总统经济恢复顾问委员会负责人，负责组织、实施经济复兴计划。奥巴马经济复苏计划的主要内容有政府节能、启动大规模基建、学校进行大规模硬件设施升级、改进医疗状况和普及宽带网。他的计划内容均属耗资极其巨大的项目，他希望该计划能化解当前的经济危机、提高就业率以及增强国家在国际上的竞争力。

在能源战略上，奥巴马倡导绿色环保概念，以节能减碳、降低污染的绿色能源环境为工作目标，并计划倾巨资努力打造。他的能源战略内容包括改善现有电网系统，将太阳能、风能、地热能并入全美统一电网，最大限度地发挥国家电网的使用效率；发展节能型车辆。他还计划将用于进口石油的资金转向发展太阳能、风能和地热能电站，以减轻对石油的依赖，如此计划顺利实现，美国的能源体系将产生革命性变化，进而改变整个美国的生产和生活方式。有媒体指出，如果他的绿色能源战略获得成功，其意义将不亚于 IT 产业革命。

奥巴马在税收政策上倾向对企业和富裕人群增税，而对于普通家庭则主张减税，认为这样能使大多数美国工薪阶层在国家税制方面受益。他的税政有两项主要内容：其一，对一些富人利用其他国家或地区相对宽松的税收环境隐瞒收入、逃避税务核查之情形，税务部门有权要求海外银行配合美国的税务调查，堵住逃税行为；其二，改变跨国公司纳税方式，使跨国公司无法在外汇收入方面逃税。

奥巴马在教育方面基本遵循布什政府的现有教育框架，但提出了“零岁至五岁教育计划”和“美国机会税收优待计划”两项教育新主张。对于布什政府的《不让一个孩子掉队》的教育法案，他对其作了多项改进，强调学生的教育质量与教师业绩挂钩，改革为考试而教学，倡导教育科目要全面，对失败学生更多关怀，增加教育经费等。他对公立学校的现有状况并不满意，要求美国各州增加对特许学校的拨款，支持特许学校的发展，但其成效还有待时间检验。另外，他认为为提高美国在国际上的长远竞争力，必须强化国民教育，提高学校教育质量，将降低高中学生辍学率作为国家的首要任务。关于教师待遇问题，他主张实行绩效工资制，提出加强实施教师聘用、培训、留任及奖励的优惠计划。

在医改方案中，他提议将医疗保险覆盖面扩大到未投保人士，并规定保费增长的上限，人们在离职和变换工作时，他们的医保权益应予保留。他的医疗改革方案，计划耗时十余年，涉及资金 9000 亿美元。该计划包括一项政府保险计划，同时鼓励民众双向选择，参与公共合作医疗保险，其主旨是降低保险成本和提高民众的健康保障质量。医改计划将每一个美国公民都纳入政府的医保范围，从而减少非法保险公司的存在。该计划包括医疗保险开支的削减和提高保险公司税负两方面。2011 年 1 月 19 日，众议院以 245 票支持，189 票反对的投票结果，将奥巴马的医改法案废除。

奥巴马移民政策的主体思路基本以 2007 年的美国移民改革法案为基础，主要内容为加强边境管制，减少非法入境；增强政府监督，对雇用非法移民的雇主进行法律制裁；为非法移民提供一条最终可以获得美国公民身份的途径；缩短合法移民的移民排期。但由于诸多因素的制约，该法案当时并未获得国会通过。2008 年 11 月，他成功当选总统，12 月提名亚利桑那州州长珍妮特·娜珀莉塔诺为国土安全部部长，以继续实施其移民改革计划。

在宗教方面，奥巴马认为宗教信仰的力量能将人民团结在一起，并能给他们带来幸福，它是美国民众生活的重要组成部分。对于美国的宗教政策，他基本沿袭上一届政府的既定方针，支持宗教机构的社区活动。美国人口来源复杂，宗教人群庞大，教种教派林立，他认为美国宗教信仰的差异性不会引起国家分裂。他不反对教人士进入国家权力机构宗，比如总统办公室，认为这样做不但不会违背美国宪法所规定的政教分离精神，反而有利于调和政府与宗教组织及宗教人士的关系。他指出不能将宗教信仰作为战争的借口，亦反对以宗教信仰的差异性来人为地制造社会隔阂。他进一步分析指出，不同的宗教念诵不同的经文、听从不同的命令，但都有共同的真理，人民不能因所信奉的教种不同而排斥异教徒，甚至萌生仇恨。

2012年5月9日，奥巴马接受美国广播公司采访时说，他改变了自己先前的反对态度，转而支持同性婚姻。他是在在与自己的下属、一些同性恋军人、夫人米歇尔及两个女儿就这一问题开展讨论后，经过思考作出这一决定的。他说，自己最终认定必须就此公开表态，支持同性婚姻。

2009年11月，奥巴马对中国展开国事访问，他认为中美关系的新发展具有战略意义，同中国的伙伴关系使美国摆脱了严重的金融危机，并强调这一关系的重要性。另一方面，他会见达赖则使中国政府非常不满。奥巴马就职以来，在与胡锦涛通电话及访问会谈中，多次表示美中发展积极合作的全面关系对两国十分重要，对世界也十分重要。发展健康稳定的美中关系符合两国长期和战略利益。美国方面确认继续奉行长期以来坚持的“一个中国”政策，承认这是中国的核心利益。2012年2月，奥巴马对访美的中华人民共和国副主席习近平表示：“美方拒绝任何台独主张”。

对于伊朗核问题，他希望联合国以决议方式敦促其弃核。对于朝鲜核问题，他认为只要朝鲜放弃核武项目，美国会在经济援助与国际关系等诸多方面给朝鲜提供帮助。

奥巴马在华盛顿举行的全球核安全峰会上指出，当今的核危机不是来自敌对国家，而是恐怖分子，因此核风险在不断加大。如果恐怖组织掌握了核武器，将发生“全球性灾难”。为此，他呼吁全球在核材料的控制上要严格，要步调一致统一行动。他还认为目前国与国之间的核对抗几率已经减小，但因为国际恐怖组织的活跃，核安全形势反而更加严峻。

奥巴马就任总统后，要求美国中央情报局将追捕基地组织首脑本·拉登作为首要任务。2010年8月，美国锁定了拉登在巴基斯坦的住所。2011年5月2日凌晨1时30分（当地时间），奥巴马下令海豹突击队对拉登住所进行突然袭击，并将其击毙。奥巴马认为击毙拉登是美国打击“基地恐怖组织”的最大成就，使“正义得到了伸张”。

奥巴马喜欢与明星交往，想借大牌明星的公众形象提升政府的形象，使自己和以自己为首的政府能像好莱坞一样，受大众欢迎。与他交往的大牌明星有《007》扮演者布鲁斯南、《律政俏佳人》主演威瑟斯彭、喜剧演员本·斯蒂勒、《钻石王老五》主演乔治·克鲁尼等，他给予这些影视明星自由出入白宫的权力。他在总统竞选期间的演讲都能得到民众，特别是年轻人的喜爱。他是一个从社会底层走出来的美国总统，所以他对于普通大众有着很强的号召力。

目 录
Contents

第一章 美国的承诺

第一节 背景介绍 / 002

第二节 奥巴马于 2007 年接受总统候选人提名时的演讲 / 004

第三节 精彩语录 / 027

第二章 无畏的希望

第一节 背景介绍 / 030

第二节 奥巴马于 2004 年在民主党全国代表大会的演讲 / 033

第三节 精彩语录 / 043

第三章 谢谢你，艾奥瓦

第一节 背景介绍 / 046

第二节 奥巴马于 2008 年在艾奥瓦州德斯莫内斯的竞选演讲 / 050

第三节 精彩语录 / 057

第四章 更加完善的联邦

第一节 背景介绍 / 062

第二节 奥巴马于 2008 年 3 月 18 日在费城国家宪法中心的演讲 / 064

第三节 精彩语录 / 086

第五章 我们所热爱的美国

第一节 背景介绍 / 090

第二节 奥巴马于 2008 年 6 月 30 日在密苏里州独立城的演讲 / 091

第三节 精彩语录 / 108

第六章 美国的变革时代已经到来

第一节 背景介绍 / 112

第二节 奥巴马于 2008 年 11 月 4 日在芝加哥格兰特公园的演讲 / 114

第三节 精彩语录 / 124

第七章 自由的新生

第一节 背景介绍 / 128

第二节 奥巴马于 2009 年 1 月 20 日在华盛顿特区国会大厦前的演讲 / 131

第三节 精彩语录 / 142

第八章 独立日演讲

第一节 背景介绍 / 146

第二节 奥巴马于 2009 年 7 月 4 日在白宫的演讲 / 147

第三节 精彩语录 / 150

第九章 民众的力量
第一节 背景介绍 / 154
第二节 奥巴马于 2013 年在白宫的第二次就职演讲 / 156
第三节 精彩语录 / 167

附 录
2010 国情咨文——2010 年 1 月 27 日美国众议院 / 170
2011 国情咨文——2011 年 1 月 25 日美国众议院 / 205
2012 国情咨文——2012 年 1 月 24 日美国众议院 / 238

第一章

美国的承诺

第一节 背景介绍

2007年2月，贝拉克·侯赛因·奥巴马二世，简称奥巴马，在伊利诺伊州宣布竞选总统，经过五个月预选后，他击败了纽约州联邦参议员希拉里，获得总统候选人提名。身为美国联邦参议员的奥巴马在民主党全国代表大会上接受总统候选人提名，成为美国历史上第一个获得主要党派总统候选人提名的少数族裔人士。

奥巴马在科罗拉多州丹佛一个能容纳七万五千人的体育场内发表演讲时说，布什政府过去八年的失败政策和国内党派斗争导致百姓生活水平下降。因此，他向民主党人、共和党人和独立派人士发出呼吁，采取变革措施，在二十一世纪“使美国的希望不灭”。

奥巴马随即向共和党竞争对手、亚利桑那州联邦参议员麦凯恩发出挑战。奥巴马说，麦凯恩在国会经常支持布什政府的政策，这足以使人对他的判断能力产生怀疑。此外，他还批评麦凯恩不了解美国民众所关注的医疗保健、教育和经济等问题。

奥巴马在演讲中重申，要对工薪家庭采取减税政策，通过发展可替代能源实现能源自给，为青少年提供世界一流水平的教育，并实现全民享有在其支付能力范围内的医疗保健服务。

针对麦凯恩批评他外交和国防经验不足，奥巴马说，民主党在罗斯福和肯尼迪担任总统时代的外交表现已经证实，该党具备处理这些事务的能力。

奥巴马还批评布什政府的外交政策让美国民主党和共和党几代人的努力“付之东流”。他说，民主党要挽回这些“遗产”，负责任地结束伊拉克战争，完成针对阿富汗塔利班和“基地”组织的战争，阻止伊朗获得核武器，建立新的伙伴关系以应对美国在二十一世纪面临的威胁。

第二节 奥巴马于2007年接受总统候选人提名时的演讲

To Chairman Dean and my great friend Dick Durbin; and to all my fellow citizens of this great nation.

With profound gratitude and great humility, I accept your nomination for the presidency of the United States.

Let me express my thanks to the historic slate of candidates who accompanied me on this journey, and especially the one who traveled the farthest—a champion for working Americans and an inspiration to my daughters and to yours—Hillary Rodham Clinton. To President Clinton, who last night made the case for change as only he can make it; to Ted Kennedy, who embodies the spirit of service; and to the next vice-president of the United States, Joe Biden, I thank you. I am grateful to finish this journey with one of the finest statesmen of our time, a man at ease with everyone from world leaders to the conductors on the Amtrak train he still takes home every night.

To the love of my life, our next first lady, Michelle Obama, and to Sasha and Malia—I love you so much, and I'm so proud of all of you.

Four years ago, I stood before you and told you my story—of the brief union between a young man from Kenya and a young woman from Kansas who weren't well-off or well-known, but shared a belief that in America, their son could achieve whatever he put his mind to.

It is that promise that has always set this country apart—that through hard work and sacrifice, each of us can pursue our individual dreams but still come together as one American family, to ensure that the next generation can pursue their dreams as well.

That's why I stand here tonight. Because for 232 years, at each moment when that promise was in jeopardy, ordinary men and women,—students and soldiers, farmers and teachers, nurses and janitors—found the courage to keep it alive.

We meet at one of those defining moments—a moment when our nation is at war, our economy is in turmoil and the American promise has been threatened once more.

Tonight, more Americans are out of work and more are working harder for less. More of you have lost your homes and even more are watching your home values plummet. More of you have cars you can't afford to drive, credit card bills you can't afford to pay and tuition that's beyond your reach. These challenges are not all of government's making. But the failure to respond is a direct result of a broken politics in Washington and the failed policies of George W. Bush.

America, we are better than these last eight years. We are a better country than this.

This country is more decent than one where a woman in Ohio, on the brink of retirement, finds herself one illness away from disaster after a lifetime of hard work.

This country is more generous than one where a man in Indiana has to pack up the equipment he's worked on for 20 years and watch it shipped off to China, and then chokes up as he explains how he felt like a failure when he went home to tell his family the news.

We are more compassionate than a government that lets veterans sleep on our streets and families slide into poverty; that sits on its hands while a major

American city drowns before our eyes.

Tonight, I say to the American people, to Democrats and Republicans and Independents across this great land—enough! This moment—this election—is our chance to keep, in the 21st century, the American promise alive. Because next week, in Minnesota, the same party that brought you two terms of George Bush and Dick Cheney will ask this country for a third. And we are here because we love this country too much to let the next four years look like the last eight. On November 4th, we must stand up and say: "Eight is enough."

Now let there be no doubt. The Republican nominee, John McCain, has worn the uniform of our country with bravery and distinction, and for that we owe him our gratitude and respect. And next week, we'll also hear about those occasions when he's broken with his party as evidence that he can deliver the change that we need.

But the record's clear: John McCain has voted with George Bush 90% of the time. Senator McCain likes to talk about judgment, but really, what does it say about your judgment when you think George Bush has been right more than 90% of the time? I don't know about you, but I'm not ready to take a 10% chance on change.

The truth is, on issue after issue that would make a difference in your lives—on healthcare and education and the economy—Senator McCain has been anything but independent. He said that our economy has made "great progress" under this president. He said that the fundamentals of the economy are strong. And when one of his chief advisers—the man who wrote his economic plan—was talking about the anxiety Americans are feeling, he said that we were just suffering from a "mental recession," and that we've become, and I quote, "a nation of whiners".

A nation of whiners? Tell that to the proud auto workers at a Michigan plant who, after they found out it was closing, kept showing up every day and working as hard as ever, because they knew there were people who counted on the brakes that they made. Tell that to the military families who shoulder their burdens silently as they watch their loved ones leave for their third or fourth or fifth tour of duty. These are not whiners. They work hard and give back and keep going without complaint. These are the Americans that I know.

Now, I don't believe that Senator McCain doesn't care what's going on in the lives of Americans. I just think he doesn't know. Why else would he define middle class as someone making under $5m a year? How else could he propose hundreds of billions in tax breaks for big corporations and oil companies but not one penny of tax relief to more than one hundred million Americans? How else could he offer a healthcare plan that would actually tax people's benefits, or an education plan that would do nothing to help families pay for college, or a plan that would privatize social security and gamble your retirement?

It's not because John McCain doesn't care. It's because John McCain doesn't get it.

For over two decades, he's subscribed to that old, discredited Republican philosophy—give more and more to those with the most and hope that prosperity trickles down to everyone else. In Washington, they call this the Ownership Society, but what it really means is—you're on your own. Out of work? Tough luck. No healthcare? The market will fix it. Born into poverty? Pull yourself up by your own bootstraps—even if you don't have boots. You're on your own.

Well it's time for them to own their failure. It's time for us to change America.

You see, we Democrats have a very different measure of what constitutes progress in this country.

We measure progress by how many people can find a job that pays the mortgage; whether you can put a little extra money away at the end of each month so you can someday watch your child receive her college diploma. We measure progress in the 23m new jobs that were created when Bill Clinton was president—when the average American family saw its income go up $7,500 instead of down $2,000 like it has under George Bush.

We measure the strength of our economy not by the number of billionaires we have or the profits of the Fortune 500, but by whether someone with a good idea can take a risk and start a new business, or whether the waitress who lives on tips can take a day off to look after a sick kid without losing her job—an economy that honors the dignity of work.

The fundamentals we use to measure economic strength are whether we are living up to that fundamental promise that has made this country great—a promise that is the only reason I am standing here tonight.

Because in the faces of those young veterans who come back from Iraq and Afghanistan, I see my grandfather, who signed up after Pearl Harbor, marched in Patton's Army, and was rewarded by a grateful nation with the chance to go to college on the GI Bill.

In the face of that young student who sleeps just three hours before working the night shift, I think about my mom, who raised my sister and me on her own while she worked and earned her degree; who once turned to food stamps but was still able to send us to the best schools in the country with the help of student loans and scholarships.

When I listen to another worker tell me that his factory has shut down, I remember all those men and women on the south side of Chicago who I stood by and fought for two decades ago after the local steel plant closed.

And when I hear a woman talk about the difficulties of starting her own business, I think about my grandmother, who worked her way up from the secretarial pool to middle management, despite years of being passed over for promotions because she was a woman. She's the one who taught me about hard work. She's the one who put off buying a new car or a new dress for herself so that I could have a better life. She poured everything she had into me. And although she can no longer travel, I know that she's watching tonight, and that tonight is her night as well.

I don't know what kind of lives John McCain thinks that celebrities lead, but this has been mine. These are my heroes. Theirs are the stories that shaped me. And it is on their behalf that I intend to win this election and keep our promise alive as president of the United States.

What is that promise?

It's a promise that says each of us has the freedom to make of our own lives what we will, but that we also have the obligation to treat each other with dignity and respect.

It's a promise that says the market should reward drive and innovation and generate growth, but that businesses should live up to their responsibilities to create American jobs, look out for American workers, and play by the rules of the road.

Ours is a promise that says government cannot solve all our problems, but what it should do is that which we cannot do for ourselves—protect us from harm and provide every child a decent education; keep our water clean and our toys safe; invest in new schools and new roads and new science and technology.

Our government should work for us, not against us. It should help us, not hurt us. It should ensure opportunity not just for those with the most money and influence, but for every American who's willing to work.

That's the promise of America—the idea that we are responsible for ourselves, but that we also rise or fall as one nation; the fundamental belief that I am my brother's keeper; I am my sister's keeper.

That's the promise we need to keep. That's the change we need right now. So let me spell out exactly what that change would mean if I am president.

Change means a tax code that doesn't reward the lobbyists who wrote it, but the American workers and small businesses who deserve it.

Unlike John McCain, I will stop giving tax breaks to corporations that ship jobs overseas, and I will start giving them to companies that create good jobs right here in America.

I will eliminate capital gains taxes for the small businesses and the start-ups that will create the high-wage, high-tech jobs of tomorrow.

I will cut taxes—cut taxes—for 95% of all working families. Because in an economy like this, the last thing we should do is raise taxes on the middle-class.

And for the sake of our economy, our security, and the future of our planet, I will set a clear goal as president: in ten years, we will finally end our dependence on oil from the Middle East.

Washington's been talking about our oil addiction for the last 30 years, and John McCain has been there for 26 of them. In that time, he's said no to higher fuel-efficiency standards for cars, no to investments in renewable energy, no to renewable fuels. And today, we import triple the amount of oil as the day that Senator McCain took office.

Now is the time to end this addiction, and to understand that drilling is a stop-gap measure, not a long-term solution. Not even close.

As president, I will tap our natural gas reserves, invest in clean coal technology and find ways to safely harness nuclear power. I'll help our auto companies re-tool, so that the fuel-efficient cars of the future are built right here in America. I'll make it easier for the American people to afford these new cars. And I'll invest $150bn dollars over the next decade in affordable, renewable sources of energy—wind power and solar power and the next generation of biofuels; an investment that will lead to new industries and 5m new jobs that pay well and can't ever be outsourced.

America, now is not the time for small plans.

Now is the time to finally meet our moral obligation to provide every child a world-class education, because it will take nothing less to compete in the global economy. Michelle and I are only here tonight because we were given a chance at an education. And I will not settle for an America where some kids don't have that chance. I'll invest in early childhood education. I'll recruit an army of new teachers, and pay them higher salaries and give them more support. And in exchange, I'll ask for higher standards and more accountability. And we will keep our promise to every young American—if you commit to serving your community or your country, we will make sure you can afford a college education.

Now is the time to finally keep the promise of affordable, accessible healthcare for every single American. If you have healthcare, my plan will lower your premiums. If you don't, you'll be able to get the same kind of coverage that members of Congress give themselves. And as someone who watched my mother argue with insurance companies while she lay in bed dying of cancer, I will make certain those companies stop discriminating against those who are sick and need care the most.

Now is the time to help families with paid sick days and better family leave, because nobody in America should have to choose between keeping their jobs and caring for a sick child or ailing parent.

Now is the time to change our bankruptcy laws, so that your pensions are protected ahead of CEO bonuses; and the time to protect social security for future generations.

And now is the time to keep the promise of equal pay for an equal day's work, because I want my daughters to have exactly the same opportunities as your sons.

Now, many of these plans will cost money, which is why I've laid out how I'll pay for every dime—by closing corporate loopholes and tax havens that don't help America grow. But I will also go through the federal budget, line by line, eliminating programs that no longer work and making the ones we do need work better and cost less—because we cannot meet 21st-century challenges with a 20th-century bureaucracy.

And Democrats, we must also admit that fulfilling America's promise will require more than just money. It will require a renewed sense of responsibility from each of us to recover what John F Kennedy called our "intellectual and moral strength". Yes, government must lead on energy independence, but each of us must do our part to make our homes and businesses more efficient. Yes, we must provide more ladders to success for young men who fall into lives of crime and despair. But we must also admit that programmes alone can't replace parents; that government can't turn off the television and make a child do her homework;

that fathers must take more responsibility for providing the love and guidance their children need.

Individual responsibility and mutual responsibility—that's the essence of America's promise.

And just as we keep our promise to the next generation here at home, so must we keep America's promise abroad. If John McCain wants to have a debate about who has the temperament, and judgment, to serve as the next commander-in-chief, that's a debate I'm ready to have.

For while Senator McCain was turning his sights to Iraq just days after 9/11, I stood up and opposed this war, knowing that it would distract us from the real threats we face. When John McCain said we could just "muddle through" in Afghanistan, I argued for more resources and more troops to finish the fight against the terrorists who actually attacked us on 9/11, and made clear that we must take out Osama bin Laden and his lieutenants if we have them in our sights. John McCain likes to say that he'll follow bin Laden to the Gates of Hell—but he won't even go to the cave where he lives.

And today, as my call for a time frame to remove our troops from Iraq has been echoed by the Iraqi government and even the Bush Administration, even after we learned that Iraq has a $79 billion surplus while we're wallowing in deficits, John McCain stands alone in his stubborn refusal to end a misguided war. That's not the judgment we need. That won't keep America safe. We need a President who can face the threats of the future, not keep grasping at the ideas of the past.

You don't defeat a terrorist network that operates in eighty countries by occupying Iraq. You don't protect Israel and deter Iran just by talking tough in Washington. You can't truly stand up for Georgia when you've strained our oldest alliances. If John McCain wants to follow George Bush with more tough talk and bad strategy, that is his choice—but it is not the change we need.

We are the party of Roosevelt. We are the party of Kennedy. So don't tell me that Democrats won't defend this country. Don't tell me that Democrats won't keep us safe. The Bush-McCain foreign policy has squandered the legacy that generations of Americans—Democrats and Republicans—have built, and we are here to restore that legacy.

As Commander-in-Chief, I will never hesitate to defend this nation, but I will only send our troops into harm's way with a clear mission and a sacred commitment to give them the equipment they need in battle and the care and benefits they deserve when they come home.

I will end this war in Iraq responsibly, and finish the fight against al Qaeda and the Taliban in Afghanistan. I will rebuild our military to meet future conflicts. But I will also renew the tough, direct diplomacy that can prevent Iran from obtaining nuclear weapons and curb Russian aggression. I will build new partnerships to defeat the threats of the 21st century: terrorism and nuclear proliferation; poverty and genocide; climate change and disease. And I will restore our moral standing, so that America is once again that last, best hope for all who are called to the cause of freedom, who long for lives of peace, and who yearn for a better future. These are the policies I will pursue. And in the weeks ahead, I look forward to debating them with John McCain.

But what I will not do is suggest that the Senator takes his positions for political purposes. Because one of the things that we have to change in our politics is the idea that people cannot disagree without challenging each other's character and patriotism.

The times are too serious, the stakes are too high for this same partisan playbook. So let us agree that patriotism has no party. I love this country, and so do you, and so does John McCain. The men and women who serve in our battlefields may be Democrats and Republicans and Independents, but they have fought together and bled together and some died together under the same proud flag. They have not served a Red America or a Blue America—they have served the United States of America.

So I've got news for you, John McCain. We all put our country first.

America, our work will not be easy. The challenges we face require tough choices, and Democrats as well as Republicans will need to cast off the worn-out ideas and politics of the past. For part of what has been lost these past eight years can't just be measured by lost wages or bigger trade deficits. What has also been lost is our sense of common purpose—our sense of higher purpose. And that's what we have to restore.

We may not agree on abortion, but surely we can agree on reducing the number of unwanted pregnancies in this country. The reality of gun ownership may be different for hunters in rural Ohio than for those plagued by gang-violence in Cleveland, but don't tell me we can't uphold the Second Amendment while keeping AK-47s out of the hands of criminals. I know there are differences on same-sex marriage, but surely we can agree that our gay and lesbian brothers and sisters deserve to visit the person they love in the hospital and to live lives free of discrimination. Passions fly on immigration, but I don't know anyone who benefits when a mother is separated from her infant child or an employer undercuts American wages by hiring illegal workers. This too is part of America's promise—the promise of a democracy where we can find the strength and grace to bridge divides and unite in common effort.

I know there are those who dismiss such beliefs as happy talk. They claim that our insistence on something larger, something firmer and more honest in our public life is just a Trojan Horse for higher taxes and the abandonment of traditional values. And that's to be expected. Because if you don't have any fresh ideas, then you use stale tactics to scare the voters. If you don't have a record to run on, then you paint your opponent as someone people should run from.

You make a big election about small things. And you know what—it's worked before. Because it feeds into the cynicism we all have about government. When Washington doesn't work, all its promises seem empty. If your hopes have been dashed again and again, then it's best to stop hoping, and settle for what you already know. I get it. I realize that I am not the likeliest candidate for this office. I don't fit the typical pedigree, and I haven't spent my career in the halls of Washington.

But I stand before you tonight because all across America something is stirring. What the nay-sayers don't understand is that this election has never been about me. It's been about you. For eighteen long months, you have stood up, one by one, and said enough to the politics of the past. You understand that in this election, the greatest risk we can take is to try the same old politics with the same old players and expect a different result. You have shown what history teaches us—that at defining moments like this one, the change we need doesn't come from Washington. Change comes to Washington. Change happens because the American people demand it—because they rise up and insist on new ideas and new leadership, a new politics for a new time.

America, this is one of those moments.

I believe that as hard as it will be, the change we need is coming. Because I've seen it. Because I've lived it. I've seen it in Illinois, when we provided health care to more children and moved more families from welfare to work. I've seen it in Washington, when we worked across party lines to open up government and hold lobbyists more accountable, to give better care for our veterans and keep nuclear weapons out of terrorist hands.

And I've seen it in this campaign. In the young people who voted for the first time, and in those who got involved again after a very long time. In the Republicans who never thought they'd pick up a Democratic ballot, but did. I've seen it in the workers who would rather cut their hours back a day than see their friends lose their jobs, in the soldiers who re-enlist after losing a limb, in the good neighbors who take a stranger in when a hurricane strikes and the floodwaters rise.

This country of ours has more wealth than any nation, but that's not what makes us rich. We have the most powerful military on Earth, but that's not what makes us strong. Our universities and our culture are the envy of the world, but that's not what keeps the world coming to our shores. Instead, it is that American spirit—that American promise—that pushes us forward even when the path is uncertain; that binds us together in spite of our differences; that makes us fix our eye not on what is seen, but what is unseen, that better place around the bend. That promise is our greatest inheritance. It's a promise I make to my daughters when I tuck them in at night, and a promise that you make to yours—a promise that has led immigrants to cross oceans and pioneers to travel west; a promise that led workers to picket lines, and women to reach for the ballot.

And it is that promise that forty five years ago today, brought Americans from every corner of this land to stand together on a Mall in Washington, before Lincoln's Memorial, and hear a young preacher from Georgia speak of his dream. The men and women who gathered there could've heard many things. They could've heard words of anger and discord. They could've been told to succumb to the fear and frustration of so many dreams deferred. But what the people heard instead—people of every creed and color, from every walk of life—is that in America, our destiny is inextricably linked. That together, our dreams can be one.

"We cannot walk alone," the preacher cried. "And as we walk, we must make the pledge that we shall always march ahead. We cannot turn back."

America, we cannot turn back. Not with so much work to be done. Not with so many children to educate, and so many veterans to care for. Not with an economy to fix and cities to rebuild and farms to save. Not with so many families to protect and so many lives to mend. America, we cannot turn back. We cannot walk alone. At this moment, in this election, we must pledge once more to march into the future. Let us keep that promise—that American promise—and in the words of Scripture hold firmly, without wavering, to the hope that we confess.

Thank you, God Bless you, and God Bless the United States of America.

首先，向迪恩主席，我的好友迪克·德宾，以及我们这个伟大国家的同胞们致意。（注：霍华德·迪恩是奥巴马所在的美国民主党全国委员会主席；迪克·德宾是美国参议院中的民主党二号人物。）

怀着深深的感激与谦恭，我接受你们的提名，成为美国总统候选人。

首先让我感谢伴随我走过初选那段征程的候选人们，特别是走得最远的那一位——为工薪阶层的美国人奋争，为你我的女儿们带来激励的候选人——希拉里·罗德姆·克林顿。感谢克林顿总统，昨晚他的演讲对美国需要变革的阐述无以伦比。感谢泰德·肯尼迪，感谢他的奉献精神。当然还有我们的下任美国副总统乔·拜登，谢谢你。有这样一位我们这个时代最优秀的政治家伴随我走完最后这段竞选之旅是我的福气。拜登平易近人，从对其他国家的领导人，到他每晚乘火车下班回家遇到的售票员都是同样的。

我还要感谢我的妻子，我们的下一任第一夫人，米歇尔·奥巴马，以及萨沙和玛丽亚，我深爱你们，你们是我的骄傲。

四年前面对你们，我讲述了自己的故事——故事起始于一对分别来自肯尼亚和（美国）堪萨斯州青年夫妇的短暂结合。（注：这里指奥巴马的父母。奥巴马的父亲来自肯尼亚，曾在美国留学；母亲是美国堪萨斯州人。）他们并不富裕、默默无闻，但他们有这样一个共同的信念，那就是在美国，他们的儿子不管有什么样的理想，都有可能实现。

正是这个美国的承诺，让我们的国家与众不同——通过努力和牺牲，我们每个人都能够追求个人的梦想，但同时又组成美国这个大家庭。并且让我们的下一代也可以追求他们的梦想。

这就是为什么今晚我会站在这里。因为在过去的二百三十二年间，每当这个美国的承诺遇到挑战之时，普普通通的男女——学生、战士、农民、教师、护士和勤杂工，都展现出他们的勇气来保卫它。

我们正处在这样一个时刻——在这一时刻，我们的国家处于战争之中，经济一团乱麻，美国的承诺又一次遇到挑战。

今夜，从未有这么多的美国人在忍受失业，他们工作更辛苦，挣的却更少。如此多的家庭失去他们的住所，更多的人则眼睁睁看着他们的房子贬值。更多的人有车却开不起，信用卡账单难以支付，孩子的学费高到无法承受。不能说这些问题都是政府的责任。但不能有效地解决这些问题，却实实在在是华盛顿的政府与乔治·W·布什政策的失败。

美国，我们的人民应当比这过去的八年过得更好。我们不该是这样的国家。

在俄亥俄，一位一生努力工作即将退休的妇女发现一场突如其来的疾病让她陷入绝境。我们的国家不该这样！

在印第安纳，一位工人把和他相伴了二十年的机器设备打包运往中国，在向家人解释这一切时，他为自己的失败泣不成声。我们的国家难道不该对我们的人民更慷慨！

老兵们流落街头，他们的家庭陷入困顿。而一座美国的重要城市眼睁睁地被洪水吞没。我们的政府难道不应当对此更有同情心！

今晚，我对美国人民、对民主党、共和党和无党派人士，对我们这个伟大国家的所有人说，够了！这一时刻，这次大选，是决定在二十一世纪我们是否仍能信守美国承诺的机会。因为下周，那个带给你们两届乔治·布什和迪克·切尼的共和党，想要带给这个国家第三届同样的货色！（注：之后的一周将是共和党全国代表大会）今天我们聚集在这里，是因为我们热爱这个国家，我们不愿意让过去的八年再上演四年。当十一月四日（注：大选投票之日）到来时，我们必须站起来说："八年已经够了。"

毫无疑问，共和党提名的总统候选人约翰·麦凯恩曾经为了我们的国家身着军装。他的勇敢和出色表现应当赢得我们的感激和尊重。而下周，我们还将听到他几次与共和党分道扬镳的陈述，让我们相信他会给我们带来这个国家所需要的改变。

但是，过去的记录清晰地表明：约翰·麦凯恩 90% 的时候都支持乔治·布什的观点。麦凯恩参议员喜欢谈论判断力，但是说真的，当你认为乔治·布什 90% 的时候都是正确的，这个时候你还有什么判断力可言？我不知道别人怎么想，但我不打算依靠这 10% 的改变几率。

事实是，在讨论我们所面对的重要问题时——从医疗到教育再到我们的经济——麦凯恩参议员都没有表达出他的独立观点。他说我们的经济在过去八年中取得了"巨大的发展"。他说经济的基础非常稳固。麦凯恩参议员的首席经济顾问——他为麦凯恩参议员撰写了经济规划——谈到美国人的焦虑感时说道，我们的国家正在经历一场"精神上的衰退"，我们已经变成了，我引用他的原话，"一个充满抱怨者的国家"。

一个充满抱怨者的国家？当密歇根州工厂自豪的汽车工人们发现工厂即将关闭，但仍然一如既往的坚持工作，只因为有人需要他们生产的刹车盘时，我们听到抱怨了吗？当一位军人的丈夫或妻子在自己的爱人又要离开家，去执行第三次、第四次甚至是第五次任务时，默默地担起了家庭的重担，我们听到抱怨了吗？他们都没有抱怨。他们仍然努力工作，仍然热爱生活，毫无怨言。这才是我所知道的美国人。

我不相信麦凯恩参议员不关心美国人的生活，我想他只是不知道。否则他怎么会将中产阶级定义为年收入少于500万美元的人呢？否则他怎么会提出上千亿美元的针对大企业和石油公司的减税计划，却不肯为超过一亿的普通美国大众减免哪怕只是一分钱？否则他怎么会提出实际加重了人民负担的医疗政策？怎么会提出对美国家庭毫无帮助的教育政策？怎么会提出社会保障的私人账户计划，这不是拿你的退休金赌博吗？

约翰·麦凯恩不是不关心，而是根本不知道。

过去的二十多年里，他一直秉承着那种陈旧、迂腐的共和党哲学——让美国人拥有更多的资产，这样每个人就可以担负自己的福利。在华盛顿，他们称之为“所有者社会”，但这种哲学背后的意思是——你只能靠你自己了。失业？你运气不好。没有医疗保险？自己去买吧。生在穷人家？你只能白手起家——即你一无所有。一切都得靠你自己。

现在，是时候让他们品尝自己的失败了。让我们来改变美国。

大家都知道，我们民主党用另外一种完全不同的方法来衡量这个国家的发展。

我们判断国家是否发展，要看有多少人能够找到工作来支付贷款；要看你是否可以每月存下一点钱为了你的孩子将来可以去读大学。判断国家是否发展，要看比尔·克林顿总统在任期间新创造的两千三百万个工作机会和美国家庭平均收入上升了7500美元，而不是乔治·布什时期的下降2000美元。

我们判断我们的经济实力并不是看亿万富翁的数目，或者财富五百强企业的利润，而是要看一个拥有非凡创意的人能否开创自己的事业，或者一个靠小费生活的服务员能不能请一天假去照顾生病的孩子而不会丢掉她的工作——我们需要一个崇尚工作尊严的经济体系。

我们用来衡量经济实力的基本原则是，我们是否真正践行了那些让国家变得更伟大的承诺——这也是我今晚站在这个台上的唯一原因。

因为在那些从伊拉克和阿富汗归来的年轻的退伍军人的脸上，我看到了我祖父的影子。珍珠港事件后他加入了军队，并在巴顿将军的部队中服役，依靠“美国退役军人权利法案”，他才有机会接受大学教育。

看到那些努力学习至深夜的年轻学生，我想起了我的母亲，她在独自抚养我和妹妹的同时还取得了学位。虽然她曾经依靠发放给穷苦人的食品券度日，却仍然可以借助学生贷款和奖学金将我们送到这个国家最好的学校去读书。

当我听到又一位工人告诉我他的工厂倒闭时，我就想起二十多年前当本地的钢厂关闭时，与我并肩作战的那些人们。

当我听到一位女性告诉我她创业的艰难时，我就会想起我的祖母从秘书到中层管理人员的奋斗历程，这用了很多年只因为她是个女性。她教育我要努力奋斗。她把买新车和新衣服的钱省下来，只为了让我过得更好。她将她的所有都给了我。虽然她不能来现场，但是我知道她一定在看着我，因为这也是属于她的夜晚。

我不知道约翰·麦凯恩认为什么样的人才是榜样，但这些就是我的榜样。他们是我的英雄，他们影响了我，塑造了我。我将代表他们赢得总统竞选，并且作为美国的总统去实现我们的诺言。

那么，我们承诺了什么？

我们承诺每个人都能自由地过上自己想要的生活，但是我们也有责任保护别人的尊严。

我们承诺市场会奖励勤奋和创新并创造增长，但是企业应当履行责任为美国人创造工作机会，保障工人权利和遵守规则。

我们承诺虽然政府不能解决所有的问题，但是可以为我们所有人谋求福利——保护我们不受伤害，让每个孩子都有接受教育的机会；保证我们喝上清洁的水，保证我们的玩具安全；投资建设新的学校，新的道路，支持科技的发展。

我们的政府应该为我们所用，而不是与我们作对。政府应该帮助我们，而不是伤害我们。政府应该保证每个人的机会平等，不能袒护那些有权或有钱的人，而是保护每一个勤奋的美国人。

这就是美国的承诺——我们每个人都要为自己负责。但我们也是一个同甘共苦的整体，我们会关爱我们的兄弟姐妹，关爱每个人。

这就是我们需要履行的承诺。这就是现在我们所需要的改变。所以，如果我能成为美国总统，我将准确诠释改变世界的真谛。

改变意味着税法不再有利于立法的政客，而是有利于美国所有的工人、中小企业家，这是他们应得的。

我不像约翰·麦凯恩，我将停止对那些将工作机会拱手送人的大公司的减税政策，并将这些优惠给予那些在这里，在美国创造良好工作机会的公司。

我将免除中小企业和初创企业的资本所得税，因为这些企业将是未来高薪、高技术工作岗位的来源。

我将减税，为95%的工薪家庭减免税赋。因为在我们的经济体系中，不到万不得已不能对中产阶级加税。

并且，为了我们的安全、我们的经济和我们这个星球的未来，我将为我的总统任期定下一个明确的目标：十年之内，我们将摆脱对中东的石油依赖。

过去三十年，华盛顿一直在谈论我们对石油的依赖，而约翰·麦凯恩在那里待了二十六年。当年，他反对更高的燃油效率标准，反对发展可再生能源，反对开发可再生燃料。现在，我们进口的石油是麦凯恩就任参议员时的三倍之多。

现在，是时候结束对石油的依赖了，并且我们要明白钻更多的油井不过是权宜之计，远非一劳永逸。

作为总统，我将鼓励开发天然气，投资研究洁净燃煤技术，发展安全、可控的核能。我将帮助我们的汽车企业改良技术，为美国生产燃油效率更高的机动车，并且让美国人能买得起这些车。未来十年，我将在廉价的可再生能源领域——风能、太阳能和新型生物燃料投资1500亿美元。这些投资将创造新的产业并提供500万个新的不可外包的高薪工作机会。

美国，现在可不是小家子气的时候。

现在，我们需要担起责任，为每个孩子提供世界一流的教育，因为这在全球经济竞争中同样重要。米歇尔和我今晚之所以能站在这里，正是因为我们受到了教育。只要还有孩子不能得到教育机会，我就不会停止脚步。我还将发展儿童早期教育。我会招募大量的新教师，给他们高薪，给他们更多的支持，同时也要求他们提供更高标准的教育。我们将坚守对每个年轻人的承诺——只要你为社会、为国家做出贡献，我们将保证你交得起学费。

我们要实现为每个美国人提供可以负担得起的医疗保障制度的承诺。如果你有医疗保险，我的计划将减少你的支出。如果你没有，你可以享受与国会议员同样的医疗保险。某些人曾亲眼看到我的母亲在身患癌症，卧床不起的时候与保险公司争论医疗保险的金额，我将确保这些公司不再歧视那些最需要保险的病人。

我们将为每个美国人提供享受带薪病假和事假的机会，因为在美国，任何人都不应在留住工作和照顾生病的孩子或父母之间做出选择。

我们将改善破产法案，优先保证你的退休金而不是 CEO 的红利。我们还将为下一代提供更好的社会保障制度。

我们将保证实现同工同酬，因为我希望我的女儿和你的儿子拥有同样的机会。

许多计划都需要投入，而我将计划好我要花出去的每一个硬币——堵死公司税务漏洞和那些对美国的增长毫无帮助的避税天堂。我也将逐字逐句地分析联邦预算，停止那些毫无意义的项目，将有限的资源投入到我们更需要的领域中去。我们不能用二十世纪的官僚体系来应对二十一世纪的挑战。

民主党人，我们必须承认实现承诺需要的不仅仅是钱。它需要我们有更多的责任感以重获约翰·F·肯尼迪总统所说的“智力和道德的力量”。不错，实现能源独立是政府的责任，但是我们每个人都有责任在生活和工作中节约能源。不错，我们需要为那些犯下罪行或者陷入绝望的年轻人提供获得成功的路径，但是我们必须承认政府的计划不可能取代父母的作用。政府不可能关掉电视，让孩子去完成家庭作业，父亲必须承担更多的责任，给孩子以必要的关爱和指导。

个体责任和共同责任——这就是美国承诺的精髓所在。

正像我们在国内的承诺一样，我们要把这些承诺扩展到美国之外的地方。如果约翰·麦凯恩想要就谁更加具有成为下一任总司令的气质和判断力展开一场辩论，我求之不得。

在“9·11”事件发生几天后，麦凯恩参议员开始关注伊拉克。而我却站起来反对这场战争，我深知这场战争会转移我们的注意力，使我们无法全力应对真正的威胁。约翰·麦凯恩说，我们在阿富汗只能草草了事。而我则主张动用更多的资源和兵力来打击“9·11”事件的真正元凶，打赢这场反恐之战。

我让人们明白：只要看到奥萨马・本・拉登和他的助手，就应该立刻把他们揪出来。约翰・麦凯恩喜欢说，即便是追到地狱门口，他也要追到本・拉登，但他甚至连本・拉登居住的洞穴都没去过。

而如今，当我发出的尽早从伊拉克撤兵的呼吁得到了伊拉克政府乃至布什政府的回应，当我们得知伊拉克拥有790亿美元的贸易顺差，而美国仍在遭遇赤字之后，约翰・麦凯恩仍然一意孤行，固执地反对停止这场错误的战争。我们需要的不是这样的判断。因为这种判断无法确保美国的安全。我们需要的是一位能够直面未来威胁的总统，他不应该死抓着昔日的想法不放。

你无法通过占领伊拉克摧毁一支活动于八十个国家的恐怖组织。你无法单凭在华盛顿发表的激烈言辞来保护以色列，遏制伊朗。你无法真正地维护格鲁吉亚的利益，在你拖垮了我们最古老的同盟者之后。如果约翰・麦凯恩想用更激烈的言辞和糟糕的策略来追随乔治・布什，那是他自己的选择。但随之而来的改变，不是我们所需要的。

我们和罗斯福同宗同源。我们和肯尼迪同宗同源。所以，别说民主党无法捍卫这个国家。别说民主党无法确保我们的安全。“布什－麦凯恩”式的外交政策已将世代美国人（民主党人和共和党人）积累的遗产挥霍掉了，而我们正是为恢复遗产而来。

作为总司令，我将义无反顾地捍卫这个国家，但是，我只会出于明确的使命让我们的军队经受战争之苦，同时，我会履行神圣的承诺：他们作战时，为他们配备必需的物资；他们战后返家时，为他们提供应有的关心和福利。

出于责任我将结束在伊拉克的战争，并击溃阿富汗的基地组织和塔利班组织。我将重建军事力量，为未来的战争做好准备。对于那种能够阻止伊朗拥有核武器，遏制俄罗斯侵略的强硬而直接的外交策略，我将对其进行革新。我将建立新的伙伴关系，以挫败二十一世纪的威胁：恐怖主义与核扩散，贫困与种族灭绝，气候改变与疾病。我还要恢复我们的道德立场，使美国再次成为向往自由、渴望和平、渴望美好未来的人们最后以及最好的圆梦之地。我将追随这些政策。我期待在几周之后与约翰・麦凯恩就此展开讨论。

然而，我建议麦凯恩参议员不要让政治目的左右他的观点。因为在政治生活中，有一点是我们必须改变的，那就是如果不对彼此的性格和爱国心做出挑衅，人们便不会发生争论。

时间紧迫，党派之争带来的代价过于高昂。所以，我们要相信爱国心没有党派之分。我爱这个国家，你也一样，约翰·麦凯恩也一样。在战场上服役的男女同胞，也许是民主党员，也许是共和党员，也许是无党派人士，但是，在同一面骄傲的旗帜下，他们一起战斗，一起流血，有些人还一起牺牲。他们不为“红色美国”服役，也不为“蓝色美国”服役——他们为美利坚合众国服役。

所以，我来告诉你，约翰·麦凯恩。我们都把国家放在第一位。

美国，我们的工作并不轻松。在挑战面前，我们必须作出艰难的选择，民主党同共和党一样，需要抛弃陈腐的观点和过时的政见。过去八年里我们丧失的部分，仅用损失的工薪和更严重的贸易逆差是无法衡量的。同样丧失的还有共同的使命感——我们更高的使命。而这正是我们必须恢复的。

我们可以不赞成流产，然而毫无疑问，我们会赞成减少这个国家的意外怀孕率。允许持枪，对俄亥俄州农村的猎户和遭受匪帮暴力威胁的克利夫兰的人们来说，不是一码事。但是，别一边禁止罪犯手拿 AK-47 步枪，一边跟我说我们不能支持宪法的第二修正案。我知道同性婚姻会有所不同，然而毫无疑问，我们会赞成那些身为同性恋的兄弟姐妹们能够去医院看望他们所爱的人，过上没有歧视的生活。反对外来移民的情绪高涨，然而，当一位母亲与尚在襁褓中的孩子分开时，当雇主通过雇用非法劳工而降低美国工资水平时，我不知道有谁能从中获益。这也在美国的承诺范围之内——一种民主的承诺，在这种承诺中，我们能够找到消除分歧、团结民众的力量与美德。

我知道有人会摒弃这些信念，把它们看做笑谈。他们宣称我们对民众生活中更庞大、更坚固和更正直的事物之坚持就如同一只特洛伊木马，只会导致更高的税收以及传统价值的流失。这是意料中的事。因为如果没有任何新鲜的想法，你只能用一些陈腐的战术去吓唬选民。如果手头没有一份记录作为谈资，你只能把对手描述成一个众叛亲离的人。

你制造了一场关乎琐碎小事的大选。而你知道吗，以前就有过这种做法。因为它是犬儒主义（我们都对政府抱有这种观点）的温床。当华盛顿不起作用时，它的所有承诺似乎都成了空谈。如果你的希望一再被击碎，那么最好别再抱有希望，接受你已经了解的事实。这一点我懂。我认识到对于这一职务，我不是最有希望的候选人。我没有显赫的家世，也没有在华盛顿工作的经历。

然而，今晚我就站在你们面前，因为整个美国都在为某件事而激动。反对者不会明白，这次选举自始至终不是关于我的，而是关于你们的。十八个月以来，你们先后站起来，针对过去的政治活动发表了足够多的言论。你们知道在这次选举中，我们最大的冒险是同样的老面孔、同样的老政策能否带来不一样的结果。你们已经展示了历史留给我们的教训，在这决定性的时刻，我们需要的改变不是“来自”华盛顿，而是“指向”华盛顿。改变因美国人民的需要而出现——因为他们站了出来，主张新观念和新领导，新时代的新政治。

美国，那样的时刻再次来临。

我坚信不管有多么艰难，我们所需的改变正在到来。因为我已经看到它了，因为我已经置身其中。我已经在伊利诺伊看到它了，我们为更多的儿童提供了保健，使更多家庭从依赖福利走向自食其力。我已经在华盛顿看到它了，我们打破党派的界线，共同努力令政府广开言路，使院外游说集团对自己的行为更负责任；给予退役军人更好的待遇；阻止恐怖主义者沾手核武器。

我在这次竞选中看到了它。它出现于那些初次参与投票的年轻选民中，也出现于那些再次参与投票的老选民中。出现于那些从没想过会为民主党投票，却给它投了票的共和党人中。我在那些情愿自己少拿薪水，也不愿看到朋友们失业的工人身上看到了它；在那些失去肢体仍再次应募的士兵身上看到了它；在那些于暴风和洪水来袭时收容陌生人的善良同胞身上看到了它。

我们国家拥有世界上最多的财富，然而让我们富有的并非是财富。我们拥有世界上最强大的军事力量，然而让我们强大的并非军事力量。我们的大学和文化受到全世界的羡慕，然而并非它们促使世界各国的人们登陆美国。相反，是美国精神——美国的承诺促使我们前行，即便前路坎坷；它将我们联系到一起，尽管我们有所不同；它让我们不要只盯着肉眼所能见到的，还要关注那些看不到的——那目力不及处的美景。那承诺是留给我们的最大的遗产。夜里给女儿掖被子的时候，我会向她们说出这个承诺；你也会向你的孩子们说出这个承诺——这个承诺引领移民者漂洋过海，引领先驱们挺进西部；这个承诺把工人们领往纠察线，让女人取得选举权。

正是这个承诺，在四十五年前的今天，把美国人从这片土地的各个角落领到一起，在华盛顿的一条林荫大道上，在林肯纪念碑前，聆听一位来自佐治亚州的年轻牧师宣讲他的梦想。聚集在那里的男男女女们，也许听到了很多东西。他们也许听到了愤怒与不和谐的言辞。也许曾有人要求他们，要他们屈从于许多被延迟的梦境带来的恐惧和失败。然而，事实与此相反，人们——各种信仰、各种肤色、各行各业的人们听到的是——在美国，我们的命运紧紧地连在一起。而我们的梦也可以成为一个共同的梦。

“我们不能独行，”牧师呼吁道。“在行走时，我们必须保证一直前行。我们不能回头。”

美国，我们不能回头。有太多的工作等着我们去完成。有太多的孩子需要教育，太多的退役军人需要关爱。经济亟待修复，城市亟待重建，农场亟待拯救。太多的家庭需要保护，太多人的生活需要改善。美国，我们不能回头。我们不能独行。在这一时刻，在这次选举中，我们必须再一次保证向未来挺进。让我们履行那个承诺吧——美国的承诺——正如圣经所指引的那样笔直前行，直到实现我们内心的希望。

感谢你们，上帝保佑你们，上帝保佑美利坚合众国。

第三节 精彩语录

It's a promise that says each of us has the freedom to make of our own lives what we will, but that we also have the obligation to treat each other with dignity and respect.

我们承诺每个人都能自由地过上自己想要的生活，但是我们也有责任保护别人的尊严。

It's a promise that says the market should reward drive and innovation and generate growth, but that businesses should live up to their responsibilities to create American jobs, look out for American workers, and play by the rules of the road.

我们承诺市场将会奖励勤奋和创新并创造增长，但是企业应当履行责任为美国人创造工作机会，保障工人权利和遵守规则。

Ours is a promise that says government cannot solve all our problems, but what it should do is that which we cannot do for ourselves—protect us from harm and provide every child a decent education; keep our water clean and our toys safe; invest in new schools and new roads and new science and technology.

我们承诺虽然政府不能解决所有的问题，但是可以为我们所有人谋求福利——保护我们不受伤害，让每个孩子都有接受教育的机会；保证我们喝上清洁的水，保证我们的玩具安全；投资建设新的学校，新的道路，支持科技的发展。

Our government should work for us, not against us. It should help us, not hurt us. It should ensure opportunity not just for those with the most money and influence, but for every American who's willing to work.

我们的政府应该为我们工作，而不是与我们作对。政府应该帮助我们，而不是伤害我们。政府应该保证每个人的机会平等，不能袒护那些有权或有钱的人，而是保护每一个勤奋的美国人。

That's the promise of America—the idea that we are responsible for ourselves, but that we also rise or fall as one nation; the fundamental belief that I am my brother's keeper; I am my sister's keeper.

这就是美国的承诺——我们每个人都要为自己负责。但我们也是一个同甘共苦的整体，我们会关爱我们的兄弟姐妹，关爱每个人。

That's the promise we need to keep. That's the change we need right now. So let me spell out exactly what that change would mean if I am president.

这就是我们需要履行的承诺。这就是现在我们所需要的改变。所以，如果我能成为美国总统，我将准确诠释改变世界的真谛。

第二章

无畏的希望

第一节 背景介绍

美国民主党全国代表大会在每隔四年的选举年举行。该大会的三个主要功能是提名总统和副总统候选人，讨论并通过党的竞选纲领，制定党的规则。来自全国五十个州、哥伦比亚特区和海外领地的代表、民主党官员以及外国要人都会出席这一会议。

1824 年，随着推选总统和副总统候选人的党团会议制度变得岌岌可危，民主党内提出举行全国代表大会的设想。1832 年，民主党首届全国代表大会在马里兰州巴尔的摩召开，来自全国各地的代表投票选举总统和副总统候选人。

近年来，民主党全国代表大会制度在本质上发生了巨大变化。由于总统候选人和副总统候选人通常在会前已经确定，代表们只是在大会上完成投票形式，而不会改变此前总统预选的结果。

通常，民主党全国代表大会持续四天。第一天用来完成一些例行事务，包括主题发言人讲话；第二天，代表们讨论并通过民主党竞选纲领和其他规定；总统竞选人在第三天获得正式提名；最后一天，副总统候选人获提名，两人随即发表接受提名的演讲。

要想获得民主党的提名是件非常困难的事情，2004 年和奥巴马一同竞争的民主党人一共有七位，其中最大的威胁莫过于布莱尔·豪尔（Blair Hull）。

豪尔是一个富有的商人，计划斥资数百万角逐提名，来势汹汹、志在必得。奥巴马则采取稳扎稳打的战术，他极力寻求非裔美国人和党内自由派人士的支持，其中包括著名的杰西·杰克逊牧师。拉什的坚定支持者也是奥巴马需要着力争取的对象，当年和拉什的选战得不偿失，许多拉什的铁杆选民至今耿耿于怀。但是，奥巴马也有自己的优势。所谓的为黑人着想、为人民服务的声誉并非靠金钱和广告堆起来的，奥巴马勤恳服务社区的记录和在州议会优异的表现，有力地证明了自己的能力和诚意。黑人群众开始相信眼前这位有着白人血统的年轻人的确是他们最好的代言人，以前的质疑烟消云散。对于白人来讲，奥巴马不是一个传统的黑人，或者简直就是一个白人。他的母亲一方祖祖辈辈都是白人，他接受过白人的精英教育。他在《哈佛法学评论》的往事被当作传奇交口传诵，他似乎就是一个集中了一切优点的选项。

最大的竞争对手豪尔后来因为个人婚姻问题一蹶不振，这给了奥巴马更大的机会。在应对其他竞争对手的威胁时，奥巴马的竞选团队发挥了巨大作用。阿克塞罗德在电视宣传方面巧妙运作，让奥巴马的公众形象不断提升，“是的，我们能！”（“Yes, we can”）一时间成为让所有人为之激动的竞选口号。奥巴马的追随者相信“是的，我们能”的确能够为美国污浊的政治空气带来一阵清风，能够为民众的生活带来实实在在的改变。

虽然选举结果揭晓之前，形势对奥巴马来说已经非常有利，但最后结果还是让许多人着实吃了一惊，95% 的黑人站在了奥巴马一边，总选票的 53% 被收入囊中，奥巴马在诸多对手中脱颖而出，一骑绝尘。在选举结束之后的庆功宴上，人群里不断发出“Yes, we can！ Yes, we can！”的呼声，这种发自内心的支持和狂热的场景是美国选举多年未见的景象。为了这一胜利奥巴马付出了很多，而且将付出更多。最大的付出莫过于如果最终当选，他将远离自己的家人，长期待在国会山。父亲当年只身前往哈佛求学的故事对于奥巴马来说不只是一种崇拜而且还是禁忌。

现在，挡在奥巴马国会参议员道路上的对手只剩下一个——共和党的杰克·瑞安。但是杰克的竞选活动一开始就不是很光彩，这也最终导致了他的失败。为了了解奥巴马的一举一动，杰克雇用了一个人全程跟踪奥巴马，还把奥巴马的言行举止用摄像机全拍了下来。这一行为显然超出了合法竞争，有侵犯隐私之嫌。奥巴马巧妙地在最恰当的时间和地点向媒体揭露了杰克的这一伎俩，如饥似渴的新闻媒体哪能放过这个机会，第二天这件事情就上了报。杰克及其竞选团队不得不公开赔礼道歉，而杰克自己更是被这件事情以及自己的婚姻危机弄得灰头土脸，与自己的参议员梦想越来越远。

风头正劲的奥巴马引起了民主党大佬们的注意。受约翰·克里（John Kerry）之邀，奥巴马出席了2004年民主党全国代表大会，并在大会上作基调演讲“无畏的希望”，这对于奥巴马来说意义非凡。基调演讲表现的是该政党、该政党的总统候选人、该代表大会想向全国观众传递的思想或政策信息。能够与前总统比尔·克林顿、杰西·杰克逊牧师和纽约州前州长马里奥·科莫同台致辞，本身就是一种至高无上的荣誉。

2004年7月27日，面对五千余名代表，奥巴马从自己的身世娓娓谈起，展望美国未来的走向，整篇演讲酣畅淋漓、妙语连珠，将大会带向了高潮。

面对美国意识形态多极化、党派政治日益突出的现状，奥巴马在演讲中称：“这里不存在一个自由派的美国和一个保守派的美国，而只有一个美利坚合众国。这里不存在黑人的美国和白人的美国、拉美裔的美国和亚洲裔的美国，而只有美利坚合众国。很多所谓的专家喜欢将我们的国家分成红色的州和蓝色的州：红州是共和党人的地盘，蓝州是民主党人的天下。但我要对他们说：我们蓝州人信仰庄严的上帝，我们红州人不喜欢联邦政府的官员在图书馆打探我们的阅读兴趣。我们蓝州人也给小棒球队做教练，我们红州人也有同性恋朋友。反对伊拉克战争的是爱国者，支持伊拉克战争的也是爱国者。我们是一个民族，所有人都宣誓效忠星条旗，所有人都捍卫美利坚合众国。”

奥巴马憧憬一个融合团结的美国，而不是一个四分五裂的美国，他大胆地说：“希望是上帝赐予我们的最好礼物，是这个民族的基石，是坚信不曾见到的前景，是坚信明天会更好。”

这种积极向上乐观的精神感染了在场的所有听众，也感染了电视机前的美国人。可以说，十七分钟的基调演讲使奥巴马一鸣惊人，成为民主党最炙手可热的政治明星，他从此迈向了全国的政治舞台。

第二节 奥巴马于2004年在民主党全国代表大会的演讲

July 27, 2004

On behalf of the great state of Illinois, crossroads of a nation, land of Lincoln, let me express my deep gratitude for the privilege of addressing this convention. Tonight is a particular honor for me because, let's face it, my presence on this stage is pretty unlikely. My father was a foreign student, born and raised in a small village in Kenya. He grew up herding goats, went to school in a tin-roof shack. His father, my grandfather, was a cook, a domestic servant.

But my grandfather had larger dreams for his son. Through hard work and perseverance my father got a scholarship to study in a magical place: America, which stood as a beacon of freedom and opportunity to so many who had come before. While studying here, my father met my mother. She was born in a town on the other side of the world, in Kansas. Her father worked on oil rigs and farms through most of the Depression. The day after Pearl Harbor he signed up for duty, joined Patton's army and marched across Europe. Back home, my grandmother raised their baby and went to work on a bomber assembly line. After the war, they studied on the GI Bill, bought a house through FHA, and moved west in search of opportunity.

And they, too, had big dreams for their daughter, a common dream, born of two continents. My parents shared not only an improbable love; they shared an abiding faith in the possibilities of this nation. They would give me an African name, Barack, or "blessed," believing that in a tolerant America your name is no barrier to success. They imagined me going to the best schools in the land, even though they weren't rich, because in a generous America you don't have to be rich to achieve your potential. They are both passed away now. Yet, I know that, on this night, they look down on me with pride.

I stand here today, grateful for the diversity of my heritage, aware that my parents' dreams live on in my precious daughters. I stand here knowing that my story is part of the larger American story, that I owe a debt to all of those who came before me, and that, in no other country on earth, is my story even possible. Tonight, we gather to affirm the greatness of our nation, not because of the height of our skyscrapers, or the power of our military, or the size of our economy. Our pride is based on a very simple premise, summed up in a declaration made over two hundred years ago, "We hold these truths to be self-evident, that all men are created equal. That, they are endowed by their Creator with certain inalienable rights. That among these are life, liberty and the pursuit of happiness."

That is the true genius of America, a faith in the simple dreams of its people, the insistence on small miracles. That we can tuck in our children at night and know they are fed and clothed and safe from harm. That we can say what we think, write what we think, without hearing a sudden knock on the door. That we can have an idea and start our own business without paying a bribe or hiring somebody's son. That we can participate in the political process without fear of retribution, and that our votes will he counted—or at least, most of the time.

This year, in this election, we are called to reaffirm our values and commitments, to hold them against a hard reality and see how we are measuring up, to the legacy of our forbearers, and the promise of future generations. And fellow Americans—Democrats, Republicans, Independents—I say to you tonight: we have more work to do. More to do for the workers I met in Illinois, who are losing their union jobs at the Maytag plant that's moving to Mexico, and now are having to compete with their own children for jobs that pay seven bucks an hour.

More to do for the father I met who was losing his job and choking back tears, wondering how he would pay $4,500 a month for the drugs his son needs without the health benefits he counted on. More to do for the young woman in East St. Louis, and thousands more like her, who has the grades, has the drive, has the will, but doesn't have the money to go to college.

Don't get me wrong. The people I meet in small towns and big cities, in diners and office parks, they don't expect government to solve all their problems. They know they have to work hard to get ahead and they want to. Go into the collar counties around Chicago, and people will tell you they don't want their tax money wasted by a welfare agency or the Pentagon. Go into any inner city neighborhood, and folks will tell you that government alone can't teach kids to learn. They know that parents have to parent, that children can't achieve unless we raise their expectations and turn off the television sets and eradicate the slander that says a black youth with a book is acting white. No, people don't expect government to solve all their problems. But they sense, deep in their bones, that with just a change in priorities, we can make sure that every child in America has a decent shot at life, and that the doors of opportunity remain open to all. They know we can do better. And they want that choice.

In this election, we offer that choice. Our party has chosen a man to lead us who embodies the best this country has to offer. That man is John Kerry. John Kerry understands the ideals of community, faith, and sacrifice, because they've defined his life. From his heroic service in Vietnam to his years as prosecutor and lieutenant governor, through two decades in the United States Senate, he has devoted himself to this country. Again and again, we've seen him make tough choices when easier ones were available. His values and his record affirm what is best in us.

John Kerry believes in an America where hard work is rewarded. So instead of offering tax breaks to companies shipping jobs overseas, he'll offer them to companies creating jobs here at home. John Kerry believes in an America where all Americans can afford the same health coverage our politicians in Washington have for themselves. John Kerry believes in energy independence, so we aren't held hostage to the profits of oil companies or the sabotage of foreign oil fields. John Kerry believes in the constitutional freedoms that have made our country the envy of the world, and he will never sacrifice our basic liberties nor use faith as a wedge to divide us. And John Kerry believes that in a dangerous world, war must be an option, but it should never be the first option.

A while back, I met a young man named Shamus at the VFW Hall in East Moline, Illinois. He was a good-looking kid, six-two or six-three, clear-eyed, with an easy smile. He told me he'd joined the Marines and was heading to Iraq the following week. As I listened to him explain why he'd enlisted, his absolute faith in our country and its leaders, his devotion to duty and service, I thought this young man was all any of us might hope for in a child. But then I asked myself: Are we serving Shamus as well as he was serving us? I thought of more than 900 service men and women, sons and daughters, husbands and wives, friends and neighbors, who will not be returning to their hometowns. I thought of families I had met who were struggling to get by without a loved one's full income, or whose loved ones had returned with a limb missing or with nerves shattered, but who still lacked long-term health benefits because they were reservists. When we send our young men and women into harm's way, we have a solemn obligation not to fudge the numbers or shade the truth about why they're going, to care for their families while they're gone, to tend to the soldiers upon their return, and to never ever go to war without enough troops to win the war, secure the peace, and earn the respect of the world.

Now let me be clear. We have real enemies in the world. These enemies must be found. They must be pursued and they must be defeated. John Kerry knows this. And just as Lieutenant Kerry did not hesitate to risk his life to protect the men who served with him in Vietnam, President Kerry will not hesitate one moment to use our military might to keep America safe and secure. John Kerry believes in America. And he knows it's not enough for just some of us to prosper. For alongside our famous individualism, there's another ingredient in the American saga.

A belief that we are connected as one people. If there's a child on the south side of Chicago who can't read, that matters to me, even if it's not my child. If there's a senior citizen somewhere who can't pay for her prescription and has to choose between medicine and the rent, that makes my life poorer, even if it's not my grandmother. If there's an Arab American family being rounded up without benefit of an attorney or due process, that threatens my civil liberties. It's that fundamental belief—I am my brother's keeper, I am my sister's keeper—that makes this country work. It's what allows us to pursue our individual dreams, yet still come together as a single American family. "Epluribus unum." Out of many, one.

Yet even as we speak, there are those who are preparing to divide us, the spin masters and negative ad peddlers who embrace the politics of anything goes. Well, I say to them tonight, there's not a liberal America and a conservative America—there's the United States of America. There's not a black America and white America and Latino America and Asian America; there's the United States of America. The pundits like to slice-and-dice our country into Red States and Blue States; Red States for Republicans, Blue States for Democrats. But I've got news for them, too. We worship an awesome God in the Blue States, and we don't like federal agents poking around our libraries in the Red States. We coach Little League in the Blue States and have gay friends in the Red States. There are patriots who opposed the war in Iraq and patriots who supported it. We are one people, all of us pledging allegiance to the stars and stripes, all of us defending the United States of America.

In the end, that's what this election is about. Do we participate in a politics of cynicism or a politics of hope? John Kerry calls on us to hope. John Edwards calls on us to hope. I'm not talking about blind optimism here—the almost willful ignorance that thinks unemployment will go away if we just don't talk about it, or the health care crisis will solve itself if we just ignore it. No, I'm talking about something more substantial. It's the hope of slaves sitting around a fire singing freedom songs; the hope of immigrants setting out for distant shores; the hope of a young naval lieutenant bravely patrolling the Mekong Delta; the hope of a millworker's son who dares to defy the odds; the hope of a skinny kid with a funny name who believes that America has a place for him, too. The audacity of hope!

In the end, that is God's greatest gift to us, the bedrock of this nation; the belief in things not seen; the belief that there are better days ahead. I believe we can give our middle class relief and provide working families with a road to opportunity. I believe we can provide jobs to the jobless, homes to the homeless, and reclaim young people in cities across America from violence and despair. I believe that as we stand on the crossroads of history, we can make the right choices, and meet the challenges that face us. America!

Tonight, if you feel the same energy I do, the same urgency I do, the same passion I do, the same hopefulness I do—if we do what we must do, then I have no doubt that all across the country, from Florida to Oregon, from Washington to Maine, the people will rise up in November, and John Kerry will be sworn in as president, and John Edwards will be sworn in as vice president, and this country will reclaim its promise, and out of this long political darkness a brighter day will come. Thank you and God bless you.

2004 年 7 月 27 日

伟大的伊利诺伊州既是全国的交通枢纽，也是林肯的故乡。作为州代表，今天我将在大会致词，并为自己能有幸获此殊荣而倍感骄傲和自豪。今晚对我而言颇不寻常，我们得承认，我能站在这里本身就已意义非凡。我父亲是一个外国留学生，他原本生于肯尼亚的一个小村庄，并在那里长大成人。他小的时候放过羊，上的学校简陋不堪，屋顶上仅有块铁皮来遮风挡雨。而他的父亲也就是我的祖父，不过是个普通的厨子，还做过家佣。

但祖父对父亲抱以厚望。凭借不懈的努力和坚韧不拔的毅力，父亲获得赴美留学的机会，而且还拿到奖学金。美国这片神奇的土地，对于很多踏上这片国土的人而言，意味着自由和机遇。在留学期间，父亲与母亲不期而遇。母亲来自完全不同的另一个世界，她生于堪萨斯的一个小镇。大萧条时期，外祖父为谋生计，曾在石油钻井打工，还曾在农场务农。日军偷袭珍珠港后的第二天，他就自愿应征入伍，在巴顿将军麾下，转战南北，横扫欧洲。在后方的家中，外祖母含辛茹苦，抚养子女，并在轰炸机装配线上找了份活计。战后，依据士兵安置法案他们上了学，安置通过联邦住宅管理局购置了一套房子，并举家西迁，谋求更大发展。

他们对自己的女儿也寄予厚望，两家人虽然身在不同的非洲和美洲大陆，却有着共同的梦想。我的父母不仅不可思议地彼此相爱，而且还对这个国家有着不变的信念。他们赐予我一个非洲名字贝拉克，意为“上天福佑”，因为他们相信，在如此包容的国度中，这样的名字不会成为成功的羁绊。尽管他们生活并不宽裕，还是想方设法让我接受当地最好的教育，因为在这样一个慷慨的国度中，无论贫富贵贱，都同样有机会发展个人的潜力。现在他们都已不在人世，不过，我知道他们的在天之灵，此时此刻正在骄傲地注视着我。

今天，我站在这里，对自己身上这种特殊的血统心怀感激，而且我知道，父母的梦想将在我的宝贝女儿身上延续；我站在这里，深知自己的经历只是千百万美国故事中的一个，更深知自己无法忘却那些更早踏上这片土地的先人，因为若不是在美国，我的故事无论如何都不可能发生。今夜，我们聚集一堂，再次证明这个国度的伟大之处，并不在于鳞次栉比的摩天大厦，也不在于傲视群雄的军事实力，更不在于稳健雄厚的经济实力。我们的自豪与荣耀来自一个非常简单的前提，两百多年前，它在一个著名的宣言中得以高度的概括：“我们认为以下真理不言而喻，人生来平等，造物主赐予他们以下不可剥夺的权利：生命、自由和对幸福的追求。”

这才是真正的美国智慧，坚信自己的国民有着朴素无华的梦想，坚信点滴的奇迹终会出现在身边。入夜，当我们为孩子掖好小被的同时，相信他们不会为缺少衣食所累，不会为安全担忧。我们可以畅所欲言，无需担心不速之客会不请自来。我们有灵感，有想法，可以去实现，去创业，无须行贿或雇佣某些人物的子女作为条件。我们可以参政议政，不必担心打击报复，我们的选票至关重要，至少多数情况下都是如此。

在今年的选举中，我们要特别重申我们主张的价值和肩负的责任，以此来应对当下的艰难现实，了解怎样才能更好秉承前辈的遗产，实现对子孙的承诺。诸位美国国民，无论你是民主党，还是共和党，抑或是无党派人士，今晚我想对大家说的是：我们需要做的事情还有很多很多。在伊利诺伊州，由于 Maytag 洗衣机厂要迁至墨西哥，很多工人将失去工作，他们现在唯一的选择就是和自己的子女去竞争每小时 7 美元的低薪工作。我曾遇到一位强忍泪水的父亲，他丢掉了工作，没有了经济来源，不知怎样才能为儿子支付得起每月 4500 美元的高昂医药费用，本可救命的医疗保险对他而言却遥不可及。在东圣路易斯市，有这样一个年轻女孩，她品学兼优，成绩出色，却因为没有钱，而与大学无缘。而像她这样的孩子还有千千万万，我们应该为他们做点什么？

请正面理解我的意思。我在城市与乡镇，在餐厅和办公楼停车场，接触过很多民众，他们并不期待由政府出面帮他们排忧解难。他们清楚地意识到，需要通过努力工作，去面对和解决所有的问题，而这也确实是他们真实的想法和愿望。走进芝加哥周边的城镇，大家会告诉你，希望自己缴纳的税款能够物尽其用，而不是让社会保障机构或五角大楼任意支配。走进市中心的街区，大家会告诉你，让孩子好好读书不能仅仅依靠政府的力量，父母也要尽职尽责，培养下一代，不能让孩子整天沉溺于电视。对于黑人而言，更要和白人一样，让子女有接受教育的权利，而不是相反。人们并不期望依赖政府来解决所有问题，但他们真诚地认为，只要政府的工作重点有所调整，就可以使每个孩子都能奋发图强，积极向上，机遇大门仍旧向每个人敞开。他们深知我们有能力做得更好，他们同样希望如此。

在本次选举中，我们提供了这样的选择。民主党已选出一国之中品行最为高尚的人作为我们的领袖，他就是约翰·克里，他深刻地领悟了社区、信念和献身精神这些崇高的理想，因为这些铸就了他生命的全部。他曾在越南英勇作战，回国后出任过检察官和副州长，在美国参议院度过了二十个春秋，把全部精力都投入到维国家工作之中。多少次他面对艰难抉择，知难而上，不畏艰险，他的阅历和品行为我们树立了榜样。

约翰·克里坚信在美国付出就会有回报，因此，对于那些在本土创造就业机会的公司，他会在税收上给与优惠，而将工作机会输送到海外的公司则不会享受到如此待遇。他坚信美国应该实现标准的医疗保险，对普通百姓和华盛顿的政治家都一视同仁。他坚信能源自主的重要性，因此我们不会再因石油公司对利润的追求，或国外油田被破坏而受到威胁。他坚信美国应该成为世人艳羡的国度，因为国民的自由受到宪法的保护。他永远都不会让大家的基本自由受到影响，更不会以信仰为借口来制造分裂。他坚信当今世界的确存在危险因素，战争在所难免，但战争永远不会成为解决争端的首选。

前不久，在伊利诺伊州东莫林市的外战老兵俱乐部里，我偶遇一个年轻人，他叫沙莫斯，身高足有两米，相貌英俊，目光清澈，笑容可掬。他说自己加入了海军陆战队，一周后就将进驻伊拉克。当我听他讲述入伍的原因时，他讲到了对我们国家和领导人的绝对信赖，对军队的忠诚以及自身强烈的责任感，这让我感受到他身上具备的优良品质正是我们对子女所期待的。然而，当我扪心自问：我们为他所做的一切，是否能与他的付出相当呢？我想到这次战争中已有九百多名军人战死沙场，他们也有自己的家人和邻友，也许已是为人父母，还有年迈的双亲，却再也无法回到这些关爱他们的人身边。我想到自己遇到的那些家庭，他们或是要应对亲人阵亡，收入锐减所带来的经济窘境，或是要面对肢体残缺，甚至精神崩溃的家人复员归来，却因其预备役军人的身份而无法享受长期的医疗保险。当这些可爱的年轻人舍身踏上征程，我们责无旁贷地要确认做出出兵决定的所有数据和理由是否确凿无误；我们责无旁贷地要替他们照顾好家人，当他们荣归故里时，要关照他们的生活；当决定要介入战争、保卫和平和赢得世界的尊重时，我们责无旁贷地要派驻足够数量的军队，以确保战士们能凯旋而归。

请允许我阐明下述观点：在世界上，确实有人与我们为敌，我们必须找到他们，并予以坚决打击。约翰·克里深知这一点，正如身为上尉的他在越南战场上出生入死，保护自己的下属一样，若他身为总统，也同样会义无反顾地运用军队力量确保国家的安全。他对美国充满信心，而且深知仅有部分公民实现生活的富足还远远不够，是与我们闻名于世的个人主义相伴的另一种元素，才使得美国史册熠熠生辉。

这就是我们作为一个民族荣辱与共的信仰。假如，芝加哥南部的一个孩子无法读书识字，即便他与我非亲非故，我也会心怀忐忑。如果有位老人因无法支付高昂的医疗费用，不得不在治病和租房之间痛苦抉择，即便她与我素未谋面，我也会如坐针毡。假如，一个阿拉伯裔的美国家庭未经律师辩护，或诉讼程序就遭受不公正待遇，同样会让我寝食难安。正是这个基本信仰让这个国家发展到今天：我们都是一家人，我们都是兄弟姐妹。正是这个信仰才让我们在实现个人梦想的同时，成为一个美利坚大家庭，合众为一。

当我们在这里聚会的时候，也有人正准备分裂我们，那些操纵舆论的人和制作负面宣传的人，他们投身没有原则和不择手段的政治。今晚，我需要对这些人讲的是，美国人没有所谓自由和保守之分，世间只存在一个美利坚合众国。没有所谓美国白人和黑人之分，拉丁裔和亚裔之分，有的只是美利坚合众国一国的国民。有评论员愿意将我们的国家分成红蓝两色，红色代表共和党，蓝色代表民主党。但我想说的是即便是民主党也都信奉万能的主，即便是共和党也不喜欢联邦警探对我们的藏书指指点点，民主党中也有人执教少年棒球联盟，共和党中也有同性恋朋友，有爱国人士支持伊拉克战争，也有爱国人士反对就伊出兵。我们都是一国之民，都效忠于伟大的星条旗，所有的人都热爱我们的祖国美利坚合众国。

说到底，这才是本次选举的意义所在：我们所参与的政治应该是愤世嫉俗还是充满希望？约翰·克里号召我们要对未来满怀希望，这并不是说要盲目乐观，以为只要不谈论失业问题，这个问题就会自行消失；认为只要无视医疗危机的存在，它也会烟消云散。我所谈的是更为根本的问题。是因为存在希望，奴隶们才会围坐在火堆边，吟唱自由之歌；是因为存在希望，才使得人们愿意远涉重洋，移民他乡；是因为希望，年轻的海军上尉才会在湄公河三角洲勇敢地巡逻；是因为希望，出身工人家庭的孩子才会敢于挑战自己所处的逆境；是因为希望，一个名字怪怪的瘦小子才相信美国这片热土上也有自己的容身之地。这就是无畏的希望。

最后，感谢上苍赐予我们最好的礼物，也就是这个国家赖以生存的基石。因为我们相信最好的东西尚未出现，更好的日子就在明天。我相信我们可以为中产阶级减负，让工人家庭走上希望之路；我相信我们可以为无业者创造就业机会，为无家可归者带来可以遮风挡雨的房屋，让美国城市中的年轻人从暴力和绝望的阴影中走出来；我相信今天的我们就站在历史的十字街头，我们可以做出正确的选择，迎接面临的挑战。

今晚，如果你能感同身受，有和我一样的的力量、急迫感、冲动和希望；如果我们都去做我们必须要做的，那么我相信，从佛罗里达到俄勒冈，从华盛顿到缅因州，全国人民将会在 11 月积极行动起来，使约翰·克里、约翰·爱德华兹分别宣誓就任总统、副总统之职，而国家也将就此走出低谷、重振旗鼓。暗夜即将过去，黎明即将到来。谢谢大家，愿上帝保佑你们。

第三节 精彩语录

The greatness of our nation, not because of the height of our skyscrapers, or the power of our military, or the size of our economy. Our pride is based on a very simple premise, summed up in a declaration made over two hundred years ago, "We hold these truths to he self-evident, that all men are created equal. That they are endowed by their Creator with certain inalienable rights. That among these are life, liberty and the pursuit of happiness."

这个国度的伟大之处，并不在于鳞次栉比的摩天大厦，也不在于傲视群雄的军事实力，更不在于稳健雄厚的经济实力。我们的自豪与荣耀来自一个非常简单的前提，两百多年前，它在一个著名的宣言中得以高度的概括："我们认为以下真理不言而喻，人生来平等，造物主赐予他们以下不可剥夺的权利：生命、自由和对幸福的追求。"

That is the true genius of America, a faith in the simple dreams of its people, the insistence on small miracles.

这才是真正的美国智慧，坚信自己的国民有着朴素无华的梦想，坚信点滴的奇迹终会出现在身边。

We have real enemies in the world. These enemies must be found. They must be pursued and they must be defeated.

在世界上，确实有人与我们为敌，我们必须找到他们，并予以坚决打击。

There's not a liberal America and a conservative America—there's the United States of America. There's not a black America and white America and Latino America and Asian America; there's the United States of America.

美国人没有所谓自由和保守之分，世间只存在一个美利坚合众国。没有所谓美国白人和黑人之分，拉丁裔和亚裔之分，有的只是美利坚合众国一国的国民。

That is God's greatest gift to us, the bedrock of this nation; the belief in things not seen; the belief that there are better days ahead. I believe we can give our middle class relief and provide working families with a road to opportunity. I believe we can provide jobs to the jobless, homes to the homeless, and reclaim young people in cities across America from violence and despair. I believe that as we stand on the crossroads of history, we can make the right choices, and meet the challenges that face us. America!

感谢上苍赐予我们最好的礼物，也就是这个国家赖以生存的基石。因为我们相信最好的东西尚未出现，更好的日子就在明天。我相信我们可以为中产阶级减负，让工人家庭走上希望之路；我相信我们可以为无业者创造就业机会，为无家可归者带来可以遮风挡雨的房屋，让美国城市中的年轻人从暴力和绝望的阴影中走出来；我相信今天的我们就站在历史的十字街头，我们可以做出正确的选择，迎接面临的挑战。

第三章

谢谢你，艾奥瓦

第一节 背景介绍

奥巴马的演讲集传道士的雄辩和推销员的机敏于一身，既激情四射、振奋人心，又言简意赅、主题突出。这样的演讲技巧，再经过媒体的放大，便能产生明星效应。奥巴马成功当选美国第四十四任总统，也是美国历史上第一位黑人总统。美国新一场变革即将来临。

奥巴马面临的金融和经济危机从程度上虽不能与罗斯福时期相比，但却是罗斯福之后历任总统所面临的危机中最为严重的一次。次贷危机引发的金融危机摧毁了很多美国家庭在过去十多年积累起来的财富，能否尽快稳定市场和稳定投资者的信心，决定了奥巴马是成为像罗斯福那样的民族英雄，还是昙花一现的黑人总统。

2008 年 11 月 5 日正午，美国作出了一个伟大的决定，历史上第一次，一个黑皮肤的人登上了世界的权力之巅。而仅仅十二年前，他还只是一介平民；是什么令他如此平步青云?

贝拉克·奥巴马于 2007 年 1 月 16 日宣布，他有意参加 2008 年的总统竞选，已于当天向美国联邦选举机构提交了有关文件，将成立一个委员会，以评估他参加总统竞选的可行性。

奥巴马 16 日在其网站上发表声明说，数月来他一直在考虑是否参加 2008

年的总统选举，但参加与否不会取决于媒体宣传和个人抱负。过去六年中，联邦政府所作的决定以及所忽视的问题使美国处于一种非常不安全的境地，美国陷入了一场本不应该发动的“不幸的、代价高昂的”战争，而身在华盛顿的领导人却不能以一种实际的方式进行合作。

而在 1 月 20 号，前总统克林顿的妻子希拉里在其个人网站上宣布参加 2008 年美国总统大选。她的竞选标语是：“我来了，为胜利而来。”

由于双方在党内支持者众多，一场激烈的抢票大战必不可免，绝不逊色于之后的总统选举。

奥巴马主攻年轻选民，特别是通过网络。2007 年 3 月，奥巴马在“Yahoo! Answers”（雅虎知识堂的美国版）发表题为《How can we engage more people in the democratic process?》（如何吸引更多人参与民主进程？）的问题，回复量超越一万七千个。之后他还在社交网站 Facebook 开了一个账户，版面很受欢迎。

而希拉里最大的优势是丈夫克林顿和其本身身为女性，容易吸引女性选民的目光。当一位民意测验专家马克・迈尔曼让十位黑人妇女选出她们心中的政治英雄时，有八个人选了希拉里。

6 月 7 日，希拉里正式宣布停止竞选，呼吁她的选民转而支持党内初选胜出者奥巴马。

2008 年美国总统选举将于当地时间 1 月 3 日晚打响第一枪，届时民主共和两党党内初选将在艾奥瓦州率先拉开大幕。艾奥瓦州民主党初选在当地时间 1 月 3 日晚上 6 时 30 分（北京时间 1 月 4 日上午 7 时 30 分）开始。半个小时后，共和党初选开始，结果最快在一至两个小时后得出。

盖洛普最新民调显示，美国选民认为，艾奥瓦州党团会议初选的结果，就民主党参选人而言，对奥巴马的影响较大，对希拉里・克林顿及爱德华兹的影响较小。盖洛普 1 月 2 日公布的民调显示，如果奥巴马在即将于 1 月 3 日举行的艾奥瓦党团会议初选中获胜，67% 的全国选民认为其将在未来的提名战中对希拉里形成“严重挑战”，只有 31% 认为是“暂时胜利”。

而如果希拉里在艾奥瓦党团会议初选中落败，则有高达 70% 的全国选民认为只是“暂时挫败”；只有 28% 认为这将对她提名之路带来麻烦。如果艾奥瓦党团会议的胜利者是爱德华兹，只有40%的全国选民认为这将对希拉里造成“严重挑战”；58%认为这只是“暂时胜利”。

经过一系列的拉票，美国当地时间2008年6月3日，美民主党总统竞选人奥巴马宣布他在该党初选中胜出，获得民主党总统候选人提名。

据悉，希拉里、奥巴马和爱德华兹均在媒体上买下广告时段或版面，为大选第一仗作最后冲刺。希拉里与奥巴马目前在不同民调中分别领先，爱德华兹则名列第三。

奥巴马在两分钟的电视广告中说：“这个国家需要一个可以把我们都团结起来的领导人，那样我们才算真正地赢得了这场选举，也只有这样我们才能解决医疗、教育、能源以及战争等问题。”

希拉里也在广告中再次发动了她的煽情攻势，她说：“如果你们支持我一个晚上（指1月3日晚），我作为总统将支持你们每一天。我将呕心沥血，把我们热爱的国家带入一个新起点，我将从第一天开始就进入状态。”

爱德华兹则请了一位名叫多格·比谢普的下岗工人做“代言人”。比谢普说：“我心目中的候选人要能坐下来，看着一个七岁孩子的眼睛告诉他：‘我会为你爸爸的工作而战。’而爱德华兹就是我的选择。”

每个选举年，艾奥瓦州都会成为全美瞩目的中心，也是每届美国选战最为激烈的战场。一项研究发现，艾奥瓦州初选获得的媒体关注是其他州的143倍。

在初选阶段，一个州的面积大小和人口多寡与该州对选举的影响力并不成正比，最重要的是它的初选日期——往往日期越早影响越大。在初选中最早获胜的候选人会得到更多的关注，在接下来的竞选过程中也会拥有更大的优势。正因如此，艾奥瓦州尽管以人口和面积而论都是小州，却在整个初选阶段具有“风向标”的作用，因此也受到各位竞选人和各路媒体的高度关注。

其次是艾奥瓦州特殊的初选制度，选民决定自己支持谁可能需要多达五小时。艾奥瓦州的初选称为Caucus，意为集会，与绝大多数州不同。在艾奥瓦州，初选其实并没有“投票”这个环节，而是选民到达投票所后，依据其支持的对象分类，一群一群地集中。然后好戏登场，参选人边喝茶吃点心边拉票，游走穿梭于各群间。既要设法把别的“群”里的选民拉到自己这个“群”里，还要防止自己“群”里的选民被别的参选人“群”拉走。这样来来往往，所以需要花费五小时才能最后确定每位候选人的得票数。

第二节 奥巴马于2008年在艾奥瓦州德斯莫内斯的竞选演讲

Thank you, Iowa.

You know, they said this day would never come. They said our sights were set too high. They said this country was too divided; too disillusioned to ever come together around a common purpose.

But on this January night—at this defining moment in history—you have done what the cynics said we couldn't do. You have done what the state of New Hampshire can do in five days. You have done what America can do in this New Year, 2008. In lines that stretched around schools and churches; in small towns and big cities; you came together as Democrats, Republicans and Independents to stand up and say that we are one nation; we are one people; and our time for change has come.

You said the time has come to move beyond the bitterness and pettiness and anger that's consumed Washington; to end the political strategy that's been all about division and instead make it about addition—to build a coalition for change that stretches through Red States and Blue States. Because that's how we'll win in November, and that's how we'll finally meet the challenges that we face as a nation.

We are choosing hope over fear. We're choosing unity over division, and sending a powerful message that change is coming to America.

You said the time has come to tell the lobbyists who think their money and their influence speak louder than our voices that they don't own this government, we do; and we are here to take it back.

The time has come for a President who will be honest about the choices and the challenges we face; who will listen to you and learn from you even when we disagree; who won't just tell you what you want to hear, but what you need to know. And in New Hampshire, if you give me the same chance that Iowa did tonight, I will be that president for America.

Thank you.

I'll be a President who finally makes health care affordable and available to every single American the same way I expanded health care in Illinois—by bringing Democrats and Republicans together to get the job done. I'll be a President who ends the tax breaks for companies that ship our jobs overseas and put a middle-class tax cut into the pockets of the working Americans who deserve it. I'll be a President who harnesses the ingenuity of farmers and scientists and entrepreneurs to free this nation from the tyranny of oil once and for all.

And I'll be a President who ends this war in Iraq and finally brings our troops home; who restores our moral standing; who understands that 9/11 is not a way to scare up votes, but a challenge that should unite America and the world against the common threats of the twenty-first century; common threats of terrorism and nuclear weapons; climate change and poverty; genocide and disease.

Tonight, we are one step closer to that vision of America because of what you did here in Iowa.

And so I'd especially like to thank the organizers and the precinct captains; the volunteers and the staff who made this all possible. And while I'm at it, on "thank yous," I think it makes sense for me to thank the love of my life, the rock of the Obama family, the closer on the campaign trail; give it up for Michelle Obama.

I know you didn't do this for me. You did this—you did this because you believed so deeply in the most American of ideas—that in the face of impossible odds, people who love this country can change it. I know this—I know this because while I may be standing here tonight, I'll never forget that my journey began on the streets of Chicago doing what so many of you have done for this campaign and all the campaigns here in Iowa—organizing, and working, and fighting to make people's lives just a little bit better. I know how hard it is. It comes with little sleep, little pay, and a lot of sacrifice.

There are days of disappointment, but sometimes, just sometimes, there are nights like this—a night—a night that, years from now, when we've made the changes we believe in; when more families can afford to see a doctor; when our children—when Malia and Sasha and your children–inherit a planet that's a little cleaner and safer; when the world sees America differently, and America sees itself as a nation less divided and more united; you'll be able to look back with pride and say that this was the moment when it all began.

This was the moment when the improbable beat what Washington always said was inevitable. This was the moment when we tore down barriers that have divided us for too long—when we rallied people of all parties and ages to a common cause; when we finally gave Americans who'd never participated in politics a reason to stand up and to do so. This was the moment when we finally beat back the politics of fear, and doubt, and cynicism; the politics where we tear each other down instead of lifting this country up. This was the moment. Years from now, you'll look back and you'll say that this was the moment—this was the place—where America remembered what it means to hope.

For many months, we've been teased, even derided for talking about hope. But we always knew that hope is not blind optimism. It's not ignoring the enormity of the task ahead or the roadblocks that stand in our path. It's not sitting on the sidelines or shirking from a fight. Hope is that thing inside us that insists, despite all evidence to the contrary, that something better awaits us if we have the courage to reach for it, and to work for it, and to fight for it.

Hope is what I saw in the eyes of the young woman in Cedar Rapids who works the night shift after a full day of college and still can't afford health care for a sister who's ill; a young woman who still believes that this country will give her the chance to live out her dreams. Hope is what I heard in the voice of the New Hampshire woman who told me that she hasn't been able to breathe since her nephew left for Iraq; who still goes to bed each night praying for his safe return.

Hope is what led a band of colonists to rise up against an empire; what led the greatest of generations to free a continent and heal a nation; what led young women and young men to sit at lunch counters and brave fire hoses and march through Selma and Montgomery for freedom's cause. Hope—hope—is what led me here today—with a father from Kenya; a mother from Kansas; and a story that could only happen in the United States of America. Hope is the bedrock of this nation; the belief that our destiny will not be written for us, but by us; by all those men and women who are not content to settle for the world as it is; who have the courage to remake the world as it should be.

That is what we started here in Iowa, and that is the message we can now carry to New Hampshire and beyond; the same message we had when we were up and when we were down; the one that can change this country brick by brick, block by block, calloused hand by calloused hand—that together, ordinary people can do extraordinary things; because we are not a collection of Red States and Blue States, we are the United States of America; and at this moment, in this election, we are ready to believe again. Thank you, Iowa.

谢谢你，艾奥瓦。

有人说这一天永远不会到来。有人说我们好高骛远。有人说这是一个分裂的国家，很难再为同一个目标风雨同舟、甘苦与共。

在这个新年的夜晚，你们让所有质疑的人闭嘴。这是个足以载入史册的时刻，五天之后新罕布什尔也会迎来同样的时刻，2008 年整个美国都将迎来这样一个欢欣鼓舞的时刻！学校和教堂旁、乡村和城市中，民主党人、共和党人抑或无党派人士，你们怀揣着不同的政治主张而来，你们发出同一个声音：我们是一个国家，我们是一个民族，我们变革的时代已经到来！

长久以来，华盛顿被斤斤计较的政治风气所笼罩，早已难堪重负。国家的未来要求我们携起手去结束这种政治的尔虞我诈，重返联邦“合众为一”的伟大理想；要求我们抛弃党派隔阂、求同存异共谋改变！只有这样，我们才能在十一月相拥而笑，共同担当起这个国家的命运。

我们用希望对抗恐惧，用联合对抗分裂，我们用有力的声音向所有人宣布，美利坚革旧维新之日已至！

你们用强有力的声音告诉那些自以为能用金钱和权势压制人民意愿的说客：“你们不配做我们的政府，我们才是国家的主人！我们来，为我们自己的政府而来！”

人们需要的是一个能够直面选择与挑战的总统，一个虚己以听、从谏如流的总统，一个直言不讳、真诚坦率的总统。谢谢你，艾奥瓦，你们的选择让新罕布什尔州的选民信心百倍，你们将使这样的总统从可能成为现实！

谢谢你们。

我会让每一个美国人都能获得医疗服务。伊利诺伊州议会的成功经验告诉我，若能摒弃党派分歧通力合作，这一目标并非遥不可及。我会让每个将工作机会转移到国外的公司付出代价，为长久以来承担了巨大社会责任的美国中产阶级减税。我会努力让农场主、科学家和企业家们坐在一起，发挥创造力，根本性地解决美国对石油的依赖。

我会结束伊拉克战争，让士兵们重回家园；我要让美国重拾自己的道德准则；我要让所有人知道“9·11”不应成为诓取选票的幌子，而应是让美国与国际社会广泛开展合作，应对诸如恐怖主义与核扩散，全球变暖与贫困，种族屠杀与疾病等二十一世纪人类共同威胁的机遇。

今夜，艾奥瓦的选择让我们距离这样一个美国又近了一步。

在此我特别要感谢选举的组织者和选区负责人、志愿者和我的竞选团队，没有你们就没有这一切。同时，我要感谢我的妻子米歇尔·奥巴马，她是全家的坚实后盾，竞选旅途她陪我一路走来。

你们这样做并非因为我，我知道。我们胸中都有一个坚定的信念，改变的道路虽然崎岖艰险，但深爱着这个国家的人民必将为它殚精竭虑。此时此刻，我之所以能站在这里，是因为芝加哥的大街小巷闪动着你们的身影，是因为艾奥瓦州的每一寸土地都渗透着你们的辛勤付出。为了人们的生活能有一丝改变，你们不吝百倍努力。即便通宵达旦、薪酬微薄，你们仍旧全身心地付出。

虽然也曾有过失望，但那仅仅只是暂时，雨过天晴之后是这样美好的夜晚。当我们多年以后最终实现改变，当每个家庭不再因为健康没有保障而犯愁，当我们的孩子在一个更美好的环境中尽情嬉戏，当整个世界对团结一心的美国刮目相看时，请回望这个夜晚。你们将会为自己曾经做出的选择感到骄傲，你们将自豪地说，梦想始于今晚！

今晚，无畏的希望越过华盛顿的高墙。今晚，不同年龄、不同党派的人们聚集在一起，长久以来的隔阂最终烟消云散。那些对政治失望已久的人们第一次走向投票站，为这个国家承担自己作为公民的责任。今晚，曾让我们四分五裂的恐惧、疑虑和犬儒主义政治终于被击败。期待已久的一刻终于来到。数年以后回望今晚，回忆此时此景，我们会更了解它对希望的意义。

几个月以来，我们饱受挖苦和嘲讽，因为我们谈论希望。希望不是盲目的乐观主义，不是对未来的困难轻描淡写，不是对可能出现的艰难险阻视若无睹，更不是袖手旁观、畏首畏尾。尽管常常事与愿违，但希望永远是我们心中的信仰，只要我们敢于寻找，希望就总在不远的前方。

我在一个来自锡达拉匹兹市的年轻女士眼中看到了希望：她白天在学校读书，晚上加班挣钱，虽然仍然不能负担妹妹的医疗费，但她没有对这个国家失去信心，她仍相信自己的梦想终将实现。我从一个来自新罕布什尔州妇女的话语中听到了希望：她说自从侄儿被派往伊拉克战场之后她就一直惴惴不安，于是夜夜祈祷，希望他能平安归来。

希望曾带领殖民地人民奋起反抗帝国暴行；希望曾带领我们的伟大先辈解放了一个大陆，救活了一个国家；希望让青年男女为了自由的事业手挽手勇敢面对高压水柱，穿越塞尔玛直至蒙哥马利。希望让我今天站在这里——他的父亲来自肯尼亚、母亲来自堪萨斯，这样的故事只可能发生在美利坚的土地上。希望是这个国家的基石和信仰，我们的命运不受别人掌握，而是在我们脚下，在那些不甘受这个世界摆布的人手中，在那些立志改变世界的人心中！

从艾奥瓦我们燃起希望，希望将从这里传向新罕布什尔，传向更远的地方。经历等于浮沉，我们手中紧握希望；一砖一瓦、一石一垒，我们用粗糙的双手一起搭建希望，所谓平凡者亦不平凡。这个国家不应有党派隔阂，不应有红蓝之分，因为我们是美利坚合众国。“纵有万千之众，我等实为一体”，此情此境之下，我们愿意再次相信这句话。谢谢你，艾奥瓦！

第三节 精彩语录

We are choosing hope over fear. We're choosing unity over division, and sending a powerful message that change is coming to America.

我们用希望对抗恐惧，用联合对抗分裂，我们用有力的声音向所有人宣布，美利坚革旧维新之日已至！

You said the time has come to tell the lobbyists who think their money and their influence speak louder than our voices that they don't own this government, we do; and we are here to take it back.

你们用强有力的声音告诉那些自以为能用金钱和权势压制人民意愿的说客："你们不配做我们的政府，我们才是国家的主人！我们来，为我们自己的政府而来！"

You did this—you did this because you believed so deeply in the most American of ideas—that in the face of impossible odds, people who love this country can change it.

我们胸中都有一个坚定的信念，改变的道路虽然崎岖艰险，但深爱着这个国家的人民必将为它殚精竭虑。

When we've made the changes we believe in; when more families can afford to see a doctor; when our children—when Malia and Sasha and your children-inherit a planet that's a little cleaner and safer; when the world sees America differently, and America sees itself as a nation less divided and more united; you'll be able to look back with pride and say that this was the moment when it all began.

当我们多年以后最终实现改变，当每个家庭不再因为健康没有保障而犯愁，当我们的孩子在一个更美好的环境中尽情嬉戏，当整个世界对团结一心的美国刮目相看时，请回望这个夜晚。你们将会为自己曾经做出的选择感到骄傲，你们将自豪地说，梦想始于今晚！

Hope is not blind optimism. It's not ignoring the enormity of the task ahead or the roadblocks that stand in our path. It's not sitting on the sidelines or shirking from a fight. Hope is that thing inside us that insists, despite all evidence to the contrary, that something better awaits us if we have the courage to reach for it, and to work for it, and to fight for it.

希望不是盲目的乐观主义，不是对未来的困难轻描淡写，不是对可能出现的艰难险阻视若无睹，更不是袖手旁观、畏首畏尾。尽管常常事与愿违，但希望永远是我们心中的信仰，只要我们敢于寻找，希望就总在不远的前方。

Hope is the bedrock of this nation; the belief that our destiny will not be written for us, but by us; by all those men and women who are not content to settle for the world as it is; who have the courage to remake the world as it should be.

希望是这个国家的基石和信仰，我们的命运不受别人掌握，而是在我们脚下，在那些不甘受这个世界摆布的人手中，在那些立志改变世界的人心中！

When we were up and when we were down; the one that can change this country brick by brick, block by block, calloused hand by calloused hand—that together, ordinary people can do extraordinary things; because we are not a collection of Red States and Blue States, we are the United States of America; and at this moment, in this election, we are ready to believe again.

经历风雨沉浮，我们手中紧握希望。一砖一瓦、一石一垒，我们用粗糙的双手一起搭建希望，所谓平凡者亦不平凡。这个国家不应有党派隔阂，不应有红蓝之分，因为我们是美利坚合众国。“纵有万千之众，我等实为一体”，此情此境之下，我们愿意再次相信这句话。

第四章

更加完善的联邦

第一节 背景介绍

奥巴马的此次演讲发表于2008年民主党总统候选人初选阶段，也是奥巴马与希拉里的角逐正酣之际。为防被抨击打种族牌，一直以来双方都沉着谨慎，避免围绕种族问题发表演讲。促使奥巴马首先就种族问题开腔的原因是，奥巴马的前牧师耶利米·赖特在布道时说出仇视白人的种族主义言论，各界纷纷要求奥巴马表态。

2008年3月18日，奥巴马选择在费城的美国宪法中心，发表了这篇长达三十多分钟的演讲。演讲中，奥巴马一方面明确谴责了赖特牧师所持的种族主义观点是扭曲的，另一方面他解释了这类观点的历史渊源，号召国民认清矛盾的真相并引导国民以发展的观点和客观的态度看问题。当时奥巴马在党内的民调还远远落后于希拉里，但这篇演讲犹如一颗定心丸，使他原有的支持者恢复了信心，更赢得了一片额外的掌声。

贝拉克·奥巴马关于种族、宗教以及他与其前牧师耶利米·赖特关系的演讲，再一次雄辩地证明了种族主义仍然是困扰美国的一大问题。奥巴马已经尖锐地指出了这个问题，现在需要的是在奥巴马以及其他总统候选人之间就这个问题展开一场平等的高层之间的讨论，以求得对这个问题的合理解决方案。

奥巴马提出一个论点：水涨船自高。他说：“政府应该在孩子们的卫生、福利以及教育上加大投入，不管他们是黑色、棕色还是白色人种。这种投入最终将促进美国的繁荣。”然而，正如奥巴马所认识到的，加大投入并不能完全消除种族之间的紧张关系。无可否认，如何解决历史遗留下来的种族歧视以及持续存在的不平等问题，仍然是美国所面临的一大考验。

奥巴马将怎样解决长期以来存在于美国学校的种族问题。例如，奥巴马曾经提到，在大学招生的时候，“我的女儿们很可能因为黑色皮肤而被优先考虑。但我认为我们应该同样考虑到处于不利地位或者家境贫穷的白人小孩。”这是否意味着他认为社会经济地位应该取代种族问题成为大学招生的考虑因素。奥巴马在担任国会参议员的时候，曾经填写过一份调查表，他在其中指出，在大学招生、职位招聘以及签约时，政府应该将种族和性别问题作为考虑的因素。2006 年，奥巴马曾经录制一段电台广告，号召密歇根州的选民反对一项投票活动，该项活动试图废除州政府在高等教育以及其他相关领域实行种族特惠，从而促进种族多元化的制度。

奥巴马在演讲中指出，大部分处于劳动者阶层以及中产阶层的白种美国人，并没有因为他们是白种人而享受特权的感觉，所以他们对积极行动计划感到愤怒。如果奥巴马当上总统，他将怎么解决这个问题或者缓和这种愤怒。奥巴马还谈到白人父母被告知他们得让他们的孩子坐公共汽车去上学时的愤怒。但是，在 2007 年，当最高法院审理一起关于两个学校将学生们按种族分组的案件的时候，奥巴马却主张积极行动计划应该得到支持。当法院判决不同意他的观点时，他公开指责“这是一份坚持错误的裁决”，并发誓将“任命懂得‘布朗案’的宪法重要性的人作为最高法院法官”（在“布朗案”中，法院最终废除了学校的种族隔离制度）。

奥巴马的演讲只是给这个问题开了个头，毕竟，正如奥巴马所说：“我相信种族问题是美国现在无法忽视的问题。”

第二节 奥巴马于2008年3月18日在费城国家宪法中心的演讲

We the people, in order to form a more perfect union.

Two hundred and twenty-one years ago, in a hall that still stands across the street, a group of men gathered and, with these simple words, launched America's improbable experiment in democracy. Farmers and scholars; statesmen and patriots who had traveled across an ocean to escape tyranny and persecution finally made real their declaration of independence at a Philadelphia convention that lasted through the spring of 1787.

The document they produced was eventually signed but ultimately unfinished. It was stained by this nation's original sin of slavery, a question that divided the colonies and brought the convention to a stalemate until the founders chose to allow the slave trade to continue for at least twenty more years, and to leave any final resolution to future generations.

Of course, the answer to the slavery question was already embedded within our Constitution—a Constitution that had at is very core the ideal of equal citizenship under the law; a Constitution that promised its people liberty, and justice, and a union that could be and should be perfected over time. And yet words on a parchment would not be enough to deliver slaves from bondage, or provide men and women of every color and creed their full rights and obligations as citizens of the United States. What would be needed were Americans in successive generations who were willing to do their part—through protests and struggle, on the streets and in the courts, through a civil war and civil disobedience and always at great risk—to narrow that gap between the promise of our ideals and the reality of their time.

This was one of the tasks we set forth at the beginning of this campaign—to continue the long march of those who came before us, a march for a more just, more equal, more free, more caring and more prosperous America. I chose to run for the presidency at this moment in history because I believe deeply that we cannot solve the challenges of our time unless we solve them together—unless we perfect our union by understanding that we may have different stories, but we hold common hopes; that we may not look the same and we may not have come from the same place, but we all want to move in the same direction—towards a better future for our children and our grandchildren.

This belief comes from my unyielding faith in the decency and generosity of the American people. But it also comes from my own American story. I am the son of a black man from Kenya and a white woman from Kansas. I was raised with the help of a white grandfather who survived a Depression to serve in Patton's Army during World War II and a white grandmother who worked on a bomber assembly line at Fort Leavenworth while he was overseas. I've gone to some of the best schools in America and lived in one of the world's poorest nations. I am married to a black American who carries within her the blood of slaves and slaveowners—an inheritance we pass on to our two precious daughters. I have brothers, sisters, nieces, nephews, uncles and cousins, of every race and every hue, scattered across three continents, and for as long as I live, I will never forget that in no other country on Earth is my story even possible. It's a story that hasn't made me the most conventional candidate. But it is a story that has seared into my genetic makeup the idea that this nation is more than the sum of its parts—that out of many, we are truly one.

Throughout the first year of this campaign, against all predictions to the contrary, we saw how hungry the American people were for this message of unity. Despite the temptation to view my candidacy through a purely racial lens, we won commanding victories in states with some of the whitest populations in the country. In South Carolina, where the Confederate Flag still flies, we built a powerful coalition of African Americans and white Americans.

This is not to say that race has not been an issue in the campaign. At various stages in the campaign, some commentators have deemed me either "too black" or "not black enough." We saw racial tensions bubble to the surface during the week before the South Carolina primary. The press has scoured every exit poll for the latest evidence of racial polarization, not just in terms of white and black, but black and brown as well.

And yet, it has only been in the last couple of weeks that the discussion of race in this campaign has taken a particularly divisive turn. On one end of the spectrum, we've heard the implication that my candidacy is somehow an exercise in affirmative action; that it's based solely on the desire of wide-eyed liberals to purchase racial reconciliation on the cheap. On the other end, we've heard my former pastor, Reverend Jeremiah Wright, use incendiary language to express views that have the potential not only to widen the racial divide, but views that denigrate both the greatness and the goodness of our nation; that rightly offend white and black alike.

I have already condemned, in unequivocal terms, the statements of Reverend Wright that have caused such controversy. For some, nagging questions remain. Did I know him to be an occasionally fierce critic of American domestic and foreign policy? Of course. Did I ever hear him make remarks that could be considered controversial while I sat in church? Yes. Did I strongly disagree with many of his political views? Absolutely—just as I'm sure many of you have heard remarks from your pastors, priests, or rabbis with which you strongly disagreed.

But the remarks that have caused this recent firestorm weren't simply controversial. They weren't simply a religious leader's effort to speak out against perceived injustice. Instead, they expressed a profoundly distorted view of this country—a view that sees white racism as endemic, and that elevates what is wrong with America above all that we know is right with America; a view that sees the conflicts in the Middle East as rooted primarily in the actions of stalwart allies like Israel, instead of emanating from the perverse and hateful ideologies of radical Islam.

As such, Reverend Wright's comments were not only wrong but divisive, divisive at a time when we need unity; racially charged at a time when we need to come together to solve a set of monumental problems—two wars, a terrorist threat, a falling economy, a chronic health care crisis and potentially devastating climate change; problems that are neither black or white or Latino or Asian, but rather problems that confront us all.

Given my background, my politics, and my professed values and ideals, there will no doubt be those for whom my statements of condemnation are not enough. Why associate myself with Reverend Wright in the first place, they may ask? Why not join another church? And I confess that if all that I knew of Reverend Wright were the snippets of those sermons that have run in an endless loop on the television and You Tube, or if Trinity United Church of Christ conformed to the caricatures being peddled by some commentators, there is no doubt that I would react in much the same way. But the truth is, that isn't all that I know of the man. The man I met more than twenty years ago is a man who helped introduce me to my Christian faith, a man who spoke to me about our obligations to love one another; to care for the sick and lift up the poor. He is a man who served his country as a U.S. Marine; who has studied and lectured at some of the finest universities and seminaries in the country, and who for over thirty years led a church that serves the community by doing God's work here on Earth—by housing the homeless, ministering to the needy, providing day care services and scholarships and prison ministries, and reaching out to those suffering from HIV/AIDS.

In my first book, *Dreams From My Father,* I described the experience of my first service at Trinity:"People began to shout, to rise from their seats and clap and cry out, a forceful wind carrying the reverend's voice up into the rafters. And in that single note—hope!—I heard something else; at the foot of that cross, inside the thousands of churches across the city, I imagined the stories of ordinary black people merging with the stories of David and Goliath, Moses and Pharaoh, the Christians in the lion's den, Ezekiel's field of dry bones. Those stories—of survival, and freedom, and hope—became our story, my story; the blood that had spilled was our blood, the tears our tears; until this black church, on this bright day, seemed once more a vessel carrying the story of a people into future generations and into a larger world. Our trials and triumphs became at once unique and universal, black and more than black; in chronicling our journey, the stories and songs gave us a means to reclaim memories that we didn't need to feel shame about... memories that all people might study and cherish—and with which we could start to rebuild."

That has been my experience at Trinity. Like other predominantly black churches across the country, Trinity embodies the black community in its entirety—the doctor and the welfare mom, the model student and the former gang-banger. Like other black churches, Trinity's services are full of raucous laughter and sometimes bawdy humor. They are full of dancing, clapping, screaming and shouting that may seem jarring to the untrained ear. The church contains in full the kindness and cruelty, the fierce intelligence and the shocking ignorance, the struggles and successes, the love and yes, the bitterness and bias that make up the black experience in America.

And this helps explain, perhaps, my relationship with Reverend Wright. As imperfect as he may be, he has been like family to me. He strengthened my faith, officiated my wedding, and baptized my children. Not once in my conversations with him have I heard him talk about any ethnic group in derogatory terms, or treat whites with whom he interacted with anything but courtesy and respect. He contains within him the contradictions—the good and the bad—of the community that he has served diligently for so many years.

I can no more disown him than I can disown the black community. I can no more disown him than I can my white grandmother—a woman who helped raise me, a woman who sacrificed again and again for me, a woman who loves me as much as she loves anything in this world, but a woman who once confessed her fear of black men who passed by her on the street, and who on more than one occasion has uttered racial or ethnic stereotypes that made me cringe. These people are a part of me. And they are a part of America, this country that I love.

Some will see this as an attempt to justify or excuse comments that are simply inexcusable. I can assure you it is not. I suppose the politically safe thing would be to move on from this episode and just hope that it fades into the woodwork. We can dismiss Reverend Wright as a crank or a demagogue, just as some have dismissed Geraldine Ferraro, in the aftermath of her recent statements, as harboring some deep-seated racial bias.

But race is an issue that I believe this nation cannot afford to ignore right now. We would be making the same mistake that Reverend Wright made in his offending sermons about America—to simplify and stereotype and amplify the negative to the point that it distorts reality. The fact is that the comments that have been made and the issues that have surfaced over the last few weeks reflect the complexities of race in this country that we've never really worked through—a part of our union that we have yet to perfect. And if we walk away now, if we simply retreat into our respective corners, we will never be able to come together and solve challenges like health care, or education, or the need to find good jobs for every American.

Understanding this reality requires a reminder of how we arrived at this point. As William Faulkner once wrote, "The past isn't dead and buried. In fact, it isn't even past." We do not need to recite here the history of racial injustice in this country. But we do need to remind ourselves that so many of the disparities that exist in the African-American community today can be directly traced to inequalities passed on from an earlier generation that suffered under the brutal legacy of slavery and Jim Crow.

Segregated schools were, and are, inferior schools; we still haven't fixed them, fifty years after Brown v. Board of Education, and the inferior education they provided, then and now, helps explain the pervasive achievement gap between today's black and white students.

Legalized discrimination—where blacks were prevented, often through violence, from owning property, or loans were not granted to African-American business owners, or black homeowners could not access FHA mortgages, or blacks were excluded from unions, or the police force, or fire departments—meant that black families could not amass any meaningful wealth to bequeath to future generations. That history helps explain the wealth and income gap between black and white, and the concentrated pockets of poverty that persists in so many of today's urban and rural communities.

A lack of economic opportunity among black men, and the shame and frustration that came from not being able to provide for one's family, contributed to the erosion of black families—a problem that welfare policies for many years may have worsened. And the lack of basic services in so many urban black neighborhoods—parks for kids to play in, police walking the beat, regular garbage pick-up and building code enforcement—all helped create a cycle of violence, blight and neglect that continue to haunt us.

This is the reality in which Reverend Wright and other African-Americans of his generation grew up. They came of age in the late fifties and early sixties, a time when segregation was still the law of the land and opportunity was systematically constricted. What's remarkable is not how many failed in the face of discrimination, but rather how many men and women overcame the odds; how many were able to make a way out of no way for those like me who would come after them. But for all those who scratched and clawed their way to get a piece of the American Dream, there were many who didn't make it—those who were ultimately defeated, in one way or another, by discrimination. That legacy of defeat was passed on to future generations—those young men and increasingly young women who we see standing on street corners or languishing in our prisons, without hope or prospects for the future. Even for those blacks who did make it, questions of race, and racism, continue to define their worldview in fundamental ways. For the men and women of Reverend Wright's generation, the memories of humiliation and doubt and fear have not gone away; nor has the anger and the bitterness of those years. That anger may not get expressed in public, in front of white co-workers or white friends. But it does find voice in the barbershop or around the kitchen table. At times, that anger is exploited by politicians, to gin up votes along racial lines, or to make up for a politician's own failings.

And occasionally it finds voice in the church on Sunday morning, in the pulpit and in the pews. The fact that so many people are surprised to hear that anger in some of Reverend Wright's sermons simply reminds us of the old truism that the most segregated hour in American life occurs on Sunday morning. That anger is not always productive; indeed, all too often it distracts attention from solving real problems; it keeps us from squarely facing our own complicity in our condition, and prevents the African-American community from forging the alliances it needs to bring about real change. But the anger is real; it is powerful; and to simply wish it away, to condemn it without understanding its roots, only serves to widen the chasm of misunderstanding that exists between the races.

In fact, a similar anger exists within segments of the white community. Most working—and middle-class white Americans don't feel that they have been particularly privileged by their race. Their experience is the immigrant experience—as far as they're concerned, no one's handed them anything, they've built it from scratch. They've worked hard all their lives, many times only to see their jobs shipped overseas or their pension dumped after a lifetime of labor. They are anxious about their futures, and feel their dreams slipping away; in an era of stagnant wages and global competition, opportunity comes to be seen as a zero sum game, in which your dreams come at my expense. So when they are told to bus their children to a school across town; when they hear that an African American is getting an advantage in landing a good job or a spot in a good college because of an injustice that they themselves never committed; when they're told that their fears about crime in urban neighborhoods are somehow prejudiced, resentment builds over time.

Like the anger within the black community, these resentments aren't always expressed in polite company. But they have helped shape the political landscape for at least a generation. Anger over welfare and affirmative action helped forge the Reagan Coalition. Politicians routinely exploited fears of crime for their own electoral ends. Talk show hosts and conservative commentators built entire careers unmasking bogus claims of racism while dismissing legitimate discussions of racial injustice and inequality as mere political correctness or reverse racism.

Just as black anger often proved counterproductive, so have these white resentments distracted attention from the real culprits of the middle class squeeze—a corporate culture rife with inside dealing, questionable accounting practices, and short-term greed; a Washington dominated by lobbyists and special interests; economic policies that favor the few over the many. And yet, to wish away the resentments of white Americans, to label them as misguided or even racist, without recognizing they are grounded in legitimate concerns—this too widens the racial divide, and blocks the path to understanding.

This is where we are right now. It's a racial stalemate we've been stuck in for years. Contrary to the claims of some of my critics, black and white, I have never been so naïve as to believe that we can get beyond our racial divisions in a single election cycle, or with a single candidacy—particularly a candidacy as imperfect as my own.

But I have asserted a firm conviction—a conviction rooted in my faith in God and my faith in the American people—that working together we can move beyond some of our old racial wounds, and that in fact we have no choice if we are to continue on the path of a more perfect union.

For the African-American community, that path means embracing the burdens of our past without becoming victims of our past. It means continuing to insist on a full measure of justice in every aspect of American life. But it also means binding our particular grievances—for better health care, and better schools, and better jobs—to the larger aspirations of all Americans—the white woman struggling to break the glass ceiling, the white man who has been laid off, the immigrant trying to feed his family. And it means taking full responsibility for own lives—by demanding more from our fathers, and spending more time with our children, and reading to them, and teaching them that while they may face challenges and discrimination in their own lives, they must never succumb to despair or cynicism; they must always believe that they can write their own destiny.

Ironically, this quintessentially American—and yes, conservative—notion of self-help found frequent expression in Reverend Wright's sermons. But what my former pastor too often failed to understand is that embarking on a program of self-help also requires a belief that society can change. The profound mistake of Reverend Wright's sermons is not that he spoke about racism in our society. It's that he spoke as if our society was static; as if no progress has been made; as if this country—a country that has made it possible for one of his own members to run for the highest office in the land and build a coalition of white and black; Latino and Asian, rich and poor, young and old—is still irrevocably bound to a tragic past. But what we know—what we have seen—is that America can change. That is true genius of this nation. What we have already achieved gives us hope—the audacity to hope—for what we can and must achieve tomorrow.

In the white community, the path to a more perfect union means acknowledging that what ails the African-American community does not just exist in the minds of black people; that the legacy of discrimination—and current incidents of discrimination, while less overt than in the past—are real and must be addressed. Not just with words, but with deeds—by investing in our schools and our communities; by enforcing our civil rights laws and ensuring fairness in our criminal justice system; by providing this generation with ladders of opportunity that were unavailable for previous generations. It requires all Americans to realize that your dreams do not have to come at the expense of my dreams; that investing in the health, welfare, and education of black and brown and white children will ultimately help all of America prosper.

In the end, then, what is called for is nothing more, and nothing less, than what all the world's great religions demand—that we do unto others as we would have them do unto us. Let us be our brother's keeper, Scripture tells us. Let us be our sister's keeper. Let us find that common stake we all have in one another, and let our politics reflect that spirit as well.

For we have a choice in this country. We can accept a politics that breeds division, and conflict, and cynicism. We can tackle race only as spectacle—as we did in the OJ trial—or in the wake of tragedy, as we did in the aftermath of Katrina—or as fodder for the nightly news. We can play Reverend Wright's sermons on every channel, every day and talk about them from now until the election, and make the only question in this campaign whether or not the American people think that I somehow believe or sympathize with his most offensive words. We can pounce on some gaffe by a Hillary supporter as evidence that she's playing the race card, or we can speculate on whether white men will all flock to John McCain in the general election regardless of his policies.

We can do that. But if we do, I can tell you that in the next election, we'll be talking about some other distraction. And then another one. And then another one. And nothing will change.

That is one option. Or, at this moment, in this election, we can come together and say, "Not this time." This time we want to talk about the crumbling schools that are stealing the future of black children and white children and Asian children and Hispanic children and Native American children. This time we want to reject the cynicism that tells us that these kids can't learn; that those kids who don't look like us are somebody else's problem. The children of America are not those kids, they are our kids, and we will not let them fall behind in a 21st century economy. Not this time.

This time we want to talk about how the lines in the Emergency Room are filled with whites and blacks and Hispanics who do not have health care; who don't have the power on their own to overcome the special interests in Washington, but who can take them on if we do it together.

This time we want to talk about the shuttered mills that once provided a decent life for men and women of every race, and the homes for sale that once belonged to Americans from every religion, every region, every walk of life. This time we want to talk about the fact that the real problem is not that someone who doesn't look like you might take your job; it's that the corporation you work for will ship it overseas for nothing more than a profit.

This time we want to talk about the men and women of every color and creed who serve together, and fight together, and bleed together under the same proud flag. We want to talk about how to bring them home from a war that never should've been authorized and never should've been waged, and we want to talk about how we'll show our patriotism by caring for them, and their families, and giving them the benefits they have earned.

I would not be running for President if I didn't believe with all my heart that this is what the vast majority of Americans want for this country. This union may never be perfect, but generation after generation has shown that it can always be perfected. And today, whenever I find myself feeling doubtful or cynical about this possibility, what gives me the most hope is the next generation—the young people whose attitudes and beliefs and openness to change have already made history in this election.

There is one story in particularly that I'd like to leave you with today—a story I told when I had the great honor of speaking on Dr. King's birthday at his home church, Ebenezer Baptist, in Atlanta.

There is a young, twenty-three year old white woman named Ashley Baia who organized for our campaign in Florence, South Carolina. She had been working to organize a mostly African-American community since the beginning of this campaign, and one day she was at a roundtable discussion where everyone went around telling their story and why they were there. And Ashley said that when she was nine years old, her mother got cancer. And because she had to miss days of work, she was let go and lost her health care. They had to file for bankruptcy, and that's when Ashley decided that she had to do something to help her mom. She knew that food was one of their most expensive costs, and so Ashley convinced her mother that what she really liked and really wanted to eat more than anything else was mustard and relish sandwiches. Because that was the cheapest way to eat. She did this for a year until her mom got better, and she told everyone at the roundtable that the reason she joined our campaign was so that she could help the millions of other children in the country who want and need to help their parents too.

Now Ashley might have made a different choice. Perhaps somebody told her along the way that the source of her mother's problems were blacks who were on welfare and too lazy to work, or Hispanics who were coming into the country illegally. But she didn't. She sought out allies in her fight against injustice.

Anyway, Ashley finishes her story and then goes around the room and asks everyone else why they're supporting the campaign. They all have different stories and reasons. Many bring up a specific issue. And finally they come to this elderly black man who's been sitting there quietly the entire time. And Ashley asks him why he's there. And he does not bring up a specific issue. He does not say health care or the economy. He does not say education or the war. He does not say that he was there because of Barack Obama. He simply says to everyone in the room, "I am here because of Ashley."

"I'm here because of Ashley." By itself, that single moment of recognition between that young white girl and that old black man is not enough. It is not enough to give health care to the sick, or jobs to the jobless, or education to our children. But it is where we start. It is where our union grows stronger. And as so many generations have come to realize over the course of the two-hundred and twenty one years since a band of patriots signed that document in Philadelphia, that is where the perfection begins.

我们合众国的人民，为了建立更加完善的联邦．

二百二十一年前，在对面街角那座至今仍旧巍然挺立的大厅中，美国自由的先驱聚集在一起，用简单的话语启动了在当时看来不可能完成的民主试验。这些为逃避暴虐与压迫而远涉重洋来到北美大陆的农场主、学者、政治家和爱国者，终于在 1787 年春天的费城会议上，将独立从宣言变为现实。

这份文件最终签署，但事实上从未完成，它被这个国家奴隶制的原罪所玷污。在那个问题（是否保留奴隶制）上，各殖民地莫衷一是，将整个会议引入僵局。联邦的创建者们选择允许奴隶制至少存在二十年，并将这个问题留给后人去最终解决。

从一开始，奴隶制问题的解决方法就已深埋于宪法之中了——我们宪法的核心就是法律之下的公民权平等理想，它保证给予其人民自由、公正，以及一个能够并且应该随着时间而不断趋向完善的联邦。但是，羊皮纸上的词句却不曾让奴隶们挣脱束缚，或完整地赋予各种肤色、各种信仰的人们作为合众国公民的权利和义务。因此，还需要一代接一代的美国公民用大街小巷的奔走抗议、用法庭上的据理力争，甚至诉诸于战争与对抗，冒着巨大的风险去缩小承诺与现实的差距。

从一开始我们就将建国先父们的美好愿望融入到了这次竞选之中——继续前人的长征，继续这场旨在建立更加公正、平等、自由、博爱、繁荣美利坚的长征。我选择在这样的历史时刻竞选总统，因为我坚信除非我们将这个时代的问题一起解决，除非我们完善这个联邦，否则美国将寸步难行。必须认识到，我们的生活故事可能不尽相同，但是我们的希望只有一个，来自五湖四海、有着不同的相貌与肤色的我们都朝着同一个方向前进，那就是子孙们更好的未来。

这一信念来自我对美国人民高尚与宽容的不可动摇的信任，也来自于我自己的美国故事。我的父亲是肯尼亚黑人，母亲是堪萨斯白人，我在外祖父和外祖母的抚养下长大。外祖父经历过大萧条、打过二战，有幸曾在巴顿将军的队伍里服役，外祖母则在里文沃斯堡的一个轰炸机生产线上工作。我既接受过美国的精英教育，也在世界上最贫困的国家生活过，最后与一个奴隶和奴隶主的后代结合，把这条血脉传给了我们的两个宝贝女儿。我的兄弟姐妹遍及世界三个大洲，他们肤色各异、种族不同。我知道像我这样的故事出现在其他任何一个国家都是不可能的，这段故事把我和其他的候选人区别开来，也在我的心中烙下了对这个国家最基本的理解——“合众为一”。

这场竞选的第一年里，所有相反的预测都被美国人民这种对于团结的渴望所打破。尽管有人试图通过种族的有色眼镜来歪曲这次竞选，我们在这个国家的白人州里所取得的压倒性胜利让所有质疑变得苍白无力。在邦联旗帜人就飘扬的南卡罗来纳州，黑人和白人联合起来，一起站在我的身后摇旗呐喊。

这并不意味着种族问题不再是这次竞选的一个议题。在整个竞选过程中，一直都有评论员说我“太黑”或“不够黑”。种族问题的泡泡在南卡罗来纳州初选的前一周浮到了表面。新闻界在每一个投票站的出口费心地搜寻着黑人和白人之间，甚至黑人和其他人种之间种族对立的证据。

但是，直到最近几个星期，有关种族的讨论才变得特别尖锐和具有攻击性。一方面，我听到了这样一种说法，即我迄今为止在竞选中所获得的一切都不过是一种安抚，不过是自由派廉价求购种族调和表象的伎俩。另一方面，我原来的牧师耶利米·耐特则使用更具煽动性和攻击性的语言来表达自己的立场。这些语言不仅有加深种族矛盾的倾向，还侮辱了这个国家的伟大和善良，使得无论黑人还是白人同样受到了冒犯。

我明确地谴责了耐特这些引发了巨大争议的言论。然而，不管我怎么表述，一些人仍不满足。我是否知道他有抨击美国内政和外交政策的记录？知道。我以前坐在教堂里时有没有听到过他发表争议性的讲话？有。我是不是从一开始就和他的政治观点保持距离？当然——正如你们中的许多人肯定都曾从牧师、神父或拉比那里听过不敢苟同的言论，我想它们的道理是一样的。

然而，这些引发铺天盖地争论的言论不仅仅是观点不同那么简单，也不仅仅是一个宗教领袖对显而易见的社会不公的大声抗议，它将这个国家彻底地、极度地扭曲。这种看法认为白人种族主义根深蒂固，把美国所有问题的根结置于这个伟大国家的种种优点之上；它还认为中东冲突的症结在于我们坚定盟友以色列的胡作非为，而非源自伊斯兰极端主义充满仇恨的意识形态。

耐特充满了种族怨怒的语言不仅是错误的而且是极端的，这个时候我们需要的是团结，是大家走到一起解决重大问题的勇气。我们面临的困难太多：两场战争、恐怖主义威胁、摇摇欲坠的经济、旷日持久的医保危机以及灾难性的气候变化。这些问题不是黑人、白人、拉美裔或者亚裔哪一群人所要面对的，也不是哪一群人能独自解决的，我们必须共同面对。

由于我个人背景、政治经历、价值观和理想的缘故，不论我怎么谴责耐特，总会有人不依不饶，对他们来说发表声明予以谴责是远远不够的。他们的问题几乎是一样的，为什么我会和如此极端一个人做了这么多年朋友？为什么我不加入另一个教会？坦白讲，如果我对耐特牧师的全部了解仅限于那些在电视和YouTube上循环播放的布道片断，如果三一联合基督教堂仅仅是某些评论者所恶意歪曲的那般模样的话，毫无疑问，我会做出同样的反应。但是据我了解，耐特并不完全是这个样子。我二十多年前认识的是这样一个人，他使我皈依了基督，教导我与众人相亲相爱，告诉我照顾病人帮助弱小的责任。他曾在美国海军陆战队为国家服役，曾在这个国家的最高学府和神学院学习并讲学。主持教堂工作三十多年间，他勤恳服务当地社区，按上帝的旨意在人间广播福祉——收留无家可归的人，救人于疾苦，提供婴幼儿日托服务，为学生提供奖学金，到监狱探视犯人并为他们祷告，还向艾滋病患者和艾滋病毒感染者伸出援助之手。

在我的第一本书《父亲的梦想》里，我描述了在三一教堂第一次参加礼拜的经历："人们开始从座位上站起来，呼喊声、掌声疾风一般将那位牧师的声音带上房椽……简单的一句'希望'掷地有声、让我从中听到一些其他的东西。十字架下，全城千百个教堂里，普通黑人在我的想象中成为了圣经故事里的角色：大卫和歌利亚的故事、摩西和法老的故事、基督徒在狮子坑的故事以及《以西结书》中满是骨骸的大地的故事。这些关于生存、自由和希望的故事，也渐渐成为了我们的故事、我的故事，故事里抛洒的热血是我们的热血，挥洒的眼泪是我们的眼泪，晴朗的天空下，这座黑人教堂就好像一艘航船，满载着一个民族的故事缓缓驶进未来的世代，驶向更加宽广的世界。我们的历史立刻变得既独特又普遍，既是黑人的又不仅仅是黑人的。自然而然地，我们将这些黑人化的圣经故事当作是自己的历史，自己的经历来学习和珍惜，有了这些故事，我们才能重建自己的过去。"

这就是我在三一教堂的经历。和全国其他地方以黑人信徒为主的教堂一样，三一教堂就是一个完整的黑人社区——有医生也有接受社会救济的母亲，有模范学生也有黑帮混混。和其他黑人教堂一样，三一教堂的礼拜充满喧闹的笑声，不时还有些粗俗的打趣。他们跳舞、拍手、尖叫或是喧闹，不常来的人还真的会受不了。这座教堂将美国黑人的一切囊括其中，仁慈与残忍、绝顶智慧与浑浑噩噩、奋争与成功、爱与恨以及痛苦与偏见。

也许这些可以更好地解释我与耐特牧师的关系。他也许并不完美，但他对我来说就像是家里的一员。他坚定了我的信仰，主持过我的婚礼，为我的女儿做了洗礼。我从来没听到过他用贬损的语言贬低其他族裔，他从来都是带着礼貌和敬意来对待与他交往的白人。他是一个矛盾的集合体——好好坏坏——就像他多年为之勤奋服务的社区一样。

和他断绝关系就等于和整个黑人社区断绝关系；和他断绝关系，就好比与抚养我长大成人的白人外祖母，一位曾为我一再做出牺牲，一位爱我胜过世界上任何人，一位曾向我坦言她在街上会对身边走过的黑人男子感到害怕，并曾经不止一次将那些令人恐惧的种族偏见挂在嘴边的亲人断绝关系。这些人都是我的一部分，也是这个我深爱着的国家的一部分。

这样说并不是在为这些不可饶恕的言论寻找托词。相信我不是这样的。在这件事情上，保全政治名誉最好的做法莫过于冷处理，让它随着时间一起慢慢淡去。我们大可将耐特看作是个思想偏激或是蛊惑人心的人，就好像某些人对待杰拉尔丁·菲拉萝那样，将他们的种族言论归因于其心中深藏的种族偏见，然后将他们当作无可救药的人抛到一边。

但是，我认为美国的种族问题已经严重到不得不直接面对的程度了。若不如此，我们就会犯和耐特一样的错误——把种族问题简单化、脸谱化，将消极面放大到足以扭曲真实的程度。实际情况是，这些过去几周浮出水面的言论和问题反映了这个国家种族问题的复杂性。这是一个我们从未完全解决的问题，也是我们的联邦需要完善的方面。如果我们现在将它搁置起来，默默地回到自己的角落，我们将永远无法再走到一起来，解决诸如医保、教育和就业等问题。

要认识这一现实，需要回顾一下我们是如何陷入今天这种困境的。威廉·福克纳曾写道："过去既没有死去也没有被埋葬。甚至它根本就还没有过去。"在这里，我们没有必要复述这个国家种族歧视的历史。但是我们需要提醒自己，今天美国非裔社区里存在的众多不公正现象可以直接追溯到奴隶制和从吉姆·克劳法时期代代遗传下来的种族问题流毒。

种族隔离的学校过去是，现在仍然是次等学校。在布朗诉教育董事会案五十年后，这些学校的情况丝毫没有改变。它们提供的次等教育，不管是在过去还是现在，都有助于解释黑人学生和白人学生在学业成就方面存在的普遍差距。

那些合法的歧视——通过暴力禁止黑人拥有财产，拒绝给非裔美国企业主放贷，黑人买房无法享受联邦住房管理局的抵押贷款，黑人被拒绝进入工会、警察局和消防队——意味着黑人家庭无法为自己的下一代积累起足够多的财产。这就解释了为什么黑人和白人在财富和收入上存在巨大差距，为什么今天许多城市和乡村社区存在大量的贫困现象。

黑人男子缺乏工作机会这一事实，以及无法供养家庭所带来的耻辱感和沮丧，让黑人家庭面临危机——在国家现有的福利政策下，这一问题日益恶化。众多城市黑人社区基本社区服务的缺乏——如小孩儿玩耍的公园、警察巡逻、按时回收垃圾和强制建筑标准——最终导致一个无法摆脱的暴力、破败和忽视的恶性循环。

耐特和与他同时代的非裔美国人就是在这样的环境下长大的。二十世纪五六十年代的时候他们开始步入社会，当时种族隔离仍然是合法制度，黑人的诸多机会被制度性地限制或剥夺。但是这些黑人并没有屈服于严酷的环境，他们携起手来披荆斩棘、克服困难，努力为自己的下一代闯出一条路来。然而，能够最终抓住机会成就自己美国梦的黑人毕竟只是少数，他们中仍然有许多人无法实现自己的梦想，不得不以这样或那样的方式屈服于种族歧视的梦魇。这种挫败感遗传到了他们的下一代那里——年轻的黑人男子和越来越多的青年女子闲站街角无所事事，或者慵懒地躺在监狱里，对未来不抱任何希望和期待。即便对那些实现了自己梦想的人来说，种族和种族问题仍旧是他们世界观的基本来源。在与耐特同时代的男男女女脑海里，羞辱、怀疑和恐惧的记忆挥之不去，愤怒和痛苦更难忘怀。这些愤怒也许不会在公开的场合表达出来，不会在白人同事或朋友的面前表达出来。但是一旦到了相对私人的空间，比如餐桌上、理发店里，这些情感就有了倾诉的场合。有时，这些黑人的愤怒被政客们所利用，他们用种族划线捞取选票，或是掩饰其个人的失误。

我们有时也会在周日教堂的讲台或是条椅上听到类似的情感表达。许多人都对耐特布道中的激烈言辞感到震惊，但是这不过再次证明了一个事实，那就是在美国周日早上的这段去教堂祷告时间，种族分裂问题最为激化。这种发泄其实没有任何实际意义，相反，还常常影响我们对实际问题的解决。它让我们无法看清自己也应对此现状负责，让非裔美国人的社区难以联合起来做出什么实际的改变。但是我要说，这种愤怒是真实而强烈的，仅仅希望它自行消失，或是对其不假思索地进行抨击，往往只能让两个种族之间误解的鸿沟越来越大。

事实上，白人社区中也存在着与此相同的情绪。美国劳工阶层和中产阶级中的很多人都觉得自己没有因为他们的种族而获得什么特权。这些人多为移民，在他们看来自己完全就是白手起家，没有拿过谁的好处受过谁的恩惠。他们勤勤恳恳、任劳任怨，但最终却眼睁睁地看着自己的工作机会被转向国外，眼睁睁地看着自己一生积攒下来的退休金缩水。他们对自己的未来感到焦虑，感觉自己距离梦想渐行渐远。在工资不变、国际竞争加剧的情况下，所谓机会实则成为了一个零和博弈，你的成功必定要以我的失败为代价。所以，当他们被告之自己的孩子得坐公交车去上学，当他们听说非裔美国人由于那些并非他们犯下的历史过错在找工作或受教育方面享受了优惠政策，当他们对社区犯罪活动的担忧被视为带有种族偏见的时候，胸中怨恨就会随着时间推移而增长。

和黑人社区的情况类似，这些怨恨绝少会在温和的日常交往中表现出来。但是它所塑造的政治景观影响了至少整整一代美国人。对福利和“反歧视行动”的不满催生出了“里根联盟”。政客们没完没了地拿人们对犯罪的恐惧做文章、捞选票。脱口秀主持人和保守的时政评论员醉心于指责种族主义的言论多么荒唐，将关于种族不公正和不平等的合理讨论归于简单的政治正确或是种族主义的另一种表现。

正如黑人们的情感宣泄常常带来消极作用，白人们的愤怒只会让他们忽略压榨中产阶级的罪魁祸首——充斥着肮脏内幕交易、问题重重的会计活动、短视贪婪逐利的公司文化；被游说者和有特别利益的人占领的华盛顿以及偏向少数利益群体的经济政策。不去成人他们的合法诉求，反而希望这些问题能够不治自愈，或是单纯地把这些人归作被误导者或是种族激进分子，同样会加剧种族矛盾，阻碍种族之间的理解与和解。

这就是我们现在的处境。我们深陷种族主义的泥潭已有多时。与那些批评我的人，不论黑人白人，所持的观点刚好相反，我从未天真地以为种族问题能够因为一次选举而药到病除，更非一次参选就能够明显改善，况且我也不是一个完美的参选者。

但是我已经坚定了自己的信念，这个信念植根于我对上帝的信仰和对美国人民的信任。携起手来我们能够治愈种族主义的顽疾，事实上，如果我们打算在建立一个更加完善联邦的路上继续前进，我们就别无选择。

对黑人社区来说，这条道路意味着勇敢地接过历史的包袱而不被历史所荼毒；意味着继续在社会的各个方面为正义而奔走疾呼；但是，这同样意味着我们必须把自己的诉求，诸如更好的医疗、更好的教育、更好的工作——与全体美国人更大的愿望联系在一起——立志打破玻璃天花板的白人妇女、失业的白人男子以及为家庭而打拼的移民；意味着我们要为自己的生活负责，对我们的父亲提出更高的要求。花更多的时间陪孩子，给他们读书，教他们如何处理可能发生在他们身上的种族歧视。告诉他们无论如何也不要自暴自弃或愤世嫉俗，要让他们坚信命运就在自己的手中。

充满讽刺意味的是，这种经典而保守的美国式的自力更生的论调，常常出现在耐特的布道之中。但是耐特忽略了一点，所谓的自力更生必须建立在对社会的信任之上，相信这个社会是可以改变的。耐特的布道最深层次错误并不在于他公开谈论种族问题，而在于他将我们的社会看的一成不变，仿佛这么多年一点进步也没有。即便这个国家已经接纳了他的教众去竞选国家的最高公职，去建立黑人与白人、拉美裔与亚裔、富人与穷人、年轻人与老人的联盟，他仍然觉得这个社会没有改变。然而，我们知道的和看到的都明白无误的告诉我们，美国可以改变。这是这个国家真正的不凡之处。这一切改变给予我们希望——无畏的希望——它为我们的将来指明方向。

对于白人来说，通向更完善联邦的道路意味着需要承认非裔美国人的痛苦并不仅仅存在于心中。种族歧视的历史是真实的，种族歧视的现状虽不及过去严重，但也依然存在，需要着手解决。解决不能仅仅停留在口头上，而应有实际的行动——包括加大对学校和社区的投入；严格执行民权法案，保证刑事司法体系公正；为这一代人提供前几代人没有的向上发展的阶梯。需要让所有美国人意识到，别人梦想的实现并不会以自己的失败为代价。在健康、福利以及惠及多种族孩子的教育上所投入的每一分钱，最终都将促进美国的繁荣昌盛。

事实上，我们所呼吁的刚好与这个世界所有宗教的理念相契合——己所不欲，勿施于人。圣经教导我们：让我们成为兄弟的守护者。那么就让我们成为兄弟姐妹的守护者，让我们通过政治途径来谋求彼此共同的利益。

在这个国家中我们总是面临选择。我们可以接受助长分裂、冲突和愤世嫉俗的政治。我们可以把种族问题导演成闹剧，就好像我们在辛普森案中所做的那样；或者亡羊补牢，悲剧发生之后再图补救，比如我们在卡特里娜飓风袭击中所做的那样；又或将种族问题交付晚间新闻，任人评说。我们可以在每个频道反复播放耐特的言论，没日没夜地放，一直放到大选，将这次竞选演变为对一个单一话题的讨论，即美国人是否认为我会在一定程度上同意耐特的激烈言辞。我们可以抓住希拉里支持者的某些不恰当言论大书特书，指责她在玩弄种族牌。我们可以推测白人男性选民最终都将把票投给约翰·麦凯恩，不管他的政策如何。

我们可以那么做。但是如果我们做了，我可以告诉你，在下次选举中，类似的话题依然会被提起，然后是下一个，一个接一个。最终什么都不会改变。

当然，那只是我们其中的一个选项。又或许我们能就此携起手来，齐声高呼："再也不能这样了。"我们这次得谈谈那些盗取黑人孩子、白人孩子、亚裔孩子、西班牙语裔孩子和土著孩子未来的日渐破落的学校。这次我们得抛弃那种认为这些孩子不可教或者那些和我们长相不同的孩子是别人的孩子的想法。美国的孩子不是别人的孩子，他们是我们所有人的孩子，不能让他们在二十一世纪的竞争中落后。这一次，再也不能这样了。

这次我们得谈谈医院急诊室的门外为何站满了没有医疗保险的白人、黑人和拉美裔。也许仅凭他们自己还无法和华盛顿的特殊利益群体抗衡，但是如果我们大家能挽起手来，定能和他们较量一番。

这次我们得谈谈那些破败的工厂，它们曾经为各个种族的男女提供体面的生活；这次我们得谈谈那些抵押待售的房屋，曾几何时，它们属于各个宗教、各个地区、各种职业的美国人。这次我们得谈谈一个基本的事实，并不是那些和你相貌不同的人可能会抢走你的饭碗，而是你所工作的公司正在将这些工作机会转移到海外，为的仅仅是利润。

这次我们得谈谈那些肤色不同、信仰各异的男男女女，他们在同一面骄傲的旗帜下一起服役、一起战斗、一起流血。我们得谈谈怎样把他们从这场本不应该授权，更不应该发动的战争中安全地送回。我们得谈谈怎样通过对他们以及他们家庭的关爱，怎样通过给予他们应得的回报来体现我们的爱国主义。

如非坚信这是大多数美国人民的心愿，我不会参加这次总统竞选。这个联邦也许永远都不会完美，但是一代又一代的美国人告诉我们，总有机会让它变得更好。每当我自己对这种可能性表示怀疑和厌倦的时候，美国的下一代给了我最多的希望——这些年轻人的态度、信仰和对变革的包容已经在这次选举中创造了历史。

今天，我有一个特别的故事想带给大家——一个马丁·路德·金博士诞辰那天，我有幸在他的教堂——亚特兰大的埃本内泽浸礼会教堂讲述多的故事。

有个二十三岁的年轻白人妇女名叫阿什利·拜亚，她在南卡罗来纳州的佛罗伦斯为我组织竞选活动。从这次竞选一开始，她大部分时间都扑在黑人社区里。有一天她参加了一个圆桌讨论会，大家围坐在一起聊自己为什么会到这儿来。阿什利说，她九岁那年妈妈得了癌症。由于没法继续上班她被解雇了，医疗保险也没了，一家只能申请破产。阿什利决定得为妈妈做点什么。她知道食物是全家最大的开销，于是阿什利让妈妈相信自己真的很喜欢吃泡菜三明治蘸芥末酱。因为这样吃最便宜。就这样阿什利吃了一年，直到妈妈病情有所好转。她告诉所有参加讨论会的人之所以加入助选活动是因为她能通过这种方式为成千上万想为父母做点事、帮点忙的孩子提供帮助。

阿什利本可以有其他的选择。也许一直都有人告诉她，她母亲之所以这样是因为那些懒惰的黑人躺在福利制度上睡大觉，或者告诉她这一切都是拉美裔的非法移民造成的。但是阿什利并没有听信这些，她选择与大家联合起来，对抗不公平。

阿什利讲完自己的故事之后，挨个儿问房间里的其他人为什么会支持这次竞选。每个人都有自己的故事和理由，有的人理由很具体。最后轮到一位年长的黑人男子，他自始至终都没怎么说过话。阿什利问他为什么来这儿。他没有重复刚刚大家说过的那些理由。他没有说医保或者经济，他没有说教育或者伊战，他也没有说来这儿是为了奥巴马。他对每一个在场的人说，“我来是因为阿什利。”

“我来是因为阿什利。”仅就这句话来讲，一个年轻白人小姑娘和一个年长黑人男子在某一刻达成的共识并不足以改变什么，它不能给生病的人送去医疗保险，不能帮失业的人找到工作，不能为孩子们提供更好的教育。但这是我们的新起点，我们的联邦将从此变得更强大。正如二百二十一年前，一群爱国者在费城签署了那份文件后，一代又一代的美国人意识到的那样，这，就是完善的起点。

第三节 精彩语录

We cannot solve the challenges of our time unless we solve them together—unless we perfect our union by understanding that we may have different stories, but we hold common hopes; that we may not look the same and we may not have come from the same place, but we all want to move in the same direction—towards a better future for our children and our grandchildren.

除非我们将这个时代的问题一起解决，除非我们完善这个联邦，否则美国将寸步难行。必须认识到，我们的生活故事可能不尽相同，但是我们的希望只有一个。来自五湖四海、有着不同的相貌与肤色的我们都朝着同一个方向前进，那就是子孙们更好的未来。

Divisive at a time when we need unity; racially charged at a time when we need to come together to solve a set of monumental problems—two wars, a terrorist threat, a falling economy, a chronic health care crisis and potentially devastating climate change; problems that are neither black or white or Latino or Asian, but rather problems that confront us all.

这个时候我们需要的是团结，是大家走到一起解决重大问题的勇气。我们面临的困难太多：两场战争、恐怖主义威胁、摇摇欲坠的经济、旷日持久的医保危机以及灾难性的气候变化。这些问题不是黑人、白人、拉美裔或者亚裔哪一群人所要面对的，也不是哪一群人能独自解决的，我们必须共同面对。

The blood that had spilled was our blood, the tears our tears; until this black church, on this bright day, seemed once more a vessel carrying the story of a people into future generations and into a larger world. Our trials and triumphs became at once unique and universal, black and more than black; in chronicling our journey, the stories and songs gave us a means to reclaim memories that we didn't need to feel shame about... memories that all people might study and cherish—and with which we could start to rebuild.

故事里抛洒的热血是我们的热血，挥洒的眼泪是我们的眼泪，晴朗的天空下，这座黑人教堂就好像一艘航船，满载着一个民族的故事缓缓驶进未来的世代，驶向更加宽广的世界。我们的历史立刻变得既独特又普遍，既是黑人的又不仅仅是黑人的。自然而然地，我们将这些黑人化的圣经故事当作是自己的历史，自己的经历来学习和珍惜，有了这些故事，我们才能重建自己的过去。

I have asserted a firm conviction—a conviction rooted in my faith in God and my faith in the American people—that working together we can move beyond some of our old racial wounds, and that in fact we have no choice if we are to continue on the path of a more perfect union.

我已经坚定了自己的信念，这个信念植根于我对上帝的信仰和对美国人民的信任。携起手来我们能够治愈种族主义的顽疾，事实上，如果我们打算在建立一个更加完善联邦的路上继续前进，我们就别无选择。

What is called for is nothing more, and nothing less, than what all the world's great religions demand—that we do unto others as we would have them do unto us. Let us be our brother's keeper, Scripture tells us. Let us be our sister's keeper. Let us find that common stake we all have in one another, and let our politics reflect that spirit as well.

我们所呼吁的刚好与这个世界所有宗教的理念相契合——一所不欲，勿施于人。圣经教导我们：让我们成为兄弟的守护者。那么就让我们成为兄弟姐妹的守护者，让我们通过政治途径来谋求彼此共同的利益。

I would not be running for President if I didn't believe with all my heart that this is what the vast majority of Americans want for this country. This union may never be perfect, but generation after generation has shown that it can always be perfected. And today, whenever I find myself feeling doubtful or cynical about this possibility, what gives me the most hope is the next generation—the young people whose attitudes and beliefs and openness to change have already made history in this election.

如非坚信这是大多数美国人民的心愿，我不会参加这次总统竞选。这个联邦也许永远都不会完美，但是一代又一代的美国人告诉我们，总有机会让它变得更好。每当我自己对这种可能性表示怀疑和厌倦的时候，美国的下一代给了我最多的希望——这些年轻人的态度、信仰和对变革的包容已经在这次选举中创造了历史。

第五章

我们所热爱的美国

第一节 背景介绍

在美国参加总统竞选，不是占美国人口多数的盎格鲁撒克逊人后代的竞选者都很容易遭到美国人民的怀疑。人们会怀疑他们是否能维护美国的利益，是否爱美国。1988 年，民主党提名的候选人希腊裔美国人杜卡基斯，由于在任马萨诸塞州州长时，曾根据美国最高法院的判决免除了该州学校学生必须举行“向国旗宣誓效忠”的仪式，共和党就利用美国人的“国旗情结”来质疑他的价值观是否跟美国的价值观相一致，质疑他是否是一个“异己分子”。本来在大选投票之前两三个月的民意调查显示，他击败老布什的可能性很大，但没想到最后还是败在共和党的抹黑手段之下。奥巴马在发现民意调查有四分之一的美国选民认为他缺乏爱国情操之后，认为不能等闲视之，必须赶快加以对付处理。于是，他选择在美国国庆节之前的几天，向人们表明他的爱国之心，同时向人们阐明何谓爱国，何谓不爱国。6 月 30 日，他在杜鲁门总统的故乡密苏里州独立城作了题为《我们所热爱的美国》的演讲。

第二节 奥巴马于2008年6月30日在密苏里州独立城的演讲

On a spring morning in April of 1775, a simple band of colonists—farmers and merchants, blacksmiths and printers, men and boys—left their homes and families in Lexington and Concord to take up arms against the tyranny of an Empire. The odds against them were long and the risks enormous—for even if they survived the battle, any ultimate failure would bring charges of treason, and death by hanging.

And yet they took that chance. They did so not on behalf of a particular tribe or lineage, but on behalf of a larger idea. The idea of liberty. The idea of God-given, inalienable rights. And with the first shot of that fateful day—a shot heard round the world—the American Revolution, and America's experiment with democracy, began.

Those men of Lexington and Concord were among our first patriots. And at the beginning of a week when we celebrate the birth of our nation, I think it is fitting to pause for a moment and reflect on the meaning of patriotism—theirs, and ours. We do so in part because we are in the midst of war—more than one and a half million of our finest young men and women have now fought in Iraq and Afghanistan; over 60,000 have been wounded, and over 4,600 have been laid to rest. The costs of war have been great, and the debate surrounding our mission in Iraq has been fierce. It is natural, in light of such sacrifice by so many, to think more deeply about the commitments that bind us to our nation, and to each other.

We reflect on these questions as well because we are in the midst of a presidential election, perhaps the most consequential in generations; a contest that will determine the course of this nation for years, perhaps decades, to come. Not only is it a debate about big issues—health care, jobs, energy, education, and retirement security—but it is also a debate about values. How do we keep ourselves safe and secure while preserving our liberties? How do we restore trust in a government that seems increasingly removed from its people and dominated by special interests? How do we ensure that in an increasingly global economy, the winners maintain allegiance to the less fortunate? And how do we resolve our differences at a time of increasing diversity?

Finally, it is worth considering the meaning of patriotism because the question of who is—or is not—a patriot all too often poisons our political debates, in ways that divide us rather than bringing us together. I have come to know this from my own experience on the campaign trail. Throughout my life, I have always taken my deep and abiding love for this country as a given. It was how I was raised; it is what propelled me into public service; it is why I am running for President. And yet, at certain times over the last sixteen months, I have found, for the first time, my patriotism challenged—at times as a result of my own carelessness, more often as a result of the desire by some to score political points and raise fears about who I am and what I stand for. So let me say at this at outset of my remarks. I will never question the patriotism of others in this campaign. And I will not stand idly by when I hear others question mine.

My concerns here aren't simply personal, however. After all, throughout our history, men and women of far greater stature and significance than me have had their patriotism questioned in the midst of momentous debates. Thomas Jefferson was accused by the Federalists of selling out to the French. The anti-Federalists were just as convinced that John Adams was in cahoots with the British and intent on restoring monarchal rule. Likewise, even our wisest Presidents have sought to justify questionable policies on the basis of patriotism. Adams' Alien and Sedition

Act, Lincoln's suspension of habeas corpus, Roosevelt's internment of Japanese Americans—all were defended as expressions of patriotism, and those who disagreed with their policies were sometimes labeled as unpatriotic.

In other words, the use of patriotism as a political sword or a political shield is as old as the Republic. Still, what is striking about today's patriotism debate is the degree to which it remains rooted in the culture wars of the 1960s—in arguments that go back forty years or more. In the early years of the civil rights movement and opposition to the Vietnam War, defenders of the status quo often accused anybody who questioned the wisdom of government policies of being unpatriotic. Meanwhile, some of those in the so-called counter-culture of the Sixties reacted not merely by criticizing particular government policies, but by attacking the symbols, and in extreme cases, the very idea, of America itself—by burning flags; by blaming America for all that was wrong with the world; and perhaps most tragically, by failing to honor those veterans coming home from Vietnam, something that remains a national shame to this day.

Most Americans never bought into these simplistic world-views—these caricatures of left and right. Most Americans understood that dissent does not make one unpatriotic, and that there is nothing smart or sophisticated about a cynical disregard for America's traditions and institutions. And yet the anger and turmoil of that period never entirely drained away. All too often our politics still seems trapped in these old, threadbare arguments—a fact most evident during our recent debates about the war in Iraq, when those who opposed administration policy were tagged by some as unpatriotic, and a general providing his best counsel on how to move forward in Iraq was accused of betrayal.

Given the enormous challenges that lie before us, we can no longer afford these sorts of divisions. None of us expect that arguments about patriotism will, or should, vanish entirely; after all, when we argue about patriotism, we are arguing about who we are as a country, and more importantly, who we should be. But surely we can agree that no party or political philosophy has a monopoly on patriotism. And surely we can arrive at a definition of patriotism that, however rough and imperfect, captures the best of America's common spirit.

What would such a definition look like? For me, as for most Americans, patriotism starts as a gut instinct, a loyalty and love for country rooted in my earliest memories. I'm not just talking about the recitations of the Pledge of Allegiance or the Thanksgiving pageants at school or the fireworks on the Fourth of July, as wonderful as those things may be. Rather, I'm referring to the way the American ideal wove its way throughout the lessons my family taught me as a child.

One of my earliest memories is of sitting on my grandfather's shoulders and watching the astronauts come to shore in Hawaii. I remember the cheers and small flags that people waved, and my grandfather explaining how we Americans could do anything we set our minds to do. That's my idea of America.

I remember listening to my grandmother telling stories about her work on a bomber assembly-line during World War II. I remember my grandfather handing me his dog-tags from his time in Patton's Army, and understanding that his defense of this country marked one of his greatest sources of pride. That's my idea of America.

I remember, when living for four years in Indonesia as a child, listening to my mother reading me the first lines of the Declaration of Independence— "We hold these truths to be self-evident, that all men are created equal. That they are endowed by their Creator with certain unalienable rights, that among these are Life, Liberty and the pursuit of Happiness." I remember her explaining how this declaration applied to every American, black and white and brown alike; how those words, and words of the United States Constitution, protected us from the injustices that we witnessed other people suffering during those years abroad. That's my idea of America.

As I got older, that gut instinct—that America is the greatest country on earth—would survive my growing awareness of our nation's imperfections: its ongoing racial strife; the perversion of our political system laid bare during the Watergate hearings; the wrenching poverty of the Mississippi Delta and the hills of Appalachia. Not only because, in my mind, the joys of American life and culture, its vitality, its variety and its freedom, always outweighed its imperfections, but because I learned that what makes America great has never been its perfection but the belief that it can be made better. I came to understand that our revolution was waged for the sake of that belief—that we could be governed by laws, not men; that we could be equal in the eyes of those laws; that we could be free to say what we want and assemble with whomever we want and worship as we please; that we could have the right to pursue our individual dreams but the obligation to help our fellow citizens pursue theirs.

For a young man of mixed race, without firm anchor in any particular community, without even a father's steadying hand, it is this essential American idea—that we are not constrained by the accident of birth but can make of our lives what we will—that has defined my life, just as it has defined the life of so many other Americans.

That is why, for me, patriotism is always more than just loyalty to a place on a map or a certain kind of people. Instead, it is also loyalty to America's ideals—ideals for which anyone can sacrifice, or defend, or give their last full measure of devotion. I believe it is this loyalty that allows a country teeming with different races and ethnicities, religions and customs, to come together as one. It is the application of these ideals that separate us from Zimbabwe, where the opposition party and their supporters have been silently hunted, tortured or killed; or Burma, where tens of thousands continue to struggle for basic food and shelter in the wake of a monstrous storm because a military junta fears opening up the country to outsiders; or Iraq, where despite the heroic efforts of our military, and the courage of many ordinary Iraqis, even limited cooperation between various factions remains far too elusive.

I believe those who attack America's flaws without acknowledging the singular greatness of our ideals, and their proven capacity to inspire a better world, do not truly understand America.

Of course, precisely because America isn't perfect, precisely because our ideals constantly demand more from us, patriotism can never be defined as loyalty to any particular leader or government or policy. As Mark Twain, that greatest of

American satirists and proud son of Missouri, once wrote, "Patriotism is supporting your country all the time, and your government when it deserves it." We may hope that our leaders and our government stand up for our ideals, and there are many times in our history when that's occurred. But when our laws, our leaders or our government are out of alignment with our ideals, then the dissent of ordinary Americans may prove to be one of the truest expression of patriotism.

The young preacher from Georgia, Martin Luther King, Jr., who led a movement to help America confront our tragic history of racial injustice and live up to the meaning of our creed—he was a patriot. The young soldier who first spoke about the prisoner abuse at Abu Ghraib—he is a patriot. Recognizing a wrong being committed in this country's name; insisting that we deliver on the promise of our Constitution—these are the acts of patriots, men and women who are defending that which is best in America. And we should never forget that—especially when we disagree with them; especially when they make us uncomfortable with their words.

Beyond a loyalty to America's ideals, beyond a willingness to dissent on behalf of those ideals, I also believe that patriotism must, if it is to mean anything, involve the willingness to sacrifice—to give up something we value on behalf of a larger cause. For those who have fought under the flag of this nation—for the young veterans I meet when I visit Walter Reed; for those like John McCain who have endured physical torment in service to our country—no further proof of such sacrifice is necessary. And let me also add that no one should ever devalue that service, especially for the sake of a political campaign, and that goes for supporters on both sides.

We must always express our profound gratitude for the service of our men and women in uniform. Indeed, one of the good things to emerge from the current conflict in Iraq has been the widespread recognition that whether you support this war or oppose it, the sacrifice of our troops is always worthy of honor.

For the rest of us—for those of us not in uniform or without loved ones in the military—the call to sacrifice for the country's greater good remains an imperative of citizenship. Sadly, in recent years, in the midst of war on two fronts, this call to service never came. After 9/11, we were asked to shop. The wealthiest among us saw their tax obligations decline, even as the costs of war continued to mount. Rather than work together to reduce our dependence on foreign oil, and thereby lessen our vulnerability to a volatile region, our energy policy remained unchanged, and our oil dependence only grew.

In spite of this absence of leadership from Washington, I have seen a new generation of Americans begin to take up the call. I meet them everywhere I go, young people involved in the project of American renewal; not only those who have signed up to fight for our country in distant lands, but those who are fighting for a better America here at home, by teaching in underserved schools, or caring for the sick in understaffed hospitals, or promoting more sustainable energy policies in their local communities.

I believe one of the tasks of the next Administration is to ensure that this movement towards service grows and sustains itself in the years to come. We should expand AmeriCorps and grow the Peace Corps. We should encourage national service by making it part of the requirement for a new college assistance program, even as we strengthen the benefits for those whose sense of duty has already led them to serve in our military.

We must remember, though, that true patriotism cannot be forced or legislated with a mere set of government programs. Instead, it must reside in the hearts of our people, and cultivated in the heart of our culture, and nurtured in the hearts of our children.

As we begin our fourth century as a nation, it is easy to take the extraordinary nature of America for granted. But it is our responsibility as Americans and as parents to instill that history in our children, both at home and at school. The loss of quality civic education from so many of our classrooms has left too many young Americans without the most basic knowledge of who our forefathers are, or what they did, or the significance of the founding documents that bear their names. Too many children are ignorant of the sheer effort, the risks and sacrifices made by previous generations, to ensure that this country survived war and depression; through the great struggles for civil, and social, and worker's rights.

It is up to us, then, to teach them. It is up to us to teach them that even though we have faced great challenges and made our share of mistakes, we have always been able to come together and make this nation stronger, and more prosperous, and more united, and more just. It is up to us to teach them that America has been a force for good in the world, and that other nations and other people have looked to us as the last, best hope of Earth. It is up to us to teach them that it is good to give back to one's community; that it is honorable to serve in the military; that it is vital to participate in our democracy and make our voices heard.

And it is up to us to teach our children a lesson that those of us in politics too often forget: that patriotism involves not only defending this country against external threat, but also working constantly to make America a better place for future generations. When we pile up mountains of debt for the next generation to absorb, or put off changes to our energy policies, knowing full well the potential consequences of inaction, we are placing our short-term interests ahead of the nation's long-term well-being. When we fail to educate effectively millions of our children so that they might compete in a global economy, or we fail to invest in the basic scientific research that has driven innovation in this country, we risk leaving behind an America that has fallen in the ranks of the world. Just as patriotism involves each of us making a commitment to this nation that extends beyond our own immediate self-interest, so must that commitment extends beyond our own time here on earth.

Our greatest leaders have always understood this. They've defined patriotism with an eye toward posterity. George Washington is rightly revered for his leadership of the Continental Army, but one of his greatest acts of patriotism was his insistence on stepping down after two terms, thereby setting a pattern for those that would follow, reminding future presidents that this is a government of and by and for the people.

Abraham Lincoln did not simply win a war or hold the Union together. In his unwillingness to demonize those against whom he fought; in his refusal to succumb to either the hatred or self-righteousness that war can unleash; in his ultimate insistence that in the aftermath of war the nation would no longer remain half slave and half free; and his trust in the better angels of our nature—he displayed the wisdom and courage that sets a standard for patriotism.

And it was the most famous son of Independence, Harry S Truman, who sat in the White House during his final days in office and said in his Farewell Address: "When Franklin Roosevelt died, I felt there must be a million men better qualified than I, to take up the Presidential task…But through all of it, through all the years I have worked here in this room, I have been well aware than I did not really work alone—that you were working with me. No President could ever hope to lead our country, or to sustain the burdens of this office, save the people helped with their support."

In the end, it may be this quality that best describes patriotism in my mind—not just a love of America in the abstract, but a very particular love for, and faith in, the American people. That is why our heart swells with pride at the sight of our flag; why we shed a tear as the lonely notes of Taps sound. For we know that the greatness of this country—its victories in war, its enormous wealth, its scientific and cultural achievements—all result from the energy and imagination of the American people; their toil, drive, struggle, restlessness, humor and quiet heroism.

That is the liberty we defend—the liberty of each of us to pursue our own dreams. That is the equality we seek—not an equality of results, but the chance of every single one of us to make it if we try. That is the community we strive to build—one in which we trust in this sometimes messy democracy of ours, one in which we continue to insist that there is nothing we cannot do when we put our mind to it, one in which we see ourselves as part of a larger story, our own fates wrapped up in the fates of those who share allegiance to America's happy and singular creed.

Thank you, God Bless you, and may God Bless the United States of America.

在1775年4月的一个春晨，一小群殖民地的居民——农民和商人、铁匠和印刷工人、成年和未成年的男人，告别了他们在列克星敦和康克尔德的家，他们拿起武器开始反对英帝国的专制统治。他们获胜的机会极小，但风险极大——即使他们在战斗中能够幸存下来，如果最终结局是失败的话，他们都将面临叛国的指控而获绞刑。

虽然如此，他们还是决定试试。他们如此做不是为了一个部族或家族，而是为了一个更大的理想。即自由的理想，上天赋予的、不可剥夺的人权的理想。在那个意义重大的日子，随着这一声响彻世界的枪响，美国大革命，即美国实行民主的试验开始了。

列克星敦和康克尔德的那些人属于我们最早的爱国者。在庆祝我们国家诞辰的这一周开始之际，我认为不妨稍息片刻来思考爱国主义的意义——先人的和今人的爱国主义。我们有这样做部分是因为我们正处于战争之中，我们一百五十多万优秀的男女青年已在伊拉克和阿富汗服过兵役，六万人受伤，四千六百多人入土长眠。战争的费用非常高昂，围绕我们在伊拉克的使命的争论也非常激烈。有这么多人付出了牺牲，我们很自然地要更深刻地思考那些我们对国家和我们相互之间应尽的义务。

我们对这些问题进行思考的另一个原因是因为我们正处于一场大选的竞选之中，这可以说是一场近几代人以来最具决定性意义的竞选，一场关系到我们国家今后几年或许几十年发展方向的竞选。我们所进行的不仅是关于许多重大问题——健康保险、就业、能源、教育和退休保障的论争，也是关于价值观的论争。我们如何在保障我们人身和国家安全的同时，保有我们的自由？我们如何恢复一个越来越远离其人民，并越来越被特殊利益集团主宰的政府的公信力？我们如何保证在一个越来越全球化的经济情势下，获胜者对那些不那么幸运的人能尽其义务？我们如何在一个日趋多样化的时代解决我们的分歧？

最后，值得我们思考的是，爱国的意义是什么，因为谁是爱国者，或者谁不是爱国者这个问题，经常毒化了我们的政治论争，其结果是分化了我们而不是团结了我们。我在这次竞选的行程中对此已深有体会。在我一生中，我一直认为我对这个国家深切和坚定不移的爱是理所当然的。它事关我如何被抚养长大，它推动我投身于为公众服务，它让我参与了总统竞选。然而，在过去十六个月的某些时间里，我第一次发现人们怀疑我的爱国心——有些时候这是因为我疏忽而造成的，更多的时候这是某些人为了在政治上多捞好处而造成的，他们想让人对我是什么样的一个人以及我所主张的是什么感到害怕。所以，我现在明确宣布，在这次竞选中，我决不会怀疑别人的爱国主义；但当其他人置疑我的爱国主义时，我也决不会置若罔闻。

我关心此事不是纯粹基于我个人的考虑。毕竟在我们历史上，有许多比我声望和地位都高得多的男士女士，他们的爱国心在至关重大的争论中也都被怀疑过。托马斯·杰斐逊被联邦党人指责过私通法国。反联邦党人同样相信约翰·亚当斯串通英国企图复辟帝制。如出一辙的是，即便我们最具智慧的总统也曾经借爱国的名义来为他们有问题的政策辩护。亚当斯颁布的客籍法与惩治煽动法、林肯中止的人身保护令、罗斯福对日裔美国人的监禁——这些都被辩解为爱国的表现，凡不同意他们政策的人有些时候被扣上了不爱国的帽子。

换句话说，利用爱国主义作为一把政治宝剑或一张政治盾牌的做法由来已久——与我们的共和国同样长久。虽然如此，今天有关爱国主义的争辩，很突出的一点是它仍起源于二十世纪六十年代的文化冲突，其所提出的论点可以追溯到四十年或更多年前。在早期民权运动与反越战时期，不想改变国家现状的人指责任何怀疑国家政策是否明智的人为不爱国。同时，那些二十世纪六十年代所谓“反主流文化”的人，对这个指责所作出的反应是不仅仅批评政府某些特定的政策，而且还攻击美国的象征，极端的例子是攻击美国观念的象征，即焚烧国旗，还把世界所有的问题都归咎于美国，也许最不幸的是，他们没有给予那些从越南退役下来的军人应有的荣誉，直到今天这仍是我们民族的一个耻辱。

大部分美国人从未附和过这种过分简单化的世界观，这种对左派与右派漫画式的界定。大部分美国人明白一个人表示出不同意见并不等于他不爱国，他们也明白一个人对美国传统与固有象征的讽刺挖苦并不一定代表他有多聪慧和高明。但是，那个时期的愤怒与动荡不安从没完全消失。我们的政治仍旧经常地陷于那些陈腐之见中，这在我们最近有关伊拉克战争的争论中特别突显出来。譬如那些反对政府政策的人被扣上了不爱国的帽子，一位将军为了在伊拉克取得胜利提出他最善良的建议却被指责为背叛之举。

考虑到我们所面临的巨大挑战，我们再也不能容忍这种分裂了。没有人会期望有关爱国主义的争吵会消失。毕竟在我们争吵有关爱国主义的时候，我们争吵的是作为一个国家我们是什么样的人，而更重要的，是我们应该是什么样的人。我们大家可以同意的是，没有任何一种党或者任何一个政治哲学可以对爱国主义思想进行垄断。我们最终也能够对爱国主义下一个体现美国共有精神中最可贵成分的定义，不管其是多么粗糙和不完美。

这个定义会是一个什么样的定义？对我和大部分美国人来说，爱国最初是一种本能感觉，这种我对国家的忠诚和热爱起源于我最早的记忆。我指的不仅仅是对‘效忠国旗宣言’的朗诵、对学校感恩节的庆典或对 7 月 4 日（美国国庆节）放烟火的记忆——尽管它们是那么美妙。我更想指出的是，我在孩提时期所受的家庭教育如何使我接纳了美国的理想。

我最早的记忆之一是坐在外公肩上观看我们的宇航员登上夏威夷海滩。我记得人们的欢呼声以及他们挥动的小旗子。我外公向我解释说我们美国人只要想做什么事就必定能做到。那就是我脑中的美国。

我记得听我外婆讲她在二战时在一个轰炸机组装线上的工作经历。我记得我外公给我看他在巴顿将军部队服役时的士兵证。他让我知道他的卫国之举是他最感光荣自豪的源泉之一。那就是我脑中的美国。

我记得我小时候在印尼住了四年。我听妈妈给我读《独立宣言》开头的几个句子：“我们认为下列真理是不言而喻的：人人生而平等，造物主赋予他们若干不可剥夺的权利，其中包括生存、自由和追求幸福。”我记得她给我解释这个宣言适用于每个美国人，黑皮肤的、白皮肤的、褐色皮肤的都适用，里头的字句，还有美国宪法的字句如何保护我们不受不公正的对待，正如那些年我和她在海外时所见到的其他人所遭受的那样。那就是我脑中的美国。

在我大了一些的时候，我这个本能感觉——美国是世界上最伟大的国家，没有由于我察觉到我们国家的种种不完善之处而有所削减：譬如持续不断的种族纠纷、在水门事件中暴露出来的我们政治制度的扭曲和密西西比河三角洲与阿巴拉契亚山脉地区令人痛心的贫困。这不仅是因为在我心里我觉得美国生活和文化中的乐趣、生命力、多样性、自由盖过其一切不完善之处，还因为我体悟到美国从来就不是由于它的完美，而是由于人们坚信它能被塑造成一个更美好的国家而变得伟大。我逐渐明白，我们先辈就是为了这个信念而发起了一场革命，为了我们受治于法而不是受治于人，为了我们可以在法律面前人人平等，为了我们可以自由言论，可以自由与他人集会，可以自由信仰我们之所爱，以及为了我们享有追求个人梦想的权利并能够帮助别人追求他们梦想。

我是一个不同种族的混血青年，在任何种族社团都没有坚实的依靠，甚至没有一只父亲的有力之手的扶助。但对我来说，就是这样一个基本的美国观念，即我们并不受我们出生的偶然性主宰，而可以凭我们的意志来塑造我们的人生，这样一个基本的美国观念决定了我的一生，就像它决定了许许多多其他美国人的一生一样。

这就是为什么对我来说，爱国的含义不仅仅是对地图上的一处地方或对某一类人们表示忠诚，实际上，爱国是对美国的理想表示忠诚——那些任何人都可以为之牺牲、献出一切的理想。我认为这样的忠诚最适合使我们这样一个多种族、多宗教、多习俗的国家合为一体。正是把这些理想付诸于实践，我们才有别于津巴布韦，在那个国家，反对党及其支持者被秘密地搜捕、折磨或杀害；才有别于缅甸，在那个国家，几十万人在一场巨大灾害面前为基本生计挣扎着，就因为一个军人政权害怕把国家对外开放；也有别于伊拉克，在那个国家，尽管我们军人已付出了巨大努力，许许多多伊拉克老百姓也表现出了勇气，不同派系之间的合作，哪怕是有限的，还是难以看到。

我认为那些攻击美国缺点的人并没有真正了解美国，他们没有认识到我们独一无二的伟大的理想以及已获得证实的能激励人们创造一个更美好世界的能力。

当然，恰恰是因为美国并不是一个完美的国家，也恰恰是因为我们的理想不断要求我们做出更多的付出，我们不能把“爱国”定义为对某一位领导人、对某一个政府或对某一种政策的忠诚。马克·吐温，这位美国最伟大的讽刺作家、让密苏里州感到自豪的儿子曾写道：“爱国就是任何时候都支持你的国家，也支持你的政府——但只在这个政府值得你支持的时候。”我们可以期望我们的领导人和我们的政府能捍卫我们的理想，这在我们国家的历史上确实发生过很多次。但是，当我们的法律、我们的领导人或者我们的政府背离了我们的理想的时候，那么普通美国老百姓发出的反对声将成为各种最真实的爱国表现之一。

马丁·路德·金，这位乔治亚州的年轻牧师曾领导过一场运动来促使美国直面其种族不公的悲剧历史中，他也立身行道，始终如一地坚守我们国家的信条——他是一位爱国者。那位首先说出阿布格莱布监狱（美军在伊拉克管治的监狱）对犯人施加虐待的年轻美国兵——他是一位爱国者。认识到以我们国家名义犯下的错误，坚持兑现我们宪法的承诺——这都是爱国者的行为，都是爱国的男男女女为了捍卫美国最可贵之处的行为。这是我们绝不能够忘却的——即使我们与他们有意见分歧，即使他们的话让我们难堪。

对美国理想的忠诚，为了这些理想而愿意发出反对声，除了这些爱国行为之外，我认为爱国若有任何意义的话，必须包含准备牺牲的意愿——准备为一个更崇高的目标而舍弃我们所珍惜的东西。对那些在我们国旗下进行过战斗的人，如我在瓦尔特·里德军医中心碰到的年轻战士以及如约翰·麦凯恩（奥巴马的竞选对手）那样的为了报效国家而甘受肉体折磨的人，我们无需他们拿出更多的证据来证明他们所作出的牺牲。让我再补充一点，不管任何人都不应该贬低他们所作出的贡献，尤其不应该是为了政治竞选而干这种事，双方阵营的支持者都应注意这一点。

对我们穿上军服的男男女女所作出的服务贡献，我们应该深深地感激。实际上，目前有关伊拉克战争的争论所显现出来的好事中有一个就是，不管你支持或反对这场战争，我们军队所作出的牺牲是永远值得尊敬的。

对我们其他人——对我们这些不穿军服或在军队里没有至亲至爱的人，为国家更大的利益做出牺牲仍然是公民的一种义不容辞的责任。可悲的是，近些年，尽管我们处在两场战争之中，这种呼唤大家作出贡献的声音已听不到。“9·11”事件之后，叫我们做的事都是去拣便宜。虽然战争的经费不断攀升，我们之中最富有的人却享有赋税义务的减免。本来我们应该通过协调合作来减少对进口石油的依赖，从而使我们在那些风云莫测的产油区面前不显得那么脆弱，但我们的能源政策却一成不变，造成我们对石油依赖性的增加。

尽管华盛顿方面的领导缺位，但我观察到新一代的美国人正响应这种呼唤，我在走到的每个地方都碰到过他们。年轻人投身于美国复兴的项目，这不仅仅有那些为了我们国家的利益而报名到遥远国家作战的人，还有那些在家乡本土为一个更美好的美国而斗争的人。他们或者到师资匮乏的学校执教，或者到医务人员短缺的医院照顾病人，或者在他们地方社区为更具可持续性能源政策做宣传。

我认为下一届政府的一个任务就是保证这么一个让人投身于服务的运动能够在未来持续发展。我们应扩大“美国队”和发展“和平队”。我们应该鼓励人们为国家服务，将它作为新的大学援助计划要求的一部分，即使我们对那些服务于军队的人已增加补助。

然而，我们必须记住的是，真正的爱国不能通过一系列政府计划强制性地或以立法方式来推行。相反，爱国思想必须常驻于我们心中，栽培于我们的文化中，培育于我们孩子的心中。

在我们作为一个国家进入第四个世纪之际，我们很容易把美国的卓越性视为理所当然。但我们的家长有责任通过家庭和学校，把美国的历史逐渐灌输到孩子的头脑中。我们很多学校缺乏良好的公民知识教育，许多美国青年不知道我们先辈的事迹，也不知道他们制定的奠定我国基础的文献的意义。先辈们全力以赴冒着风险做出牺牲，使我国打赢了战争，度过了经济萧条，获得了争取民权、社会权利和工人权利的伟大斗争的胜利，而许多儿童却对这一切一无所知。

我们需要教育孩子，让他们知道尽管我们面临严重的挑战，尽管我们犯过错误，我们一定能团结起来，使我国变得更加强大，更加兴旺，更加团结，更加公平。我们需要教育他们，美国已成为世界上一支追求美好的力量，被其他国家和民族视为地球上最终的希望。我们需要教育他们，返回自己社区服务是好事，在军队服役很光荣，参与民主政治活动发出自己的声音至关紧要。

我们需要教育孩子，使他们明白一个从政者经常忘记的道理：爱国主义不仅包括保卫我国不受外来威胁，还包括坚持工作，使子孙后代有一个更美好的美国。我们把债务积累如山，等待下一代去偿还，或者明知后果而拒不改变能源政策，这都是把短期利益置于国家长远福利之上。如果我们不能通过教育使上百万美国儿童在全球化经济中具有竞争力，或者不能投资基础科学研究以推动我国的科技创新，我们就可能使美国在世界排名中后退。正如爱国主义要求我们所有人把国家利益置于个人的眼前利益之上，它还要求我们把子孙后代的利益置于我们自己的利益之上。

我们的最伟大的领袖们明白这个道理。他们对爱国主义的定义着眼于未来。乔治．华盛顿因为领导大陆军而得到尊敬，但他的一项最伟大的爱国行动就是在担任两届总统之后坚决离职，为后来的总统树立一个模式，并提醒后来的总统，这是一个为人民所有、受人民统治和为人民谋利益的政府。（注：旧译为民有、民治、民享）

亚伯拉罕·林肯不仅打赢了一场战争，捍卫了美国的统一，而且不愿妖魔化他的战场对手，拒绝屈从于战争带来的仇恨或自以为是，坚持战后的美国不能继续保持那种一半奴隶一半自由人的制度。他相信我们天性中较好的一面，他的智慧与勇气为我们树立了一个爱国主义的典范。

哈里·杜鲁门离职前在白宫的告别演说中说：“富兰克林·罗斯福逝世时，我感觉应该有一百万人比我更有资格担任总统。但经过了所有这一切，经过我在这间办公室工作的所有岁月，我清楚地认识到我确实不是一个人在工作，你们在与我一道工作。没有人民的帮助和支持，任何总统都不能指望领导这个国家，或者承担这个职务的重担。”

最后，最能准确描述我心目中的爱国主义的可能是下列品质——不仅抽象地爱美国，而且对美国人民有一种特别的爱和信心。我一看见我们的国旗就豪情满怀，一听到悲哀孤寂的葬礼号声就热泪盈眶，原因就在于此。因为我们知道我们国家的伟大，它在战争中的凯旋，它巨大的财富，它在科技与文化上的成就，这一切都是美国人民的精力与想象力的结晶；是他们的辛劳，他们的勇往直前，他们的奋斗，他们的不懈努力，幽默感和默默无闻的英雄主义精神的结晶。

这就是我们要捍卫的自由——我们每个人追求自己梦想的自由。这就是我们要追求的平等——不是结果的平等，而是让每个人有平等的机会去尝试获得成功。这就是我们要努力建设的社会——一个让我们抱有信心但有时候有点混乱的民主的社会，一个让我们坚信有志者事竟成的社会，一个让我们看到我们每个人都是一项伟大事业的组成部分，我们以及那些同样宣誓效忠于美国幸福和其独一无二信念的人们的命运休戚与共的社会。

谢谢大家。愿上帝保佑您，愿上帝保佑美利坚共和国。

第三节 精彩语录

Finally, it is worth considering the meaning of patriotism because the question of who is—or is not—a patriot all too often poisons our political debates, in ways that divide us rather than bringing us together.

最后，值得我们思考的是，爱国的意义是什么，因为谁是爱国者，或者谁不是爱国者这个问题，经常毒化了我们的政治论争，其结果是分化了我们而不是团结了我们。

Patriotism is always more than just loyalty to a place on a map or a certain kind of people. Instead, it is also loyalty to America's ideals——ideals for which anyone can sacrifice, or defend, or give their last full measure of devotion. I believe it is this loyalty that allows a country teeming with different races and ethnicities, religions and customs, to come together as one.

爱国的含义不仅仅是对地图上的一处地方或对某一类人们表示忠诚，实际上，爱国是对美国的理想表示忠诚——那些任何人都可以为之牺牲、献出一切的理想。我认为这样的忠诚最适合使我们这样一个多种族、多宗教、多习俗的国家合为一体。

For the rest of us——for those of us not in uniform or without loved ones in the military——the call to sacrifice for the country's greater good remains an imperative of citizenship.

对我们其他人——对我们这些不穿军服或在军队里没有至亲至爱的人，为国家更大的利益做出牺牲仍然是公民的一种义不容辞的责任。

And it is up to us to teach our children a lesson that those of us in politics too often forget: that patriotism involves not only defending this country against external threat, but also working constantly to make America a better place for future generations.

真正的爱国不能通过一系列政府计划强制性地或以立法方式来推行。相反，爱国思想必须常驻于我们心中，栽培于我们的文化中，培育于我们孩子的心中。

That is the liberty we defend——the liberty of each of us to pursue our own dreams. That is the equality we seek——not an equality of results, but the chance of every single one of us to make it if we try. That is the community we strive to build——one in which we trust in this sometimes messy democracy of ours, one in which we continue to insist that there is nothing we cannot do when we put our mind to it, one in which we see ourselves as part of a larger story, our own fates wrapped up in the fates of those who share allegiance to America's happy and singular creed.

这就是我们要捍卫的自由——我们每个人追求自己梦想的自由。这就是我们要追求的平等——不是结果的平等，而是让我们每个人有平等的机会去尝试获得成功。这就是我们要努力建设的社会——一个让我们抱有信心但有时候有点混乱的民主的社会，一个让我们坚信有志者事竟成的社会，一个让我们看到我们每个人都是一项伟大事业的组成部分，我们以及那些同样宣誓效忠于美国幸福和其独一无二信念的人们的命运休戚与共的社会。

第六章

美国的变革时代已经到来

第一节 背景介绍

2008年11月4日，美国诞生了历史上第一位黑人总统——奥巴马。

一时间兴奋、期待、希望、疑惑……各种复杂的情感交织在了一起，其中变革的希望似乎更让人翘首以盼。因为这个时代已经被赋予了太多的无奈，面对机遇和挑战，变革则是必由之路。而奥巴马的横空出世，不仅使“我们需要变革”成了他的最佳广告，而且他的思想、他的作为也已经成了变革的“符号”。

根据已公布的四十八个州和华盛顿特区计票结果，奥巴马攻下二十七个州和华盛顿特区共349张选举人票，远超出中选所需的270张选举人票，共和党对手麦凯恩拿下二十一个州共163张选举人票。两人在北卡罗来纳州和密苏里州票数接近，成绩有待分晓。这两个州加起来共有26张选举人票。

选票方面，奥巴马得票率52%，麦凯恩47%。

麦凯恩在美国东部时间4日午夜前确定大势已去之后，从老家阿利桑那州打电话祝贺奥巴马当选。然后向支持者发表演说，表示尊重国人的选择及理解这场胜利对美国黑人的意义，并表明会协助奥巴马应付未来的挑战。

布什总统则从白宫打电话向奥巴马道贺，保证顺利移交政权，并邀请奥巴马和家人及早到白宫做客。

奥巴马当选消息传开之后，群众纷纷走上街头欢庆胜利，许多人在白宫外面集合，庆祝不得人心的布什政府即将下台。

在芝加哥，奥巴马在如潮般的掌声和呼唤声中，带着妻子和两个女儿出现在竞选总部的舞台上，向二十万支持者发表胜利演说，声称："虽然等待了很长时间，但在今晚这一决定性时刻，由于我们在这次选举中的努力，美国终于迎来了变革。"

2008年11月4日晚，新上任的美国总统奥巴马在故乡芝加哥发表胜选感言。他说，美国目前主要面临三大挑战：伊拉克和阿富汗战争，百年一遇的经济危机以及全球环境问题。

关于未来，奥巴马说："未来的路还很长，而且我们正在艰难地攀登在陡峭的山坡上，我们未必能够在一年或是一个总统任期内达到目标，但美国肯定可以。我们肯定可以达到目标，此前我从未有今天晚上的如此信心，我向你们承诺，我们肯定可以。"

"是的，我们可以。"台下支持者高喊口号，回答奥巴马。

奥巴马说，未来他还有很多艰巨的任务需要完成，如解决金融危机，结束伊拉克战争，给更多人提供健康保险，给孩子们修建更多学校等。

奥巴马在选举中保住了民主党候选人克里在上届大选中拿下的各州，并夺下布什在上届大选赢得的俄亥俄州、佛罗里达州、弗吉尼亚州、艾奥瓦州、新墨西哥州、内华达州和科罗拉多州，奠定胜局，麦凯恩守土无功，饮恨沙场。

奥巴马和民主党控制的新国会面对强大压力，为实现竞选诺言，奥巴马曾许诺当选后和盟国密切合作，恢复美国在世界舞台的领导地位，在十六个月内从伊拉克撤军和增兵阿富汗。

但他最急切的要务是应对金融危机。他建议通过另一轮耗资1750亿美元的经济刺激配套，整顿经济，包括拨款兴建基础设施和进一步减税。

一切都在紧张而急切地等待着奥巴马的领导与抉择。

第二节 奥巴马于2008年11月4日在芝加哥格兰特公园的演讲

If there is anyone out there who still doubts that America is a place where all things are possible, who still wonders if the dream of our founders is alive in our time, who still questions the power of our democracy, tonight is your answer.

It's the answer told by lines that stretched around schools and churches in numbers this nation has never seen, by people who waited three hours and four hours, many for the very first time in their lives, because they believed that this time must be different, that their voice could be that difference.

It's the answer spoken by young and old, rich and poor, Democrat and Republican, black, white, Latino, Asian, Native American, gay, straight, disabled and not disabled—Americans who sent a message to the world that we have never been a collection of Red States and Blue States: we are, and always will be, the United States of America.

It's the answer that led those who have been told for so long by so many to be cynical, and fearful, and doubtful of what we can achieve to put their hands on the arc of history and bend it once more toward the hope of a better day.

It's been a long time coming, but tonight, because of what we did on this day, in this election, at this defining moment, change has come to America.

I just received a very gracious call from Senator McCain. He fought long and hard in this campaign, and he's fought even longer and harder for the country he loves. He has endured sacrifices for America that most of us cannot begin to imagine, and we are better off for the service rendered by this brave and selfless leader. I congratulate him and Governor Palin for all they have achieved, and I look forward to working with them to renew this nation's promise in the months ahead.

I want to thank my partner in this journey, a man who campaigned from his heart and spoke for the men and women he grew up with on the streets of Scranton and rode with on that train home to Delaware, the Vice President-elect of the United States, Joe Biden.

I would not be standing here tonight without the unyielding support of my best friend for the last sixteen years, the rock of our family and the love of my life, our nation's next First Lady, Michelle Obama. Sasha and Malia, I love you both so much, and you have earned the new puppy that's coming with us to the White House. And while she's no longer with us, I know my grandmother is watching, along with the family that made me who I am. I miss them tonight, and know that my debt to them is beyond measure.

To my campaign manager David Plouffe, my chief strategist David Axelrod, and the best campaign team ever assembled in the history of politics—you made this happen, and I am forever grateful for what you've sacrificed to get it done.

But above all, I will never forget who this victory truly belongs to—it belongs to you.

I was never the likeliest candidate for this office. We didn't start with much money or many endorsements. Our campaign was not hatched in the halls of Washington—it began in the backyards of Des Moines and the living rooms of Concord and the front porches of Charleston.

It was built by working men and women who dug into what little savings they had to give five dollars and ten dollars and twenty dollars to this cause. It grew strength from the young people who rejected the myth of their generation's apathy, who left their homes and their families for jobs that offered little pay and less sleep; from the not-so-young people who braved the bitter cold and scorching heat to knock on the doors of perfect strangers; from the millions of Americans who volunteered, and organized, and proved that more than two centuries later, a government of the people, by the people and for the people has not perished from this Earth. This is your victory.

I know you didn't do this just to win an election and I know you didn't do it for me. You did it because you understand the enormity of the task that lies ahead. For even as we celebrate tonight, we know the challenges that tomorrow will bring are the greatest of our lifetime—two wars, a planet in peril, the worst financial crisis in a century. Even as we stand here tonight, we know there are brave Americans waking up in the deserts of Iraq and the mountains of Afghanistan to risk their lives for us. There are mothers and fathers who will lie awake after their children fall asleep and wonder how they'll make the mortgage, or pay their doctor's bills, or save enough for college. There is new energy to harness and new jobs to be created; new schools to build and threats to meet and alliances to repair.

The road ahead will be long. Our climb will be steep. We may not get there in one year or even one term, but America—I have never been more hopeful than I am tonight that we will get there. I promise you—we as a people will get there.

There will be setbacks and false starts. There are many who won't agree with every decision or policy I make as President, and we know that government can't solve every problem. But I will always be honest with you about the challenges we face. I will listen to you, especially when we disagree. And above all, I will ask you join in the work of remaking this nation the only way it's been done in America for two-hundred and twenty-one years—block by block, brick by brick, calloused hand by calloused hand.

What began twenty-one months ago in the depths of winter must not end on this autumn night. This victory alone is not the change we seek—it is only the chance for us to make that change. And that cannot happen if we go back to the way things were. It cannot happen without you.

So let us summon a new spirit of patriotism, of service and responsibility where each of us resolves to pitch in and work harder and look after not only ourselves, but each other. Let us remember that if this financial crisis taught us anything, it's that we cannot have a thriving Wall Street while Main Street suffers—in this country, we rise or fall as one nation, as one people.

Let us resist the temptation to fall back on the same partisanship and pettiness and immaturity that has poisoned our politics for so long. Let us remember that it was a man from this state who first carried the banner of the Republican Party to the White House—a party founded on the values of self-reliance, individual liberty, and national unity. Those are values we all share, and while the Democratic Party has won a great victory tonight, we do so with a measure of humility and determination to heal the divides that have held back our progress. As Lincoln said to a nation far more divided than ours, "We are not enemies, but friends though passion may have strained it must not break our bonds of affection." And to those Americans whose support I have yet to earn—I may not have won your vote, but I hear your voices, I need your help, and I will be your President too.

And to all those watching tonight from beyond our shores, from parliaments and palaces to those who are huddled around radios in the forgotten corners of our world—our stories are singular, but our destiny is shared, and a new dawn of American leadership is at hand. To those who would tear this world down—we will defeat you. To those who seek peace and security—we support you. And to all those who have wondered if America's beacon still burns as bright—tonight we proved once more that the true strength of our nation comes not from the might of our arms or the scale of our wealth, but from the enduring power of our ideals: democracy, liberty, opportunity, and unyielding hope.

For that is the true genius of America—that America can change. Our union can be perfected. And what we have already achieved gives us hope for what we can and must achieve tomorrow.

This election had many firsts and many stories that will be told for generations.

But one that's on my mind tonight is about a woman who cast her ballot in Atlanta. She's a lot like the millions of others who stood in line to make their voice heard in this election except for one thing—Ann Nixon Cooper is 106 years old. She was born just a generation past slavery, a time when there were no cars on the road or planes in the sky, when someone like her couldn't vote for two reasons—because she was a woman and because of the colour of her skin.

And tonight, I think about all that she's seen throughout her century in America—the heartache and the hope, the struggle and the progress, the times we were told that we can't, and the people who pressed on with that American creed: Yes we can.

At a time when women's voices were silenced and their hopes dismissed, she lived to see them stand up and speak out and reach for the ballot. Yes we can.

When there was despair in the dust bowl and depression across the land, she saw a nation conquer fear itself with a New Deal, new jobs and a new sense of common purpose. Yes we can.

When the bombs fell on our harbor and tyranny threatened the world, she was there to witness a generation rise to greatness and a democracy was saved. Yes we can.

She was there for the buses in Montgomery, the hoses in Birmingham, a bridge in Selma, and a preacher from Atlanta who told a people that "We Shall Overcome." Yes we can.

A man touched down on the moon, a wall came down in Berlin, a world was connected by our own science and imagination. And this year, in this election, she touched her finger to a screen, and cast her vote, because after 106 years in America, through the best of times and the darkest of hours, she knows how America can change. Yes we can.

America, we have come so far. We have seen so much. But there is so much more to do. So tonight, let us ask ourselves—if our children should live to see the next century, if my daughters should be so lucky to live as long as Ann Nixon

Cooper, what change will they see? What progress will we have made?

This is our chance to answer that call. This is our moment. This is our time, to put our people back to work and open doors of opportunity for our kids; to restore prosperity and promote the cause of peace; to reclaim the American Dream and reaffirm that fundamental truth, that, out of many, we are one; that while we breathe, we hope, and where we are met with cynicism, and doubts, and those who tell us that we can't, we will respond with that timeless creed that sums up the spirit of a people: Yes We Can.

Thank you, God bless you, and may God Bless the United States of America.

美国是否暗藏一切皆有可能的巨大潜力？美国是否已经实现开国者锻造的美国梦？民主信仰是否具有强大力量？如果还有人对此报以怀疑，那么今晚这里发生的一切就是答案。

学校旁、教堂边无数人都在排队投票，这一情景我们已经多年未见；三个小时、四个小时他们为此而等候良久，这是很多同胞有生以来的第一次。因为他们相信，这一次将不同以往，这一次他们的呼声有所不同。

无论老少贫富，无论共和党抑或民主党，不管是黑人、白人、拉丁后裔、亚裔子孙还是本土美国人，无论性向如何，不管健康抑或残疾，所有的美国人民都向全世界传递出这样一条信息：我们从来都不是红蓝阵营的政治堆砌，我们是，而且永远是，美利坚合众国。

长期以来，很多人缺乏信心，对自己所能取得的成就畏首畏尾、疑心重重。如今，我们走在历史的长河里，挺起胸膛，勾勒出美好明天的光辉画卷。

此情此景，等待尤长。然而，就在今晚，在这个大选的日子，在这个具有历史性意义的时刻，由于你们的付出，美国终于迎来了变革。

刚刚我接到了麦凯恩参议员很有风度的祝贺电话。为了此次竞选，他奋战良久、竭尽所能；为了他所深爱的美国，他曾作出了更长久、更努力的奉献。麦凯恩参议员为美国所作出的牺牲是大部分人难以想象的，他这种英勇无私的奉献改善了我们的生活。对于麦凯恩参议员和佩林州长所取得的成就，我对他们致以祝贺。在接下来的几个月里，以重振美国为目标，我期待着与他们的合作。

在此，我想感谢一路陪伴我的竞选搭档，他就是我们即将上任的副总统乔·拜登。为了让美国广大的工人阶层发出自己的声音，他毫无私心地全身心投入竞选，因为他和那些宾夕法尼亚州斯克兰顿城街头的人们一样，出身平凡，一切白手起家。

如果没有米歇尔·奥巴马，美国准第一夫人的坚定支持，今晚，我就不会站在这儿了。我们相伴走过了十六个春秋，她是我们整个家庭的顶梁柱，我一生的挚爱。还有萨沙和玛利亚，我爱你们，你们姊妹俩终于可以带着你们的新宠物狗入主白宫了。我知道就像我的其他已故亲属一样，外祖母一定也在某处注视着我，虽然她已经不在人世。是他们造就了今天的我。今晚我很想念他们，我对他们的亏欠无以计量。

我想对我的竞选经理大卫·普劳夫、首席战略师大卫·阿克塞尔罗德以及我们这个史上最佳的竞选团队说，是你们让这一切成为了现实，对于你们为此所作的牺牲和付出我永远感怀在心。

然而，有一点是最重要的，那就是我永远都不会忘记，真正拥有这个胜利的是你们，你们所有人！

对于入主白宫，我从来都不是最热候选人。竞选伊始，我们的资金并不充裕，获得的支持也不多。我们的竞选班子并非始于华府，而是一路从艾奥瓦州的得梅因酒店后院辗转北卡罗莱纳州的康克酒店客房，后来会首在西弗吉尼亚州查尔斯顿酒店的主厅。

我们的胜利来自于广大工薪阶级，正是他们从仅有的微薄存款里掏出5美元、10美元或者20美元来支持我们的竞选。我们的力量来自于摘下冷漠面罩的年轻一代，来自于夜以继日奋力工作以维持生计的下层百姓，来自于冒着严寒酷暑、户户敲门宣传的团队中流砥柱，更来自于成千上万的大选志愿者。他们用出色的奉献精神和组织能力证明了一个民有、民治、民享的政府在两百年后仍然保持着生命力。这就是你们的胜利！

我明白你们所做的这些，并不仅仅是为了赢得这次竞选，也不单单只是为了我本人。你们之所以这么做，是因为你们懂得前方任务的艰巨。即使我们今晚沉浸于庆祝的喜悦之中，我们也深知明天面临的将是我们这辈子最为艰巨的挑战：两场战争、濒临危险的地球和百年一遇的金融危机；即使今晚我们安然站在此处，我们也深知那些深陷伊拉克沙漠和阿富汗山区的英勇美国战士，是为了我们而冒着生命危险。还有那些孩子早已熟睡、自己却辗转反侧的人父人母，他们夜不能寐，想着如何还清房贷、如何支付医药费以及给孩子存下大学经费。我们要掌握新能源，创造就业岗位，建造新校舍，正视存在的威胁，并修复与盟友的关系。

前方的道路很漫长，我们将步履维艰。我们也许无法在一年内，甚至是一个任期内，达成我们的目标。但是，今晚，我比任何时候都对此更有信心。我承诺，我们所有人将作为一个整体顺利地到达目的地。

我们将不可避免地遭遇许多挫折，也许开头并不会一帆风顺。我们需要弄明白一点，那就是政府无法解决所有的问题，也许有很多人不会同意我上台执政后制定的政策。不过，我将坦诚地接受各方的批评，直面我们的挑战。我将倾听你们的意见，尤其是不同的政见。总之，我邀请各位一同投入到国家的建设中来，用我们勤劳的双手堆砌建设这个国家所需的砖瓦。正是这一方式，使美国在二百二十一年的建国道路上不断前行。

我在二十一个月前的深冬开始为竞选做出的努力并不会在今晚画上句号。我们所追求的并不是这场选举的胜利，这仅仅是为我们提供了一个做出变革的机会。如果回到过去的老路，我们将无法做出任何改变。当然，如果没有你们，一切都无法发生。

所以，让我们一同唤醒自己的爱国心，唤醒为国效力的责任感。我们将一起披星戴月，披荆斩棘向前行进，我们需要照顾的不再只有我们自己，而是每一个人。这次的金融危机让我们认识到一个事实，如果大众受苦受难，华尔街就不可能繁华似锦。我们必须携手与共、共同经历这个国家的荣辱兴衰。

长期以来，两党隔阂以及不成熟的狭隘主义造成了我们现在的失败政策，所以让我们一同抵制住这种倾向，避免回到那条老路。请记住，这个国家有一个民主党人将第一次手扛民主和共和两党旗帜迈向白宫。充满自信，崇尚个人自由，维护国家团结将是我们共同追求的价值观。尽管民主党在今晚取得了压倒性的胜利，但是我们将继续带着谦卑前行，愈合这个国家因分裂受到的创伤。社会的分裂曾经阻碍我们国家前行的脚步。正如林肯总统在 1861 年的反国家分裂的演说中说道："我们不是敌人而是朋友，我们决不能成为敌人。尽管目前的情绪有些紧张，但决不能容许它使我们之间的亲密情感纽带破裂。”我要告诉那些没有将选票投给我的朋友，也许我没有赢得你们的选票，但我将聆听你们的声音，我需要你们的帮助，因为我同样将成为你们的总统。

我要告诉那些在美国大陆以外关注今晚选举的人们，也许你们在一个被世界遗忘的角落通过收音机了解今晚的选举，尽管我们的国情不一样，但是我们的命运是紧紧联系在一起的。一个全新的美国领导层即将呼之欲出。我要告诉那些试图破坏这个世界的人们，我们将打败你们！我要告诉那些追求和平和安全的人们，我们将全力支持你们！我要告诉那些对美国的未来持怀疑态度的人们，今晚，我们再次证明了一个事实，那就是这个国家拥有强大的力量，这并不是因为我们拥有众多的武器和财富。民主、自由、机遇、坚定不屈的希望才是这个国家保持强大的持久力量！

美国强大的真谛在于它能够做出改变，我们的国家可以变得更加完美。我们过去所达到的成就让我们看到了前进的希望。

本届选举创造了多项历史之最，有许多故事将代代相传。但此时此刻，我脑海中想起的是一名来自亚特兰大的选民，这位名叫安妮·尼克松·库珀的女性和千千万万的选民一样，静静地站在投票队伍之中，投出自己的选票，表达自己的声音。不过，与众不同的是，她已经一百零六岁高龄了。在她出生的年代，公路上没有汽车，天空中没有飞机。像她一样的人仅仅因为肤色和性别就被挡在参与投票的大门之外。

今晚，我由此联想到了她一个世纪以来，在美国见证的一切：困苦与希望，奋斗与进步。那是一个让人无能为力的年代，但人们必须不断告诉自己美国的伟大信条：是的，我们可以！

曾经，女性无法表达自己的意见，她们的希望成为幻影。如今，她终于见证了这一幕，和她一样有着悲惨遭遇的人们成功地投出了自己的选票。是的，我们可以！

当整个美国大陆都笼罩在经济大萧条的绝望之中时，她见证了一个国家战胜自身恐惧重新崛起，罗斯福总统推行的“新政”不仅给美国带来了新的就业机会，更给美国人民带来了共同的价值观。是的，我们可以！

当敌人的炮弹投向我们的港口，当世界被暴政所威胁，她见证了一个崛起的民族，民主重获新生。是的，我们可以！

她看到蒙哥马利通了公共汽车、伯明翰接上了水管、塞尔马建了桥，而后，来自亚特兰大的民权先驱告诉人们："我们可以战胜这一切"。是的，我们可以！

而后，人类登月，柏林墙倒塌，世界重新集结在科学和想象力的号角下。现在，在这场选举中她终于用自己的指尖触碰到投票屏幕，郑重地投下选票。饱经一百零六年的沧桑变化，穿越岁月的风云变迁，她知道美国能做出怎样的改变。是的，我们可以！

美国，我们风雨兼程一路走来。我们经历了太多，但前方仍有许多梦想等待着我们去实现。今晚，让我们大声地问自己，如果我们的孩子能看到下一个世纪；如果我可爱的女儿能和安妮·尼克松·库珀一样幸运，享受漫长的人生，他们将看到怎样的变革？我们将取得怎样的进步？

这是我们给出答案的机会。这是属于我们的时刻。这是我们的时代：让人们有事可做；为我们的孩子打开机遇之门；推动世界和平与繁荣；再次锻造美国梦，重申这一不可动摇的事实——虽然我们每个人不尽相同，但我们是一个整体，只要我们呼吸尚存，希望就永不磨灭。我们将用那历经时间考验的不朽信条掷地有声地直面质疑："是的，我们可以！"

谢谢！上帝保佑你们，保佑美利坚合众国！

第三节 精彩语录

But I will always be honest with you about the challenges we face. I will listen to you, especially when we disagree. And, above all, I will ask you to join in the work of remaking this nation, the only way it's been done in America for 221 years—block by block, brick by brick, calloused hand by calloused hand.

但我也会向你们诚恳地交待我们所面临的挑战。我会认真听从你们的建议，尤其是意见不一致的时候。总之，我邀请你们加入到国家的重建工作之中。二百二十一年来，我们的国家就是这样一砖一瓦，一点一滴地建造起来的。

So let us summon a new spirit of patriotism, of responsibility, where each of us resolves to pitch in and work harder and look after not only ourselves, but each other.

所以，让我们一同唤醒自己的爱国心，唤醒为国效力的责任感。我们将一起披星戴月，披荆斩棘向前行进，我们需要照顾的不再只有我们自己，而是每一个人。

This is our time, to put our people back to work and open doors of opportunity for our kids; to restore prosperity and promote the cause of peace; to reclaim the American dream and reaffirm that fundamental truth, that, out of many, we are one; that while we breathe, we hope. And where we are met with cynicism, and doubts and those who tell us that we can't, we will respond with that timeless creed that sums up the spirit of a people: Yes, we can.

这是我们的时代：让人们有事可做；为我们的孩子打开机遇之门；推动世界和平与繁荣；再次锻造美国梦，重申这一不可动摇的事实——虽然我们每个人不尽相同，但我们是一个整体，只要我们呼吸尚存，希望就永不磨灭。我们将用那历经时间考验的不朽信条掷地有声地直面质疑：“是的，我们可以！”

第七章

自由的新生

第一节 背景介绍

2007 年至 2009 年的环球金融危机，又称世界金融危机、次贷危机、信用危机，并于 2008 年起名为金融海啸及华尔街海啸等，是一场在 2007 年 8 月 9 日开始浮现的金融危机。自次级房屋信贷危机爆发后，投资者开始对按揭证券的价值失去信心，引发流动性危机。即使多国中央银行多次向金融市场注入巨额资金，也无法阻止这场金融危机的爆发。直到 2008 年 9 月 9 日，这场金融危机开始失控，并导致多家大型金融机构倒闭或被政府接管。

由次债危机引发的美国金融危机愈演愈烈，到目前为止已经有数家大型投行及金融机构在危机中轰然倒塌或被对手兼并，华尔街人人自危。美国金融危机不仅引发美国国内的金融恐慌，也引起世界主要金融市场的担忧和震荡。人们担心这场金融危机可能会导致二十世纪三十年代那场经济大萧条悲剧重演，把美国乃至世界的经济推向动荡深渊。

出于此种担忧，华盛顿高层，从布什总统到财政部长鲍尔森，以及联邦储备委员会主席伯南特，一致希望采取紧急措施应对危机进行“救市”。除去鲍尔森大手笔进行救助的几家金融机构外，最近在布什总统的支持下他又抛出了 7000 亿美元的救市计划。

华尔街的金融动荡除了引起美国政府高层的高度关注与积极行动，也影响到当时正在紧张进行的总统大选。共和党总统候选人麦凯恩甚至一度宣布中断总统竞选回到国会商讨应对金融危机的对策，展示其“领导能力和责任感”。在定于9月26日（美国时间）的首场总统候选人的辩论前夕，麦凯恩甚至一度表示为了应对危机，不惜不参加首场辩论。当然最后麦凯恩还是如期赴会，参加了首场总统辩论。民主党总统候选人奥巴马在一开始本来拒绝中断总统竞选，表示“作为总统意味着能够同时处理几件事”，但在麦凯恩已经中断竞选回到国会山，小布什又亲自致电要求两位总统候选人赴国会共商国事的情况下，只得如期赴会。

不过，这次“三巨头”聚会国会山并没有取得预期效果。虽然布什在最后不厌其烦地向国会议员渲染此次金融危机的严峻性，表示如果不采取紧急救市计划，美国经济将面临严重危机，给美国人的生活造成严重影响。众议院多数党领袖民主党人佩洛西以及少数党领袖共和党人约翰博纳也在众议院投票表决前进行动员，但在9月29日（美国时间）举行的众议院投票表决中，结果以228对205票挫败了布什总统的7000亿美元救市计划。在进行投票的众议员中，投赞成票的，民主党共140票，共和党只有65票。

这样的投票结果，不仅让布什总统深感失望，也导致人们对于国会议员的一片指责。投票结束后，美国国会就收到如雪片般飞来的电子邮件与电话，其中绝大多数是对美国国会议员的指责与质问，指责他们不负责任。在10月1日发行的《华盛顿邮报》中，有一篇文章对此投票结果作出评价，认为这不仅仅是救市计划的失败，也意味着布什总统、财政部长、国会两党主席的失败，甚至是两位总统候选人，特别是麦凯恩的失败。布什总统的救市计划遭到主要是本党议员的反对和挫败，说明这位“跛脚鸭”已经基本上失去本党的支持，毫无威信可言，这也表明本党议员对布什总统非常不满与失望，这次投票在某种意义上也算是对布什执政的打分投票。这投票似乎也与布什在民调中的结果相呼应，在《华盛顿邮报》与ABC新闻举行的联合调查中，对布什的支持率仅为26%，而不支持率占70%，后者在美国历史上绝无仅有。

救市计划受挫也是国会共和、民主党两位主席的失败，因为尽管两者在投票前都对本党及对方进行了宣传演说并做了大量工作，但投票结果却不啻是一记耳光，说明他们各自对本党的影响力极其有限。同时这也是麦凯恩的失败，因为此前他曾中断选举要进行救市，但却未能对投票结果有任何影响，甚至未能改变来自他本州的共和党议员的投票倾向，后者全部投反对票。当然这也是财政部长鲍尔森的失败，表明至少他没有把救市计划向国会议员和美国民众说明清楚，让后者认为救市计划是拿纳税人的钱挽救那些贪得无厌、不负责任的华尔街高管，是劫贫济富，使那些有可能打算投票支持的议员投鼠忌器，不敢投赞成票。

众议院的投票结果加剧了人们的恐慌心理，就在投票结果出来的当天，美国道琼斯股指暴跌778点，下挫7%，甚至超过9·11恐怖袭击对美国股市的重创。美国股市的重挫还波及全球，导致全球主要股市巨幅下挫。这一结果对美国大选议题设置、选民投票偏好无疑会产生影响。民调显示，民众更为关心哪位总统候选人能够处理好美国的经济问题。而在经济议题上，民主党人奥巴马无疑占据优势，因为选民认为民主党更会处理经济问题，民调结果表明，民众认为奥巴马更理解美国的经济问题。

2009年年初，在总统就职演讲中，奥巴马宣称美国在迎接一个新的责任时代的到来。实际上，很多美国人也确实认为新时代到来了。但通过对密执安大学社会研究所最新发布的《美国全国选举研究》关于2008年总统选举前后的民意测验资料进行分析，可以发现决定奥巴马当选的社会政治背景并没有超出自罗斯福新政以来所形成的社会政治势力基本格局，经济、群体关系和国家安全仍然是围绕美国总统选举的三个长期性主题。

1月19日，在美国首都华盛顿，国会山和国家广场一带的人流熙熙攘攘。奥巴马将于1月20日在国会山宣誓就任美国第五十六届（第四十四任）总统，大批民众连日来从四面八方涌入首都，见证奥巴马就职。

第二节 奥巴马于2009年1月20日在华盛顿特区国会大厦前的演讲

My fellow citizens:

I stand here today humbled by the task before us, grateful for the trust you have bestowed, mindful of the sacrifices borne by our ancestors. I thank President Bush for his service to our nation, as well as the generosity and cooperation he has shown throughout this transition.

Forty-four Americans have now taken the presidential oath. The words have been spoken during rising tides of prosperity and the still waters of peace. Yet, every so often the oath is taken amidst gathering clouds and raging storms. At these moments, America has carried on not simply because of the skill or vision of those in high office, but because we the people have remained faithful to the ideals of our forebears, and true to our founding documents.

So it has been. So it must be with this generation of Americans.

That we are in the midst of crisis is now well understood. Our nation is at war, against a far-reaching network of violence and hatred. Our economy is badly weakened, a consequence of greed and irresponsibility on the part of some, but also our collective failure to make hard choices and prepare the nation for a new age.

Homes have been lost, jobs shed, businesses shuttered. Our health care is too costly, our schools fail too many, and each day brings further evidence that the ways we use energy strengthen our adversaries and threaten our planet.

These are the indicators of crisis, subject to data and statistics. Less measurable but no less profound is a sapping of confidence across our land, a nagging fear that America's decline is inevitable, and that the next generation must lower its sights.

Today I say to you that the challenges we face are real. They are serious and they are many. They will not be met easily or in a short span of time. But know this, America, they will be met.

On this day, we gather because we have chosen hope over fear, unity of purpose over conflict and discord.

On this day, we come to proclaim an end to the petty grievances and false promises, the recriminations and worn out dogmas, that for far too long have strangled our politics.

We remain a young nation, but in the words of *Scripture*, the time has come to set aside childish things. The time has come to reaffirm our enduring spirit; to choose our better history; to carry forward that precious gift, that noble idea, passed on from generation to generation: the God-given promise that all are equal, all are free and all deserve a chance to pursue their full measure of happiness.

In reaffirming the greatness of our nation, we understand that greatness is never a given. It must be earned. Our journey has never been one of shortcuts or settling for less. It has not been the path for the faint-hearted, for those who prefer leisure over work, or seek only the pleasures of riches and fame. Rather, it has been the risk-takers, the doers, the makers of things—some celebrated but more often men and women obscure in their labor, who have carried us up the long, rugged path towards prosperity and freedom.

For us, they packed up their few worldly possessions and traveled across oceans in search of a new life. For us, they toiled in sweatshops and settled the West, endured the lash of the whip and plowed the hard earth. For us, they fought and died, in places like Concord and Gettysburg; Normandy and Khe Sahn.

Time and again these men and women struggled and sacrificed and worked till their hands were raw so that we might live a better life. They saw America as bigger than the sum of our individual ambitions, greater than all the differences of birth or wealth or faction.

This is the journey we continue today. We remain the most prosperous, powerful nation on Earth. Our workers are no less productive than when this crisis began. Our minds are no less inventive, our goods and services no less needed than they were last week or last month or last year. Our capacity remains undiminished. But our time of standing pat, of protecting narrow interests and putting off unpleasant decisions—that time has surely passed. Starting today, we must pick ourselves up, dust ourselves off, and begin again the work of remaking America.

For everywhere we look, there is work to be done. The state of the economy calls for action, bold and swift, and we will act, not only to create new jobs, but to lay a new foundation for growth. We will build the roads and bridges, the electric grids and digital lines that feed our commerce and bind us together. We will restore science to its rightful place, and wield technology's wonders to raise health care's quality and lower its cost. We will harness the sun and the winds and the soil to fuel our cars and run our factories. And we will transform our schools and colleges and universities to meet the demands of a new age. All this we can do. And all this we will do.

Now, there are some who question the scale of our ambitions, who suggest that our system cannot tolerate too many big plans. Their memories are short. For they have forgotten what this country has already done, what free men and women can achieve when imagination is joined to common purpose, and necessity to courage.

What the cynics fail to understand is that the ground has shifted beneath them, that the stale political arguments that have consumed us for so long no longer apply. The question we ask today is not whether our government is too big or too small, but whether it works, whether it helps families find jobs at a decent wage, care they can afford, a retirement that is dignified. Where the answer is yes, we intend to move forward. Where the answer is no, programs will end. And those of us who manage the public's dollars will be held to account, to spend wisely, reform bad habits, and do our business in the light of day, because only then can we restore the vital trust between a people and their government.

Nor is the question before us whether the market is a force for good or ill. Its power to generate wealth and expand freedom is unmatched, but this crisis has reminded us that without a watchful eye, the market can spin out of control, and that a nation cannot prosper long when it favors only the prosperous. The success of our economy has always depended not just on the size of our gross domestic product, but on the reach of our prosperity, on our ability to extend opportunity to every willing heart, not out of charity, but because it is the surest route to our common good.

As for our common defense, we reject as false the choice between our safety and our ideals. Our founding fathers, faced with perils we can scarcely imagine, drafted a charter to assure the rule of law and the rights of man, a charter expanded by the blood of generations. Those ideals still light the world, and we will not give them up for expedience's sake. And so to all other peoples and governments who are watching today, from the grandest capitals to the small village where my father was born: know that America is a friend of each nation and every man, woman, and child who seeks a future of peace and dignity, and that we are ready to lead once more.

Recall that earlier generations faced down fascism not just with missiles and tanks, but with sturdy alliances and enduring convictions. They understood that our power alone cannot protect us, nor does it entitle us to do as we please. Instead, they knew that our power grows through its prudent use; our security emanates from the justness of our cause, the force of our example, the tempering qualities of humility and restraint.

We are the keepers of this legacy. Guided by these principles once more, we can meet those new threats that demand even greater effort, even greater cooperation and understanding between nations. We will begin to responsibly leave Iraq to its people, and forge a hard-earned peace in Afghanistan. With old friends and former foes, we will work tirelessly to lessen the nuclear threat, and roll back the specter of a warming planet. We will not apologize for our way of life, nor will we waver in its defense, and for those who seek to advance their aims by inducing terror and slaughtering innocents, we say to you now that our spirit is stronger and cannot be broken; you cannot outlast us, and we will defeat you.

For we know that our patchwork heritage is a strength, not a weakness. We are a nation of Christians and Muslims, Jews and Hindus, and non-believers. We are shaped by every language and culture, drawn from every end of this Earth; and because we have tasted the bitter swill of civil war and segregation, and emerged from that dark chapter stronger and more united, we cannot help but believe that the old hatreds shall someday pass; that the lines of tribe shall soon dissolve; that as the world grows smaller, our common humanity shall reveal itself; and that America must play its role in ushering in a new era of peace.

As we consider the road that unfolds before us, we remember with humble gratitude those brave Americans who, at this very hour, patrol far-off deserts and distant mountains. They have something to tell us today, just as the fallen heroes who lie in Arlington whisper through the ages.

We honor them not only because they are guardians of our liberty, but because they embody the spirit of service; a willingness to find meaning in something greater than themselves. And yet, at this moment, a moment that will define a generation, it is precisely this spirit that must inhabit us all.

For as much as government can do and must do, it is ultimately the faith and determination of the American people upon which this nation relies. It is the kindness to take in a stranger when the levees break, the selflessness of workers who would rather cut their hours than see a friend lose their job which sees us through our darkest hours. It is the firefighter's courage to storm a stairway filled with smoke, but also a parent's willingness to nurture a child, that finally decides our fate.

Our challenges may be new. The instruments with which we meet them may be new. But those values upon which our success depends—hard work and honesty, courage and fair play, tolerance and curiosity, loyalty and patriotism—these things are old. These things are true. They have been the quiet force of progress throughout our history. What is demanded then is a return to these truths. What is required of us now is a new era of responsibility, a recognition, on the part of every American, that we have duties to ourselves, our nation, and the world, duties that we do not grudgingly accept but rather seize gladly, firm in the knowledge that there is nothing so satisfying to the spirit, so defining of our character, than giving our all to a difficult task. This is the price and the promise of citizenship.

This is the source of our confidence, the knowledge that God calls on us to shape an uncertain destiny. This is the meaning of our liberty and our creed, why men and women and children of every race and every faith can join in celebration across this magnificent mall, and why a man whose father less than sixty years ago might not have been served at a local restaurant can now stand before you to take a most sacred oath.

So let us mark this day with remembrance, of who we are and how far we have traveled. In the year of America's birth, in the coldest of months, a small band of patriots huddled by dying campfires on the shores of an icy river. The capital was abandoned. The enemy was advancing. The snow was stained with blood. At a moment when the outcome of our revolution was most in doubt, the father of our nation ordered these words be read to the people: "Let it be told to the future world... that in the depth of winter, when nothing but hope and virtue could survive... that the city and the country, alarmed at one common danger, came forth to meet (it)."

America, in the face of our common dangers, in this winter of our hardship, let us remember these timeless words. With hope and virtue, let us brave once more the icy currents, and endure what storms may come. Let it be said by our children's children that when we were tested we refused to let this journey end, that we did not turn back nor did we falter; and with eyes fixed on the horizon and God's grace upon us, we carried forth that great gift of freedom and delivered it safely to future generations.

我的同胞们：

今天我站在这里，看到眼前面临的重大任务深感卑微。我感谢你们对我的信任，也知道先辈们为了这个国家所做的牺牲。我要感谢布什总统为国家做出的贡献，以及感谢他在两届政府过渡期间给予的慷慨协作。

迄今为止，已经有 44 个美国总统宣誓就职。总统的宣誓有时面对的是国家的和平繁荣，但通常面临的是乌云密布的紧张形势。在紧张的形势中，支持美国前进的不仅仅是领导人的能力和远见，也在于美国人民对国家先驱者理想的信仰，以及对美国立国文件的忠诚。

前辈们如此，我们这一代美国人也要如此。

现在我们都深知，我们身处危机之中。我们的国家在战斗，对手是影响深远的暴力和憎恨；国家的经济也受到严重的削弱，原因虽是一些人的贪婪和不负责任，但更为重要的是我们作为一个整体在一些重大问题上决策失误，同时也未能做好应对新时代的准备。

我们的人民正在失去家园，失去工作，而且很多企业要倒闭。社会的医疗过于昂贵，学校教育让许多人失望，而且每天都会有新的证据显示，我们利用能源的方式助长了我们的敌对势力，同时也威胁着我们的星球。

统计数据的指标传达着危机的消息。危机难以测量，但更难以测量的是其对美国人国家自信的侵蚀。现在一种认为美国衰落不可避免，我们的下一代必须低调的言论正在吞噬着人们的自信。

今天我要说，我们的确面临着很多严峻的挑战，而且在短期内不大可能轻易解决。但是我们要相信，我们一定会渡过难关。

今天，我们在这里齐聚一堂，因为我们战胜恐惧选择了希望，摒弃了冲突和矛盾而选择了团结。

今天，我们宣布要为无谓的摩擦、不实的承诺和指责画上句号，我们要打破牵制美国政治发展的若干陈旧教条。

美国仍是一个年轻的国家，借用《圣经》的话说，“放弃幼稚的时代已经到来了”。重拾坚韧精神的时代已经到来，我们要为历史作出更好的选择，我们要秉承历史赋予的宝贵权利，秉承那种代代相传的高贵理念：上帝赋予我们每个人以平等和自由，以及每个人尽全力去追求幸福的机会。

在重申我们国家伟大之处的同时，我们深知伟大从来不是上天赐予的，伟大需要努力赢得。（我们的民族一路走来），这旅途之中从未有过捷径或者妥协，这旅途也不适合胆怯之人，或者爱安逸胜过爱工作之人，或者单单追求名利之人。这条路是勇于承担风险者之路，是实干家、创造者之路。这其中有一些人名留青史，但是更多的人却在默默无闻地工作着。正是这些人带领我们走过了漫长崎岖的旅行，带领我们走向富强和自由。

为了我们，先辈们带着微薄的细软，横渡大洋寻找新生活；为了我们，先辈们忍辱负重，用血汗浇铸工厂；为了我们，先辈们在荒芜的西部大地辛勤耕作，定居他乡；为了我们，先辈们奔赴（独立战争中的）康科德城和葛底斯堡、（二战中的）诺曼底、（越战中的）溪山，他们征战死去。

一次又一次，我们的先辈们战斗着、牺牲着、操劳着，只为了我们可以生活得更好。在他们看来，美国的强盛与伟大超越了个人雄心，也超越了个人的出身、贫富和派别差异。

今天我们继续先辈们的旅途。美国依然是地球上最富裕、最强大的国家。同危机初露端倪之时相比，美国人民的生产力依然旺盛。与上周、上个月或者去年相比，我们的头脑依然富于创造力，我们的商品和服务依然很有市场，我们的实力不曾削弱。但是，可以肯定的是，轻歌曼舞的时代、保护狭隘利益的时代以及对艰难决定犹豫不决的时代已经过去了。从今天开始，我们必须跌倒后爬起来，拍拍身上的泥土，重新开始工作，重塑美国。

我目之所及都有工作有待完成。国家的经济情况要求我们采取大胆且快速的行动，我们的确是要行动，不仅是要创造就业，更要为（下一轮经济）增长打下新的基础。我们将造桥铺路，为企业铺设电网和数字线路，将我们联系在一起。我们将回归科学，运用科技的奇迹提高医疗质量，降低医疗费用。我们将利用风能、太阳能和土壤驱动车辆，为工厂提供能源。我们将改革中小学以及大专院校，以适应新时代的要求。这一切，我们都能做到，而且我们都将会做到。

现在，有一些人开始质疑我们的野心是不是太大了，他们认为我们的体制承载不了太多的宏伟计划。他们是健忘了，他们已经忘了这个国家取得的成就，他们已经忘了当创造力与共同目标以及必要的勇气结合起来时，自由的美国人民所能发挥的能量。

这些怀疑论者的错误在于，他们没有意识到政治现实已经发生了变化，长期以来耗掉我们太多精力的陈腐政治论争已经不再适用。今天，我们的问题不在于政府的大小，而在于政府能否起作用。政府能否帮助家庭找到薪水合适的工作，给他们可以负担得起的医疗保障并让他们体面地退休。哪个方案能给与肯定的答案，我们就推进哪个方案。哪个方案的答案是否定的，我们就选择终止。而掌管纳税人税金的人应当承担起责任，合理支出，摒弃陋习，磊落做事，只有这样才能在政府和人民之间重建至关重要的相互信任。

我们面临的问题也不是市场好坏的问题。市场创造财富、拓展自由的能力无可匹敌，但是这场危机提醒我们，如果没有监管市场很可能就会失去控制，而且偏袒富人国家的繁荣无法持久。国家经济的成败不仅仅取决于国内生产总值的大小，而且取决于繁荣的覆盖面，取决于我们是否有能力让所有有意愿的人都有机会走向富裕。我们这样做不是慈善，而是因为这是确保实现共同利益的途径。

就共同防御而言，我们认为国家安全与国家理想的只能选其一的排他选择是错的。面对我们几乎无法想象的危险，我们的先辈们起草了确保法治和个人权利的宪章。一代代人民的鲜血夯实了这一宪章。宪章中的理想依然照亮着世界，我们不能以经验之谈放弃这些理想。因此我想对正在观看这一仪式的其他国家的人民和政府说，不论他们在各国伟大的首府还是在如同我父亲出生地一般的小村落，我想让他们知道：对于每个追求和平和自尊的国家和个人而言，美国都是朋友，我们愿意再次领导大家踏上追寻之旅。

回想先辈们在抵抗法西斯主义之时，他们不仅依靠手中的导弹或坦克，他们还依靠稳固的联盟和坚定的信仰。他们深知单凭自己的力量我们无法保护自己，他们也深知我们的力量并不足以使我们有权利为所欲为。他们明白正是因为谨慎，我们的实力才不断增强；正是因为我们的事业是公正的，我们为世界树立了榜样；因为我们的谦卑和节制，我们才安全。

我们继承了这些遗产。在这些原则的再次领导下，我们有能力应对新的威胁，我们需要付出更多的努力，进行国家间更广泛的合作以及增进国家间的理解。首先，我们将以负责任的态度，将伊拉克交还给伊拉克人民，同时巩固阿富汗来之不易的和平。对于老朋友和老对手，我们将继续努力，不遗余力地削弱核威胁，遏制全球变暖的幽灵。我们不会为我们的生活方式感到抱歉，我们会不动摇地捍卫我们的生活方式。对于那些企图通过恐怖主义或屠杀无辜平民达成目标的人，我们要对他们说：我们的信仰更加坚定，不可动摇，你们不可能拖垮我们，我们定将战胜你们。

因为我们知道，我们的多元化遗产是一个优势而非劣势。我们国家里有基督徒也有穆斯林，有犹太教徒也有印度教徒，同时也有非宗教信徒。我们民族的成长受到许多语言和文化的影响，我们吸取了这个星球上任何一个角落的有益成分。正是因为我们民族曾亲尝过内战和种族隔离的苦酒，并且在经历了这些黑色的篇章之后变得更加强大更加团结，因此我们不由自主地相信一切仇恨终有一天都会成为过去，种族的划分不久就会消失，而且随着世界变得越来越小，我们相信终有一天人类共有的人性品德将会自动显现。在迎接新的和平时代到来的过程中，美国需要发挥自己的作用。

思索前方的路，我们无时无刻不在铭记那些远征沙漠和偏远山区的英勇美国战士，对他们充满了感激之情，他们和那些安息在阿灵顿国家公墓之下的战争英雄们一样，给与我们启示。

我们尊敬他们，不仅因为他们是自由的守护者，还因为他们代表的是为国家服务的精神，他们致力于追寻比自身的价值更伟大的意义。此时此刻，在这个要塑造一代人的时刻，我们需要的正是这样一种精神。

因为无论美国政府能做多少，必须做多少，美国国家的立国之本最终还是美国人的决心和信念。于防洪堤坝决堤之时收留陌生受难者的善意，于经济不景气时宁愿减少自己工时也不肯看着朋友失业的无私，正是他们支撑我们走过黑暗的时刻。消防队员冲入满是浓烟的楼梯抢救生命的勇气，父母养育孩子的坚持，正是这些决定了我们的命运。

我们面临的挑战也许是新的，我们应对挑战的措施也许也是新的，但那些长期以来指导我们成功的价值观——勤奋、诚实、勇气、公平竞争、包容以及对世界保持好奇心，还有对国家的忠诚和爱国主义却是历久弥新。这些价值观是可靠的，他们是创造美国历史的无声力量，我们现在需要的就是回归这些古老的价值观。我们需要一个新的负责任的时代，一个觉醒的时代，每个国人都应意识到我们对自己、对国家和世界负有责任，我们不应该不情愿地接受这些责任，而应该快乐地承担起这些责任。我们应该坚定这一认识，没有什么比全身心投入一项艰巨的工作更能锻炼我们的性格，更能获得精神上的满足。这是公民应尽的义务，应做出的承诺。

我们自信源于对上帝的信仰，上帝号召我们要掌握自己的命运。这就是我们自由和信仰的意义，这也是为何不同种族、不同信仰、不同性别和年龄的人可以同聚一堂在此欢庆的原因，也是我今天能站在这里庄严宣誓的原因，而在五十多年前我的父亲甚至都不能成为地方餐馆的服务生。

所以，让我们铭记自己的身份，镌刻自己的足迹。在美国诞生的时代，那最寒冷的岁月里，一群勇敢的爱国人士围着篝火在冰封的河边取暖。首都被占领，敌人在挺进，冬天的雪被鲜血染成了红色。在美国大革命最受质疑的时刻，我们的国父们这样说：“我们要让未来的世界知道……在深冬的严寒里，唯有希望和勇气才能让我们存活……面对共同的危险时，我们的城市和国家要勇敢地上前去面对。”

今天的美国也在严峻的寒冬中面对共同的挑战，让我们记住国父们不朽的语言。带着希望和勇气，让我们再一次勇敢地面对寒流，迎接可能会发生的风暴。我们要让我们的子孙后代记住，在面临挑战的时候，我们没有屈服，我们没有逃避也没有犹豫，我们脚踏实地、心怀信仰，秉承了宝贵的自由权利并将其安全地交到了下一代的手中。

第三节 精彩语录

In reaffirming the greatness of our nation, we understand that greatness is never a given. It must be earned. Our journey has never been one of shortcuts or settling for less. It has not been the path for the faint-hearted—for those who prefer leisure over work, or seek only the pleasures of riches and fame. Rather, it has been the risk-takers, the doers, the makers of things—some celebrated but more often men and women obscure in their labor, who have carried us up the long, rugged path towards prosperity and freedom.

在重申我们国家伟大之处的同时，我们深知伟大从来不是上天赐予的，伟大需要努力赢得。(我们的民族一路走来)，这旅途之中从未有过捷径或者妥协，这旅途也不适合胆怯之人，或者爱安逸胜过爱工作之人，或者单单追求名利之人。这条路是勇于承担风险者之路，是实干家、创造者之路。这其中有一些人名留青史，但是更多的人却在默默无闻地工作着。正是这些人带领我们走过了漫长崎岖的旅行，带领我们走向富强和自由。

This is the journey we continue today. We remain the most prosperous, powerful nation on Earth. Our workers are no less productive than when this crisis began. Our minds are no less inventive, our goods and services no less needed than they were last week or last month or last year. Our capacity remains undiminished. But our time of standing pat, of protecting narrow interests and putting off unpleasant decisions—that time has surely passed. Starting today, we must pick ourselves up, dust ourselves off, and begin again the work of remaking America.

今天我们继续先辈们的旅途。美国依然是地球上最富裕、最强大的国家。同危机初露端倪之时相比，美国人民的生产力依然旺盛。与上周、上个月或者去年相比，我们的头脑依然富于创造力，我们的商品和服务依然很有市场，我们的实力不曾削弱。但是，可以肯定的是，轻歌曼舞的时代、保护狭隘利益的时代以及对艰难决定犹豫不决的时代已经过去了。从今天开始，我们必须跌倒后爬起来，拍拍身上的泥土，重新开始工作，重塑美国。

Our challenges may be new. The instruments with which we meet them may be new. But those values upon which our success depends—hard work and honesty, courage and fair play, tolerance and curiosity, loyalty and patriotism—these things are old. These things are true. They have been the quiet force of progress throughout our history. What is demanded then is a return to these truths. What is required of us now is a new era of responsibility, a recognition, on the part of every American, that we have duties to ourselves, our nation, and the world, duties that we do not grudgingly accept but rather seize gladly, firm in the knowledge that there is nothing so satisfying to the spirit, so defining of our character, than giving our all to a difficult task.

我们面临的挑战也许是新的，我们应对挑战的措施也许也是新的，但那些长期以来指导我们成功的价值观——勤奋、诚实、勇气、公平竞争、包容以及对世界保持好奇心，还有对国家的忠诚和爱国主义却是历久弥新。这些价值观是可靠的，他们是创造美国历史的无声力量，我们现在需要的就是回归这些古老的价值观。我们需要一个新的负责任的时代，一个觉醒的时代，每个国人都应意识到我们对自己、对国家和世界负有责任，我们不应该不情愿地接受这些责任，而应该快乐地承担起这些责任。我们应该坚定这一认识，没有什么比全身心投入一项艰巨的工作更能锻炼我们的性格，更能获得精神上的满足。

America, in the face of our common dangers, in this winter of our hardship, let us remember these timeless words. With hope and virtue, let us brave once more the icy currents, and endure what storms may come. Let it be said by our children's children that when we were tested we refused to let this journey end, that we did not turn back nor did we falter; and with eyes fixed on the horizon and God's grace upon us, we carried forth that great gift of freedom and delivered it safely to future generations.

今天的美国也在严峻的寒冬中面对共同的挑战，让我们记住国父们不朽的语言。带着希望和勇气，让我们再一次勇敢地面对寒流，迎接可能会发生的风暴。我们要让我们的子孙后代记住，在面临挑战的时候，我们没有屈服，我们没有逃避也没有犹豫，我们脚踏实地、心怀信仰，秉承了宝贵的自由权利并将其安全地交到了下一代的手中。

第八章

独立日演讲

第一节 背景介绍

美国总统奥巴马在7月4日，即美国“独立日”发表电视演讲时说，美国目前正面临严峻挑战，国民需要重树“美国精神”。

奥巴马说，美国目前正面临前所未有的挑战——伊拉克和阿富汗这两场战争、经济危机、医保开销不断上升、学校数量缺乏以及对外国石油的依赖。而应对这些挑战需要每个美国人付出努力。

奥巴马说，美国人应该发挥先辈们的“顽强”精神，“创造”未来而非“惧怕”未来。正是不屈不挠的美国精神使得我们成为了美国人。它引领了先辈们进行了西进运动；它引领了我的祖辈一代人坚强地面对大萧条，并战胜了暴政；它引领了一代代美国工人建立起举世无匹的工业化经济体系。这种精神总是引领着我们美国人民不畏艰难，勇于面对所有的考验与挑战，让我们知道我们每个人都在书写美国的未来。那就是我们应该再次展现的美国精神。

第二节 奥巴马于 2009 年 7 月 4 日在白宫的演讲

Today, we are called upon to remember not only the day our country was born, but also the indomitable spirit of the first American citizens who made that day possible. We are called to remember how unlikely it was that our American experiment would succeed at all; that a small band of patriots would declare independence from a powerful empire; and that they would form, in the new world, what the old world had never known—a government of, by, and for the people.

That unyielding spirit is what defines us as Americans. It is what led generations of pioneers to blaze a westward trail. It is what led my grandparents' generation to persevere in the face of a depression and triumph in the face of tyranny. It is what led generations of American workers to build an industrial economy unrivaled around the world. It is what has always led us, as a people, not to wilt or cower at a difficult moment, but to face down any trial and rise to any challenge, understanding that each of us has a hand in writing America's destiny.

On this day, we also remember that during our most defining moments, it was brave and selfless men and women in uniform who defended and served our country with honor—waging war so that we might know peace; braving hardship so that we might know opportunity; and at times, paying the ultimate price so that we might know freedom. This service—the service of Soldiers, Sailors, Airmen, Marines, and Coast Guardsmen—makes our annual celebration of this day possible. This service proves that our founding ideals remain just as powerful and alive in our third century as a nation as they did on the first July 4. This service guarantees that the United States of America shall forever remain the last, best hope on Earth.

All of us must call on this spirit of service and sacrifice to meet the challenges of our time. We are waging two wars. We are battling a deep recession. Our economy—and our nation itself—are endangered by festering problems we have kicked down the road for far too long: spiraling health care costs, inadequate schools, and a dependence on foreign oil.

Meeting these extraordinary challenges will require an extraordinary effort on the part of every American. It will require us to remember that we did not get to where we are as a nation by standing pat in a time of change. We did not get here by doing what was easy. That is not how a cluster of 13 colonies became the United States of America.

We are not a people who fear the future. We are a people who make it. On this July 4, we need to summon once more the spirit that inhabited Independence Hall two hundred and thirty-three years ago today. That is how this generation of Americans will make its mark on history. That is how we will make the most of this extraordinary moment. And that is how we will write the next chapter in the great American story.

I wish you all the best for a happy Fourth of July.

今天，我们受到这个日子的感召，不仅纪念我国诞生的那一天，而且需要继承建国初期美国公民不屈不挠的精神，是他们使这一天成为值得纪念的日子。我们应该记住，当年的这一切多么来之不易。我们进行创建美国的试验，结果获得了成功。为数不多的爱国者宣布独立，脱离了帝国强权的统治。他们还在新世界建立了旧世界不可思议的事物——一个民有、民治、民享的政府。

正是这种顽强的精神构筑了美国人的特征。正是这种精神指引一代又一代先驱者开拓西进之路。正是这种精神指引我们的祖祖辈辈，以坚韧不拔的毅力渡过了大萧条，战胜了专制暴政。正是这种精神指引世世代代的美国劳动者建成全世界无可比拟的工业经济。正是这种精神始终指引全体美国人民在时局艰难的时刻永不气馁，永不退缩，敢于经受任何考验，迎接任何挑战，因为我们知道美国的命运需要我们每一个人为之努力。

在这一天到来的时候，我们还不应该忘记，在我国最紧要的关头，勇敢无私的男女军人不辱使命，保卫我们的国家，忠心为国效力——为实现和平奔赴战场，为赢得机会不辞劳苦，有时还为捍卫自由付出极为高昂的代价。正因为他们为国效力——陆军、海军、空军、海军陆战队和海岸警卫队士兵做出的奉献，我们才有可能每年庆祝这个节日。这种为国效力的精神说明，在进入建国后第三个百年之际，我国的建国理想仍然长盛不衰，生气勃勃，永远保持第一个 7 月 4 日的活力。这种为国效力的精神保证美利坚合众国永远是地球上最后、最大的希望。

为了迎接我们这个时代的挑战，我们大家都必须发扬这种为国效力和献身的精神。我们正在参与两场战争，同时我们也在抗击严重的衰退。我们长期拖延了旷日持久的问题：持续上升的医疗成本、学校设施的欠缺和对外国石油的依赖，这导致问题日益恶化，我国经济以及国家本身正面临着危难。

迎接这些巨大的挑战要求每一位美国人付出巨大的努力。我们应该牢记，我们作为一个国家取得这样的成就是因为我们在变革的时期没有固步自封，我们取得这样的成就是因为我们没有避难就易。正是因为如此，原来的十三个殖民地才能共建美利坚合众国。

我国人民敢于面对未来，我国人民敢于创造未来。在今年 7 月 4 日到来之际，我们必须再次振奋 233 年前独立厅凝聚的精神。唯有如此，这一代美国人才能在历史上留下自己的印记。唯有如此，我们才能最有效地把握当前的重要关头。唯有如此，我们才能为伟大的美国历史书写新的篇章。

我谨祝愿大家 7 月 4 日节日愉快。

第三节 精彩语录

We are called to remember how unlikely it was that our American experiment would succeed at all; that a small band of patriots would declare independence from a powerful empire; and that they would form, in the new world, what the old world had never known—a government of, by, and for the people.

我们应该记住，当年的这一切多么来之不易。我们进行创建美国的试验，结果获得了成功。为数不多的爱国者宣布独立，脱离了帝国强权的统治。他们还在新世界建立了旧世界不可思议的事物——一个民有、民治、民享的政府。

All of us must call on this spirit of service and sacrifice to meet the challenges of our time. We are waging two wars. We are battling a deep recession. Our economy—and our nation itself—are endangered by festering problems we have kicked down the road for far too long: spiraling health care costs, inadequate schools, and a dependence on foreign oil.

为了迎接我们这个时代的挑战，我们大家都必须发扬这种为国效力和献身的精神。我们正在参与两场战争，同时我们也在抗击严重的衰退。我们长期拖延了旷日持久的问题：持续上升的医疗成本、学校设施的欠缺和对外国石油的依赖，这导致问题日益恶化，我国经济以及国家本身正面临着危难。

We are not a people who fear the future. We are a people who make it. On this July 4, we need to summon once more the spirit that inhabited Independence Hall two hundred and thirty-three years ago today.

我国人民敢于面对未来，我国人民敢于创造未来。在今年 7 月 4 日到来之际，我们必须再次振奋 233 年前独立厅凝聚的精神。

第九章

民众的力量

第一节 背景介绍

2013年1月21日，奥巴马在美国首都华盛顿宣誓就职。奥巴马四年前首度入主白宫时美国经济陷入深重衰退，第二任期的奥巴马仍面临经济疲软、失业率高企和迫在眉睫的财政危机。因此，在开始新的任期后，奥巴马的首要任务仍然是处理经济问题。

目前美国财政状况正在逐步恶化。美国财政部17日公布的年度政府资产和负债评估报告显示，美国政府2012财年的财政赤字从前一年的1.313万亿美元扩大至1.316万亿美元。

中国人民大学国际关系学院美国研究中心主任时殷宏表示，就美国选民希望来看，特别是就美国面临的最重要的问题来看，毫无疑问，美国的政策关注重点仍然是国内。总的来说主要取决于三大背景：经济背景、金融背景、社会背景。

经济背景方面，虽然美国的经济早已开始复苏，但是数年来复苏乏力，特别是直到今天失业率居高不下，产业复兴缺乏市场，技术创新除了在能源页岩方面的利用好像有新的技术革命的苗头外，总体来说还不是那么强劲，经济的复兴是一个非常艰巨的任务。

金融背景方面，美国的国债已经到了非常严重的程度，再加上由于白宫和国会、共和党人党派斗争，广义的财政危险、财政虚弱是非常突出的。在一定意义上来讲，解决美国的金融问题，使它基本改观，要比振兴美国经济还要困难。

而社会背景比较复杂，但是目前来看，奥巴马遇到的新的困难，就是他大力主张管制枪支在国内引起很多争论和批评。另外移民方面，恐怕很多问题也很难解决，而且社会问题是同党派政治斗争联合在一起的，所以这个问题也非常复杂。

奥巴马当天指出美国仍未摆脱经济危机的影响，所以目前的首要任务是增加就业、促进经济发展、壮大中产阶级。在谈到财政危机时，奥巴马表示，他欢迎妥协和新的意见，并认为应当能够在为大部分美国人减税的情况下增加财政收入。但是他说，最富有的美国人应该多缴税。

奥巴马还称议员们应承诺削减联邦预算，并呼吁大家能够放下分歧一起合作，努力战胜这些挑战。

第二节 奥巴马于 2013 年在白宫的第二次就职演讲

Thank you. Thank you so much. Vice President Biden, Mr. Chief Justice, Members of the United States Congress, distinguished guests, and fellow citizens:

Each time we gather to inaugurate a president, we bear witness to the enduring strength of our Constitution. We affirm the promise of our democracy. We recall that what binds this nation together is not the colors of our skin or the tenets of our faith or the origins of our names. What makes us exceptional—what makes us American—is our allegiance to an idea, articulated in a declaration made more than two centuries ago: "We hold these truths to be self-evident, that all men are created equal, that they are endowed by their Creator with certain unalienable rights, that among these are Life, Liberty, and the pursuit of Happiness."

Today we continue a never-ending journey, to bridge the meaning of those words with the realities of our time. For history tells us that while these truths may be self-evident, they have never been self-executing; that while freedom is a gift from God, it must be secured by His people here on Earth. The patriots of 1776 did not fight to replace the tyranny of a king with the privileges of a few or the rule of a mob. They gave to us a Republic, a government of, and by, and for the people, entrusting each generation to keep safe our founding creed. For more than two hundred years, we have.

Through blood drawn by lash and blood drawn by sword, we learned that no union founded on the principles of liberty and equality could survive half-slave and half-free. We made ourselves anew, and vowed to move forward together.

Together, we determined that a modern economy requires railroads and highways to speed travel and commerce, schools and colleges to train our workers.

Together, we discovered that a free market only thrives when there are rules to ensure competition and fair play.

Together, we resolved that a great nation must care for the vulnerable, and protect its people from life's worst hazards and misfortune.

Through it all, we have never relinquished our skepticism of central authority, nor have we succumbed to the fiction that all society's ills can be cured through government alone. Our celebration of initiative and enterprise; our insistence on hard work and personal responsibility, these are constants in our character.

But we have always understood that when times change, so must we; that fidelity to our founding principles requires new responses to new challenges; that preserving our individual freedoms ultimately requires collective action. For the American people can no more meet the demands of today's world by acting alone than American soldiers could have met the forces of fascism or communism with muskets and militias. No single person can train all the math and science teachers we'll need to equip our children for the future, or build the roads and networks and research labs that will bring new jobs and businesses to our shores. Now, more than ever, we must do these things together, as one nation, and one people.

This generation of Americans has been tested by crises that steeled our resolve and proved our resilience. A decade of war is now ending. An economic recovery has begun. America's possibilities are limitless, for we possess all the qualities that this world without boundaries demands: youth and drive; diversity and openness; an endless capacity for risk and a gift for reinvention. My fellow

Americans, we are made for this moment, and we will seize it—so long as we seize it together.

For we, the people, understand that our country cannot succeed when a shrinking few do very well and a growing many barely make it. We believe that America's prosperity must rest upon the broad shoulders of a rising middle class. We know that America thrives when every person can find independence and pride in their work; when the wages of honest labor liberate families from the brink of hardship. We are true to our creed when a little girl born into the bleakest poverty knows that she has the same chance to succeed as anybody else, because she is an American, she is free, and she is equal, not just in the eyes of God but also in our own.

We understand that outworn programs are inadequate to the needs of our time. We must harness new ideas and technology to remake our government, revamp our tax code, reform our schools, and empower our citizens with the skills they need to work harder, learn more, and reach higher. But while the means will change, our purpose endures: a nation that rewards the effort and determination of every single American. That is what this moment requires. That is what will give real meaning to our creed.

We, the people, still believe that every citizen deserves a basic measure of security and dignity. We must make the hard choices to reduce the cost of health care and the size of our deficit. But we reject the belief that America must choose between caring for the generation that built this country and investing in the generation that will build its future. For we remember the lessons of our past, when twilight years were spent in poverty, and parents of a child with a disability had nowhere to turn. We do not believe that in this country, freedom is reserved for the lucky, or happiness for the few. We recognize that no matter how responsibly we live our lives, any one of us, at any time, may face a job loss, or a sudden illness, or a home swept away in a terrible storm. The commitments we make to each other—through Medicare and Medicaid and Social Security, these things do not sap our initiative; they strengthen us. They do not make us a nation of takers; they free us to take the risks that make this country great.

We, the people, still believe that our obligations as Americans are not just to ourselves, but to all posterity. We will respond to the threat of climate change, knowing that the failure to do so would betray our children and future generations. Some may still deny the overwhelming judgment of science, but none can avoid the devastating impact of raging fires, and crippling drought, and more powerful storms. The path towards sustainable energy sources will be long and sometimes difficult. But America cannot resist this transition, we must lead it. We cannot cede to other nations the technology that will power new jobs and new industries, we must claim its promise. That is how we will maintain our economic vitality and our national treasure—our forests and waterways; our croplands and snowcapped peaks. That is how we will preserve our planet, commanded to our care by God. That's what will lend meaning to the creed our fathers once declared.

We, the people, still believe that enduring security and lasting peace do not require perpetual war. Our brave men and women in uniform, tempered by the flames of battle, are unmatched in skill and courage. Our citizens, seared by the memory of those we have lost, know too well the price that is paid for liberty. The knowledge of their sacrifice will keep us forever vigilant against those who would do us harm. But we are also heirs to those who won the peace and not just the war, who turned sworn enemies into the surest of friends, and we must carry those lessons into this time as well.

We will defend our people and uphold our values through strength of arms and rule of law. We will show the courage to try and resolve our differences with other nations peacefully—not because we are naive about the dangers we face, but because engagement can more durably lift suspicion and fear. America will remain the anchor of strong alliances in every corner of the globe; and we will renew those institutions that extend our capacity to manage crisis abroad, for no one has a greater stake in a peaceful world than its most powerful nation. We will support democracy from Asia to Africa, from the Americas to the Middle East, because our interests and our conscience compel us to act on behalf of those who long for freedom. And we must be a source of hope to the poor, the sick, the marginalized, the victims of prejudice—not out of mere charity, but because peace in our time requires the constant advance of those principles that our common creed describes: tolerance and opportunity; human dignity and justice.

We, the people, declare today that the most evident of truths—that all of us are created equal—is the star that guides us still; just as it guided our forebears through Seneca Falls, and Selma, and Stonewall; just as it guided all those men and women, sung and unsung, who left footprints along this great Mall, to hear a preacher say that we cannot walk alone; to hear a King proclaim that our individual freedom is inextricably bound to the freedom of every soul on Earth.

It is now our generation's task to carry on what those pioneers began. For our journey is not complete until our wives, our mothers, and daughters can earn a living equal to their efforts. Our journey is not complete until our gay brothers and sisters are treated like anyone else under the law—for if we are truly created equal, then surely the love we commit to one another must be equal as well. Our journey is not complete until no citizen is forced to wait for hours to exercise the right to vote. Our journey is not complete until we find a better way to welcome the striving, hopeful immigrants who still see America as a land of opportunity; until bright young students and engineers are enlisted in our workforce rather than expelled from our country. Our journey is not complete until all our children, from the streets of Detroit to the hills of Appalachia to the quiet lanes of Newtown, know that they are cared for, and cherished, and always safe from harm.

That is our generation's task—to make these words, these rights, these values of Life, and Liberty, and the Pursuit of Happiness—real for every American. Being true to our founding documents does not require us to agree on every contour of life; it does not mean we will all define liberty in exactly the same way, or follow the same precise path to happiness. Progress does not compel us to settle centuries-long debates about the role of government for all time, but it does require us to act in our time.

For now decisions are upon us, and we cannot afford delay. We cannot mistake absolutism for principle, or substitute spectacle for politics, or treat name-calling as reasoned debate. We must act, knowing that our work will be imperfect.

We must act, knowing that today's victories will be only partial, and that it will be up to those who stand here in four years, and forty years, and four hundred years hence to advance the timeless spirit once conferred to us in a spare Philadelphia hall.

My fellow Americans, the oath I have sworn before you today, like the one recited by others who serve in this Capitol, was an oath to God and country, not party or faction, and we must faithfully execute that pledge during the duration of our service. But the words I spoke today are not so different from the oath that is taken each time a soldier signs up for duty, or an immigrant realizes her dream. My oath is not so different from the pledge we all make to the flag that waves above and that fills our hearts with pride. They are the words of citizens, and they represent our greatest hope.

You and I, as citizens, have the power to set this country's course. You and I, as citizens, have the obligation to shape the debates of our time—not only with the votes we cast, but with the voices we lift in defense of our most ancient values and enduring ideals.

Let each of us now embrace, with solemn duty and awesome joy, what is our lasting birthright. With common effort and common purpose, with passion and dedication, let us answer the call of history, and carry into an uncertain future that precious light of freedom.

Thank you, God Bless you, and may He forever bless these United States of America.

谢谢，非常感谢大家。拜登副总统、首席大法官先生、国会议员们、尊敬的各位嘉宾、亲爱的公民们：

每一次我们集会庆祝总统就职都是在见证美国宪法的持久力量，都是在肯定美国民主的承诺。我们重申将这个国家紧密联系在一起的不是我们的肤色，也不是我们信仰的教条，更不是我们名字的来源。让我们与众不同，让我们成为美国人的是我们对于一种理念的恪守。二百多年前，这一理念在一篇宣言中被清晰阐述："我们认为下述真理是不言而喻的，人人生而平等。造物主赋予他们若干不可剥夺的权利，包括生存、自由和追求幸福的权利。"

今天，我们继续着这一未竟的征程，架起这些理念与我们时代现实之间的桥梁。因为历史告诉我们，即便这些真理是不言而喻的，它们也从来不会自动生效。因为虽然自由是上帝赋予的礼物，但仍需要世间的子民去捍卫。1776年，美国的爱国先驱们不是只为了推翻国王的暴政而战，也不是为赢得少数人的特权，建立暴民的统治。先驱们留给我们一个共和国，一个民有、民治、民享的政府。他们委托每一代美国人捍卫我们的建国信条。在过去的二百多年里，我们做到了。

从奴役的血腥枷锁和刀剑的血光厮杀中我们懂得了，建立在自由与平等原则之上的联邦不能永远维持半奴隶和半自由的状态。我们赢得了新生，誓言共同前进。

我们共同努力，建立起现代的经济体系。架设铁路与高速公路，加速了旅行和商业交流。建立学校与大学，培训我们的工人。

我们一起发现，自由市场的繁荣只能建立在保障竞争与公平竞争的原则之上。

我们共同决定让这个伟大的国家远离危险，保护她的人民不受生命威胁和不幸的侵扰。

一路走来，我们从未放弃对集权的质疑。我们同样不屈服于这一谎言：一切的社会弊端都只能够靠政府来解决。我们对积极向上与奋发进取的赞扬，我们对努力工作与个人责任的坚持，这些都是美国精神的基本要义。

我们也理解时代在变化，我们同样需要变革。对建国精神的忠诚，需要我们肩负起新的责任，迎接新的挑战。保护我们的个人自由，最终需要所有人的共同努力。因为美国人不能再独力迎接当今世界的挑战，正如美国士兵们不能再像先辈一样，用步枪和民兵同敌人作战。一个人无法培训所有的数学与科学老师，我们需要他们为了未来去教育孩子们。一个人无法建设道路、铺设网络、建立实验室来为国内带来新的工作岗位和商业机会。现在，与以往任何时候相比，我们都更需要团结合作。作为一个国家，一个民族团结起来。

这一代美国人经历了危机的考验，经济危机坚定了我们的决心，证明了我们的恢复力。长达十年的战争正在结束，经济的复苏已经开始。美国的可能性是无限的，因为我们拥有当今没有边界的世界所需要的所有品质：年轻与活力、多样性与开放、无穷的冒险精神以及创造的天赋才能。我亲爱的同胞们，我们正是为此刻而生，我们更要在此刻团结一致，抓住当下的机会。

因为我们——美国人民清楚，如果只有越来越少的群体获得成功，而大多数人不能成功，那么我们的国家就无法成功。我们相信，美国的繁荣必须建立在不断壮大的中产阶级的宽阔臂膀之上，我们知道只有这样美国的繁荣才能实现。只有当每个人都能找到工作中的独立与自豪时才能实现。只有当诚实劳动获得的薪水足够让家庭摆脱困苦的悬崖时才能实现。我们忠诚于我们的事业，保证让一个出生于最贫穷环境中的小女孩都能知道，她有同其他所有人一样的成功机会。因为她是一个美国人，她是自由的、平等的。她的自由平等不仅由上帝来见证，更由我们亲手保护。

我们知道，我们已然陈旧的程序不足以满足时代的需要。我们必须应用新理念和新技术重塑我们的政府，改进我们的税法，改革我们的学校，让我们的公民拥有他们所需要的技能，更加努力地工作，学更多的知识，向更高处发展。尽管这意味着变革，但我们的目标是不变的：建设可以奖励每个美国人的努力和果断的国家。这是现在需要的。这将给我们的信条赋予真正的意义。

我们——美国人民仍然认为，每个公民都应当获得基本的安全和尊严。我们必须做出艰难抉择，降低医疗成本，缩减赤字规模。但我们拒绝在照顾建设国家的这一代和投资即将建设国家的下一代间做出选择。因为我们记得过去的教训：老年人的夕阳时光在贫困中度过，家有残障儿童的父母无处求助。我们相信，在这个国家，自由不只是那些幸运儿的专属，或者说幸福只属于少数人。我们知道，不管我们怎样负责任地生活，我们任何人在任何时候都可能面临失业、突发疾病或住房被可怕的飓风摧毁的风险。我们通过医疗保险、联邦医疗补助计划、社会保障项目向每个人做出承诺，这些不会让我们的创造力衰竭，而是会让我们更强大。这些不会让我们成为充满不劳而获者的国度，这些让我们敢于承担风险，让国家伟大。

我们——美国人民仍然相信，我们作为美国人的义务不只是对我们自己而言，还包括对子孙后代。我们将应对气候变化的威胁，认识到不采取措施应对气候变化就是对我们的孩子和后代的背叛。一些人可能仍在否定科学界的压倒性判断，但没有人能够避免熊熊火灾、严重旱灾、更强力风暴带来的灾难性打击。通向可再生能源利用的道路是漫长的，有时是困难的。但美国不能抵制这种趋势，我们必须引领这种趋势。我们不能把制造新就业机会和新行业的技术让给其他国家，我们必须明确这一承诺。这是我们保持经济活力和国家财富（我们的森林和航道，我们的农田与雪峰）的方法。这将是我们保护我们星球的办法，上帝把这个星球托付给我们。这将给我们的建国之父们曾宣布的信条赋予意义。

我们——美国人民仍然相信，持久的安全与和平不需要持续的战争。我们勇敢的士兵经受了战火的考验，他们的技能和勇气是无可匹敌的。我们的公民依然铭记着那些阵亡者，他们非常清楚我们为自由付出的代价。明白他们的牺牲将让我们永远对那些试图伤害我们的势力保持警惕。但我们也是那些赢得和平而不只是战争的人们的后代，他们将仇敌转变成最可靠的朋友，我们也必须把这些经验带到这个时代。

我们将通过强大的军力和法制保护我们的人民，捍卫我们的价值观。我们将展现试图和平解决与其他国家分歧的勇气，但这不是因为我们对面临的危险持幼稚的态度，而是因为接触能够更持久地化解疑虑和恐惧。美国将在全球保持强大的联盟，我们将更新这些能扩展我们应对海外危机能力的机制。因为作为世界上最强大的国家，我们在世界和平方面拥有最大的利益。我们将支持从亚洲到非洲、从美洲至中东的民主国家，因为我们的利益和良心驱使我们代表那些想获得自由的人们采取行动。我们必须成为贫困者、病患者、被边缘化的人士、异见受害者的希望来源，不仅仅是出于慈善，也是因为这个时代的和平需要不断推进我们共同信念中的原则：宽容和机遇，人类尊严与正义。

我们——美国人民，今天昭示的最明白的事实是——我们所有人都是生而平等的，这是依然引领我们的恒星。它引领我们的先辈穿越纽约塞尼卡瀑布城（女权抗议事件）、塞尔马（黑人权力事件）和石墙骚乱（同性恋与警察发生的暴力事件）；引领着所有的男性和女性，留下姓名和没留姓名的人，在伟大的征程中一路上留下足迹的人。他们来听牧师宣讲，我们不能独自前行。马丁·路德·金说，我们个人的自由与地球上每个灵魂的自由不可分割。

继续先辈开创的事业是我们这代人的任务。我们的征途不会结束，直到我们的妻子、母亲和女儿的所得能够与她们的努力付出相称。我们的征途不会结束，我们要让同性恋的兄弟姐妹在法律之下得到与其他人同样的待遇。如果我们真正是生而平等的，那么我们对彼此的爱也应该是平等的。我们的征途不会结束，直到没有公民需要等待数个小时去行使投票权。我们的征途不会结束，直到我们找到更好的方法迎接有憧憬的移民，他们依旧视美国是一块充满机会的土地，直到聪颖年轻的学生和工程师为我们所用，而不是被逐出美国。我们的征途不会结束，直到我们所有的儿童，从底特律的街道到阿巴拉契亚的山岭，再到康涅狄格州纽镇安静的小巷，直到他们得到关心和珍视，永远避免受到伤害。

那是我们这一代的任务——让生存、自由和追求幸福的言语、权力和价值切实体现在每个美国人的身上。我们的立国文件根本没有要求我们将每个人的生活一致化。这并不意味着，我们会以完全一样的方式去定义自由，沿着同样的道路通向幸福。进步不会终止几个世纪以来一直纠结的关于政府角色的争论，但这要求我们现在就采取行动。

目前是由我们决策，我们不能拖延。我们不能将绝对主义当作原则，或者以表象代替政治，或将中伤视作理性的辩论。我们必须行动，要意识到我们的工作并不完美。我们必须行动，意识到今天的胜利是并不完全的。这些将有赖于未来四年、四十年或是四百年致力于这项事业的人，去推进当年在费城制宪会议大厅传承给我们的永恒精神。

我的美国同胞，我今天在你们面前宣读的誓词，如同在国会山服务的其他人曾宣读过的誓词一样，是对上帝和国家的誓词，不是对党派或是派别的，我们必须在任期内忠实地履行这些承诺。但我今天宣读的誓词与士兵报名参军或者是移民实现梦想时所宣读的誓词没有多少差别。我的誓词与我们所有的人向我们头顶飘扬的、让我们心怀自豪的国旗所表达的誓言没有多大差别。这些是公民的誓词，代表着我们最伟大的希望。

你和我作为公民，都有为这个国家设定道路的权力。你和我作为公民，都有义务塑造我们时代的辩题，不仅是通过我们的选票，而且要为捍卫悠久的价值观和持久的理想发声。

现在让我们相互拥抱，怀着庄严的职责和无比的快乐，这是我们永恒的与生俱来的权利。有共同的努力和共同的目标，用热情与奉献，让我们回应历史的召唤，将珍贵的自由之光带入并不确定的未来。

感谢你们，上帝保佑你们，愿上帝永远保佑美利坚合众国。

第三节 精彩语录

Through blood drawn by lash and blood drawn by sword, we learned that no union founded on the principles of liberty and equality could survive half-slave and half-free. We made ourselves anew, and vowed to move forward together.

从奴役的血腥枷锁和刀剑的血光厮杀中我们懂得了，建立在自由与平等原则之上的联邦不能永远维持半奴隶和半自由的状态。我们赢得了新生，誓言共同前进。

Through it all, we have never relinquished our skepticism of central authority, nor have we succumbed to the fiction that all society's ills can be cured through government alone. Our celebration of initiative and enterprise; our insistence on hard work and personal responsibility, these are constants in our character.

一路走来，我们从未放弃对集权的质疑。我们同样不屈服于这一谎言：一切的社会弊端都能够只靠政府来解决。我们对积极向上与奋发进取的赞扬，我们对努力工作与个人责任的坚持，这些都是美国精神的基本要义。

For we, the people, understand that our country cannot succeed when a shrinking few do very well and a growing many barely make it. We believe that America's prosperity must rest upon the broad shoulders of a rising middle class. We know that America thrives when every person can find independence and pride in their work; when the wages of honest labor liberate families from the brink of hardship.

因为我们——美国人民清楚，如果只有越来越少的群体获得成功，而大多数人不能成功，那么我们的国家就无法成功。我们相信，美国的繁荣必须建立在不断壮大的中产阶级的宽阔臂膀之上，我们知道只有这样美国的繁荣才能实现。只有当每个人都能找到工作中的独立与自豪时才能实现。只有当诚实劳动获得的薪水足够让家庭摆脱困苦的悬崖时才能实现。

We, the people, still believe that enduring security and lasting peace do not require perpetual war. Our brave men and women in uniform, tempered by the flames of battle, are unmatched in skill and courage. Our citizens, seared by the memory of those we have lost, know too well the price that is paid for liberty. The knowledge of their sacrifice will keep us forever vigilant against those who would do us harm. But we are also heirs to those who won the peace and not just the war, who turned sworn enemies into the surest of friends, and we must carry those lessons into this time as well.

我们——美国人民，仍然相信持久的安全与和平不需要持续的战争。我们勇敢的士兵经受了战火的考验，他们的技能和勇气是无可匹敌的。我们的公民依然铭记着那些阵亡者，他们非常清楚我们为自由付出的代价。明白他们的牺牲将让我们永远对那些试图伤害我们的势力保持警惕。但我们也是那些赢得和平而不只是战争的人们的后代，他们将仇敌转变成最可靠的朋友，我们也必须把这些经验带到这个时代。

附 录

2010 国情咨文——2010 年 1 月 27 日美国众议院

Madam Speaker, Vice President Biden, members of Congress, distinguished guests, and fellow Americans:

Our Constitution declares that from time to time, the President shall give to Congress information about the state of our union. For 220 years, our leaders have fulfilled this duty. They've done so during periods of prosperity and tranquility. And they've done so in the midst of war and depression; at moments of great strife and great struggle.

It's tempting to look back on these moments and assume that our progress was inevitable—that America was always destined to succeed. But when the Union was turned back at Bull Run, and the Allies first landed at Omaha Beach, victory was very much in doubt.

When the market crashed on Black Tuesday, and civil rights marchers were beaten on Bloody Sunday, the future was anything but certain. These were the times that tested the courage of our convictions, and the strength of our union. And despite all our divisions and disagreements, our hesitations and our fears, America prevailed because we chose to move forward as one nation, as one people.

Again, we are tested. And again, we must answer history's call.

One year ago, I took office amid two wars, an economy rocked by a severe recession, a financial system on the verge of collapse, and a government deeply in debt. Experts from across the political spectrum warned that if we did not act, we might face a second depression. So we acted immediately and aggressively. And one year later, the worst of the storm has passed. But the devastation remains. One in 10 Americans still cannot find work. Many businesses have shuttered. Home values have declined. Small towns and rural communities have been hit especially hard. And for those who'd already known poverty, life has become that much harder.

This recession has also compounded the burdens that America's families have been dealing with for decades—the burden of working harder and longer for less; of being unable to save enough to retire or help kids with college. So I know the anxieties that are out there right now. They're not new. These struggles are the reason I ran for President. These struggles are what I've witnessed for years in places like Elkhart, Indiana; Galesburg, Illinois. I hear about them in the letters that I read each night. The toughest to read are those written by children—asking why they have to move from their home, asking when their mom or dad will be able to go back to work.

For these Americans and so many others, change has not come fast enough. Some are frustrated; some are angry. They don't understand why it seems like bad behavior on Wall Street is rewarded, but hard work on Main Street isn't; or why Washington has been unable or unwilling to solve any of our problems. They're tired of the partisanship and the shouting and the pettiness. They know we can't afford it. Not now.

So we face big and difficult challenges. And what the American people hope—what they deserve—is for all of us, Democrats and Republicans, to work through our differences; to overcome the numbing weight of our politics. For while the people who sent us here have different backgrounds, different stories, different beliefs, the anxieties they face are the same. The aspirations they hold are shared: a job that pays the bills; a chance to get ahead; most of all, the ability to give their children a better life.

You know what else they share? They share a stubborn resilience in the face of adversity. After one of the most difficult years in our history, they remain busy building cars and teaching kids, starting businesses and going back to school. They're coaching Little League and helping their neighbors. One woman wrote to me and said, "We are strained but hopeful, struggling but encouraged."

It's because of this spirit—this great decency and great strength—that I have never been more hopeful about America's future than I am tonight. Despite our hardships, our union is strong. We do not give up. We do not quit. We do not allow fear or division to break our spirit. In this new decade, it's time the American people get a government that matches their decency; that embodies their strength.

And tonight, tonight I'd like to talk about how together we can deliver on that promise.

It begins with our economy.

Our most urgent task upon taking office was to shore up the same banks that helped cause this crisis. It was not easy to do. And if there's one thing that has unified Democrats and Republicans, and everybody in between, it's that we all hated the bank bailout. I hated it, I hated it. You hated it. It was about as popular as a root canal. But when I ran for President, I promised I wouldn't just do what was popular—I would do what was necessary. And if we had allowed the meltdown of the financial system, unemployment might be double what it is today. More businesses would certainly have closed. More homes would have surely been lost.

So I supported the last administration's efforts to create the financial rescue program. And when we took that program over, we made it more transparent and more accountable. And as a result, the markets are now stabilized, and we've recovered most of the money we spent on the banks. Most but not all. To recover the rest, I've proposed a fee on the biggest banks. Now, I know Wall Street isn't keen on this idea. But if these firms can afford to hand out big bonuses again, they can afford a modest fee to pay back the taxpayers who rescued them in their time of need.

Now, as we stabilized the financial system, we also took steps to get our economy growing again, save as many jobs as possible, and help Americans who had become unemployed. That's why we extended or increased unemployment benefits for more than 18 million Americans; made health insurance 65 percent cheaper for families who get their coverage through COBRA; and passed 25 different tax cuts.

Now, let me repeat: We cut taxes. We cut taxes for 95 percent of working families. We cut taxes for small businesses. We cut taxes for first-time homebuyers. We cut taxes for parents trying to care for their children. We cut taxes for 8 million Americans paying for college.

I thought I'd get some applause on that one.

As a result, millions of Americans had more to spend on gas and food and other necessities, all of which helped businesses keep more workers. And we haven't raised income taxes by a single dime on a single person. Not a single dime.

Because of the steps we took, there are about two million Americans working right now who would otherwise be unemployed. Two hundred thousand work in construction and clean energy; 300,000 are teachers and other education workers. Tens of thousands are cops, firefighters, correctional officers, first responders. And we're on track to add another one and a half million jobs to this total by the end of the year.

The plan that has made all of this possible, from the tax cuts to the jobs, is the Recovery Act. That's right—*the Recovery Act*, also known as the *stimulus bill*. Economists on the left and the right say this bill has helped save jobs and avert disaster. But you don't have to take their word for it.

Talk to the small business in Phoenix that will triple its workforce because of *the Recovery Act*. Talk to the window manufacturer in Philadelphia who said he used to be skeptical about *the Recovery Act*, until he had to add two more work shifts just because of the business it created. Talk to the single teacher raising two kids who was told by her principal in the last week of school that because of *the*

Recovery Act, she wouldn't be laid off after all.

There are stories like this all across America. And after two years of recession, the economy is growing again. Retirement funds have started to gain back some of their value. Businesses are beginning to invest again, and slowly some are starting to hire again.

But I realize that for every success story, there are other stories, of men and women who wake up with the anguish of not knowing where their next paycheck will come from; who send out resumes week after week and hear nothing in response. That is why jobs must be our number-one focus in 2010, and that's why I'm calling for a new jobs bill tonight.

Now, the true engine of job creation in this country will always be America's businesses. But government can create the conditions necessary for businesses to expand and hire more workers.

We should start where most new jobs do—in small businesses, companies that begin when—companies that begin when an entrepreneur—when an entrepreneur takes a chance on a dream, or a worker decides it's time she became her own boss. Through sheer grit and determination, these companies have weathered the recession and they're ready to grow. But when you talk to small businessowners in places like Allentown, Pennsylvania, or Elyria, Ohio, you find out that even though banks on Wall Street are lending again, they're mostly lending to bigger companies. Financing remains difficult for small businessowners across the country, even those that are making a profit.

So tonight, I'm proposing that we take $30 billion of the money Wall Street banks have repaid and use it to help community banks give small businesses the credit they need to stay afloat. I'm also proposing a new small business tax credit—one that will go to over one million small businesses who hire new workers or raise wages. While we're at it, let's also eliminate all capital gains taxes on small business investment, and provide a tax incentive for all large businesses and all small businesses to invest in new plants and equipment.

Next, we can put Americans to work today building the infrastructure of tomorrow. From the first railroads to the Interstate Highway System, our nation has always been built to compete. There's no reason Europe or China should have the fastest trains, or the new factories that manufacture clean energy products.

Tomorrow, I'll visit Tampa, Florida, where workers will soon break ground on a new high-speed railroad funded by *the Recovery Act.* There are projects like that all across this country that will create jobs and help move our nation's goods, services, and information.

We should put more Americans to work building clean energy facilities and give rebates to Americans who make their homes more energy-efficient, which supports clean energy jobs. And to encourage these and other businesses to stay within our borders, it is time to finally slash the tax breaks for companies that ship our jobs overseas, and give those tax breaks to companies that create jobs right here in the United States of America.

Now, the House has passed a jobs bill that includes some of these steps. As the first order of business this year, I urge the Senate to do the same, and I know they will. They will. People are out of work. They're hurting. They need our help. And I want a jobs bill on my desk without delay.

But the truth is, these steps won't make up for the seven million jobs that we've lost over the last two years. The only way to move to full employment is to lay a new foundation for long-term economic growth, and finally address the problems that America's families have confronted for years. We can't afford another so-called economic "expansion" like the one from the last decade—what some call the "lost decade"—where jobs grew more slowly than during any prior expansion; where the income of the average American household declined while the cost of health care and tuition reached record highs; where prosperity was built on a housing bubble and financial speculation.

From the day I took office, I've been told that addressing our larger challenges is too ambitious; such an effort would be too contentious. I've been told that our political system is too gridlocked, and that we should just put things on hold for a while. For those who make these claims, I have one simple question: How long should we wait? How long should America put its future on hold?

You see, Washington has been telling us to wait for decades, even as the problems have grown worse. Meanwhile, China is not waiting to revamp its economy. Germany is not waiting. India is not waiting. These nations—they're not standing still. These nations aren't playing for second place. They're putting more emphasis on math and science. They're rebuilding their infrastructure. They're making serious investments in clean energy because they want those jobs.

Well, I do not accept second place for the United States of America.

As hard as it may be, as uncomfortable and contentious as the debates may become, it's time to get serious about fixing the problems that are hampering our growth.

Now, one place to start is serious financial reform. Look, I am not interested in punishing banks. I'm interested in protecting our economy. A strong, healthy financial market makes it possible for businesses to access credit and create new jobs. It channels the savings of families into investments that raise incomes. But that can only happen if we guard against the same recklessness that nearly brought down our entire economy.

We need to make sure consumers and middle-class families have the information they need to make financial decisions. We can't allow financial institutions, including those that take your deposits, to take risks that threaten the whole economy.

Now, the House has already passed financial reform with many of these changes. And the lobbyists are trying to kill it. But we cannot let them win this fight. And if the bill that ends up on my desk does not meet the test of real reform, I will send it back until we get it right. We've got to get it right.

Next, we need to encourage American innovation. Last year, we made the largest investment in basic research funding in history—an investment that could lead to the world's cheapest solar cells or treatment that kills cancer cells but leaves healthy ones untouched. And no area is more ripe for such innovation than energy. You can see the results of last year's investments in clean energy—in the North Carolina company that will create 1,200 jobs nationwide helping to make advanced batteries; or in the California business that will put a thousand people to work making solar panels.

But to create more of these clean energy jobs, we need more production, more efficiency, more incentives. And that means building a new generation of safe, clean nuclear power plants in this country. It means making tough decisions about opening new offshore areas for oil and gas development. It means continued investment in advanced biofuels and clean coal technologies. And, yes, it means passing a comprehensive energy and climate bill with incentives that will finally make clean energy the profitable kind of energy in America.

I am grateful to the House for passing such a bill last year. And this year I'm eager to help advance the bipartisan effort in the Senate.

I know there have been questions about whether we can afford such changes in a tough economy. I know that there are those who disagree with the overwhelming scientific evidence on climate change. But here's the thing—even if you doubt the evidence, providing incentives for energy-efficiency and clean energy are the right thing to do for our future—because the nation that leads the clean energy economy will be the nation that leads the global economy. And America must be that nation.

Third, we need to export more of our goods. Because the more products we make and sell to other countries, the more jobs we support right here in America. So tonight, we set a new goal: We will double our exports over the next five years, an increase that will support two million jobs in America. To help meet this goal, we're launching a National Export Initiative that will help farmers and small businesses increase their exports, and reform export controls consistent with national security.

We have to seek new markets aggressively, just as our competitors are. If America sits on the sidelines while other nations sign trade deals, we will lose the chance to create jobs on our shores. But realizing those benefits also means enforcing those agreements so our trading partners play by the rules. And that's why we'll continue to shape a Doha trade agreement that opens global markets, and why we will strengthen our trade relations in Asia and with key partners like South Korea and Panama and Colombia.

Fourth, we need to invest in the skills and education of our people. Now, this year, we've broken through the stalemate between left and right by launching a national competition to improve our schools. And the idea here is simple: Instead of rewarding failure, we only reward success. Instead of funding the status quo, we only invest in reform—reform that raises student achievement; inspires students to excel in math and science; and turns around failing schools that steal the future of too many young Americans, from rural communities to the inner city. In the 21st century, the best anti-poverty program around is a world-class education. And in this country, the success of our children cannot depend more on where they live than on their potential.

When we renew *the Elementary and Secondary Education Act*, we will work with Congress to expand these reforms to all 50 states. Still, in this economy, a high school diploma no longer guarantees a good job. That's why I urge the Senate to follow the House and pass a bill that will revitalize our community colleges, which are a career pathway to the children of so many working families.

To make college more affordable, this bill will finally end the unwarranted taxpayer subsidies that go to banks for student loans. Instead, let's take that money and give families a $10,000 tax credit for four years of college and increase Pell Grants. And let's tell another one million students that when they graduate, they will be required to pay only 10 percent of their income on student loans, and all of their debt will be forgiven after 20 years—and forgiven after 10 years if they choose a career in public service, because in the United States of America, no one should go broke because they chose to go to college. And by the way, it's time for colleges and universities to get serious about cutting their own costs—because they, too, have a responsibility to help solve this problem.

Now, the price of college tuition is just one of the burdens facing the middle class. That's why last year I asked Vice President Biden to chair a task force on middle-class families. That's why we're nearly doubling the child care tax credit, and making it easier to save for retirement by giving access to every worker a retirement account and expanding the tax credit for those who start a nest egg. That's why we're working to lift the value of a family's single largest investment—their home. The steps we took last year to shore up the housing market have allowed millions of Americans to take out new loans and save an average of $1,500 on mortgage payments. This year, we will step up refinancing so that homeowners can move into more affordable mortgages.

And it is precisely to relieve the burden on middle-class families that we still need health insurance reform. Yes, we do. Now, let's clear a few things up. I didn't choose to tackle this issue to get some legislative victory under my belt. And by now it should be fairly obvious that I didn't take on health care because it was good politics. I took on health care because of the stories I've heard from Americans with preexisting conditions whose lives depend on getting coverage; patients who've been denied coverage; families—even those with insurance—who are just one illness away from financial ruin.

After nearly a century of trying—Democratic administrations, Republican administrations—we are closer than ever to bringing more security to the lives of so many Americans. The approach we've taken would protect every American from the worst practices of the insurance industry. It would give small businesses and uninsured Americans a chance to choose an affordable health care plan in a competitive market. It would require every insurance plan to cover preventive care.

And by the way, I want to acknowledge our First Lady, Michelle Obama, who this year is creating a national movement to tackle the epidemic of childhood obesity and make kids healthier. Thank you. She gets embarrassed.

Our approach would preserve the right of Americans who have insurance to keep their doctor and their plan. It would reduce costs and premiums for millions of families and businesses. And according to the Congressional Budget Office—the independent organization that both parties have cited as the official scorekeeper for Congress—our approach would bring down the deficit by as much as $1 trillion over the next two decades.

Still, this is a complex issue, and the longer it was debated, the more skeptical people became. I take my share of the blame for not explaining it more clearly to the American people. And I know that with all the lobbying and horse-trading, the process left most Americans wondering, "What's in it for me?"

But I also know this problem is not going away. By the time I'm finished speaking tonight, more Americans will have lost their health insurance. Millions will lose it this year. Our deficit will grow. Premiums will go up. Patients will be denied the care they need. Small business owners will continue to drop coverage altogether. I will not walk away from these Americans, and neither should the people in this chamber.

So, as temperatures cool, I want everyone to take another look at the plan we've proposed. There's a reason why many doctors, nurses, and health care experts who know our system best consider this approach a vast improvement over the status quo. But if anyone from either party has a better approach that will bring down premiums, bring down the deficit, cover the uninsured, strengthen Medicare for seniors, and stop insurance company abuses, let me know. Let me know. Let me know. I'm eager to see it.

Here's what I ask Congress, though: Don't walk away from reform. Not now. Not when we are so close. Let us find a way to come together and finish the job for the American people. Let's get it done. Let's get it done.

Now, even as health care reform would reduce our deficit, it's not enough to dig us out of a massive fiscal hole in which we find ourselves. It's a challenge that makes all others that much harder to solve, and one that's been subject to a lot of political posturing. So let me start the discussion of government spending by setting the record straight.

At the beginning of the last decade, the year 2000, America had a budget surplus of over $200 billion. By the time I took office, we had a one-year deficit of over $1 trillion and projected deficits of $8 trillion over the next decade. Most of this was the result of not paying for two wars, two tax cuts, and an expensive prescription drug program. On top of that, the effects of the recession put a $3 trillion hole in our budget. All this was before I walked in the door.

Now—just stating the facts. Now, if we had taken office in ordinary times, I would have liked nothing more than to start bringing down the deficit. But we took office amid a crisis. And our efforts to prevent a second depression have added another $1 trillion to our national debt. That, too, is a fact. I'm absolutely convinced that was the right thing to do. But families across the country are tightening their belts and making tough decisions. The federal government should do the same. So tonight, I'm proposing specific steps to pay for the trillion dollars that it took to rescue the economy last year.

Starting in 2011, we are prepared to freeze government spending for three years. Spending related to our national security, Medicare, Medicaid, and Social Security will not be affected. But all other discretionary government programs will. Like any cash-strapped family, we will work within a budget to invest in what we need and sacrifice what we don't. And if I have to enforce this discipline by veto, I will. We will continue to go through the budget, line by line, page by page, to eliminate programs that we can't afford and don't work. We've already identified $20 billion in savings for next year. To help working families, we'll extend our middle-class tax cuts. But at a time of record deficits, we will not continue tax cuts for oil companies, for investment fund managers, and for those making over $250,000 a year. We just can't afford it.

Now, even after paying for what we spent on my watch, we'll still face the massive deficit we had when I took office. More importantly, the cost of Medicare, Medicaid, and Social Security will continue to skyrocket. That's why I've called for a bipartisan fiscal commission, modeled on a proposal by Republican Judd Gregg and Democrat Kent Conrad. This can't be one of those Washington gimmicks that lets us pretend we solved a problem. The commission will have to provide a specific set of solutions by a certain deadline.

Now, yesterday, the Senate blocked a bill that would have created this commission. So I'll issue an executive order that will allow us to go forward, because I refuse to pass this problem on to another generation of Americans. And when the vote comes tomorrow, the Senate should restore the pay-as-you-go law that was a big reason for why we had record surpluses in the 1990s.

Now, I know that some in my own party will argue that we can't address the deficit or freeze government spending when so many are still hurting. And I agree—which is why this freeze won't take effect until next year—when the economy is stronger. That's how budgeting works. But understand—understand if we don't take meaningful steps to rein in our debt, it could damage our markets, increase the cost of borrowing, and jeopardize our recovery—all of which would have an even worse effect on our job growth and family incomes.

From some on the right, I expect we'll hear a different argument—that if we just make fewer investments in our people, extend tax cuts including those for the wealthier Americans, eliminate more regulations, maintain the status quo on health care, our deficits will go away. The problem is that's what we did for eight years. That's what helped us into this crisis. It's what helped lead to these deficits. We can't do it again. Rather than fight the same tired battles that have dominated Washington for decades, it's time to try something new. Let's invest in our people without leaving them a mountain of debt. Let's meet our responsibility to the citizens who sent us here. Let's try common sense. (Laughter.) A novel concept.

To do that, we have to recognize that we face more than a deficit of dollars right now. We face a deficit of trust—deep and corrosive doubts about how Washington works that have been growing for years. To close that credibility gap we have to take action on both ends of Pennsylvania Avenue—to end the outsized influence of lobbyists; to do our work openly; to give our people the government they deserve.

That's what I came to Washington to do. That's why—for the first time in history—my administration posts on our White House visitors online. That's why we've excluded lobbyists from policymaking jobs, or seats on federal boards and commissions. But we can't stop there. It's time to require lobbyists to disclose each contact they make on behalf of a client with my administration or with Congress. It's time to put strict limits on the contributions that lobbyists give to candidates for federal office.

With all due deference to separation of powers, last week the Supreme Court reversed a century of law that I believe will open the floodgates for special interests—including foreign corporations—to spend without limit in our elections. I don't think American elections should be bankrolled by America's most powerful interests, or worse, by foreign entities. They should be decided by the American people. And I'd urge Democrats and Republicans to pass a bill that helps to correct some of these problems.

I'm also calling on Congress to continue down the path of earmark reform. Democrats and Republicans. Democrats and Republicans. You've trimmed some of this spending, you've embraced some meaningful change. But restoring the public trust demands more. For example, some members of Congress post some earmark requests online. Tonight, I'm calling on Congress to publish all earmark requests on a single Web site before there's a vote, so that the American people can see how their money is being spent.

Of course, none of these reforms will even happen if we don't also reform how we work with one another.

Now, I'm not naïve. I never thought that the mere fact of my election would usher in peace and harmony—and some post-partisan era. I knew that both parties have fed divisions that are deeply entrenched. And on some issues, there are simply philosophical differences that will always cause us to part ways. These disagreements, about the role of government in our lives, about our national priorities and our national security, they've been taking place for over 200 years. They're the very essence of our democracy.

But what frustrates the American people is a Washington where every day is Election Day. We can't wage a perpetual campaign where the only goal is to see who can get the most embarrassing headlines about the other side—a belief that if you lose, I win. Neither party should delay or obstruct every single bill just because they can. The confirmation of—I'm speaking to both parties now. The confirmation of well-qualified public servants shouldn't be held hostage to the pet projects or grudges of a few individual senators.

Washington may think that saying anything about the other side, no matter how false, no matter how malicious, is just part of the game. But it's precisely such politics that has stopped either party from helping the American people. Worse yet, it's sowing further division among our citizens, further distrust in our government. So, no, I will not give up on trying to change the tone of our politics. I know it's an election year. And after last week, it's clear that campaign fever has come even earlier than usual. But we still need to govern.

To Democrats, I would remind you that we still have the largest majority in decades, and the people expect us to solve problems, not run for the hills. And if the Republican leadership is going to insist that 60 votes in the Senate are required to do any business at all in this town—a supermajority—then the responsibility to govern is now yours as well. Just saying no to everything may be good short-term politics, but it's not leadership. We were sent here to serve our citizens, not our ambitions. So let's show the American people that we can do it together. This week, I'll be addressing a meeting of the House Republicans. I'd like to begin monthly meetings with both Democratic and Republican leadership. I know you can't wait.

Throughout our history, no issue has united this country more than our security. Sadly, some of the unity we felt after 9/11 has dissipated. We can argue all we want about who's to blame for this, but I'm not interested in re-litigating the past. I know that all of us love this country. All of us are committed to its defense. So let's put aside the schoolyard taunts about who's tough. Let's reject the false choice between protecting our people and upholding our values. Let's leave behind the fear and division, and do what it takes to defend our nation and forge a more hopeful future—for America and for the world.

That's the work we began last year. Since the day I took office, we've renewed our focus on the terrorists who threaten our nation. We've made substantial investments in our homeland security and disrupted plots that threatened to take American lives. We are filling unacceptable gaps revealed by the failed Christmas attack, with better airline security and swifter action on our intelligence. We've prohibited torture and strengthened partnerships from the Pacific to South Asia to the Arabian Peninsula. And in the last year, hundreds of al Qaeda's fighters and affiliates, including many senior leaders, have been captured or killed—far more than in 2008.

And in Afghanistan, we're increasing our troops and training Afghan security forces so they can begin to take the lead in July of 2011, and our troops can begin to come home. We will reward good governance, work to reduce corruption, and support the rights of all Afghans—men and women alike. We're joined by allies and partners who have increased their own commitments, and who will come together tomorrow in London to reaffirm our common purpose. There will be difficult days ahead. But I am absolutely confident we will succeed.

As we take the fight to al Qaeda, we are responsibly leaving Iraq to its people. As a candidate, I promised that I would end this war, and that is what I am doing as President. We will have all of our combat troops out of Iraq by the end of this August. We will support the Iraqi government—we will support the Iraqi government as they hold elections, and we will continue to partner with the Iraqi people to promote regional peace and prosperity. But make no mistake: This war is ending, and all of our troops are coming home.

Tonight, all of our men and women in uniform—in Iraq, in Afghanistan, and around the world—they have to know that we—that they have our respect, our gratitude, our full support. And just as they must have the resources they need in war, we all have a responsibility to support them when they come home. That's why we made the largest increase in investments for veterans in decades—last year. That's why we're building a 21st century VA. And that's why Michelle has joined with Jill Biden to forge a national commitment to support military families.

Now, even as we prosecute two wars, we're also confronting perhaps the greatest danger to the American people—the threat of nuclear weapons. I've embraced the vision of John F. Kennedy and Ronald Reagan through a strategy that reverses the spread of these weapons and seeks a world without them. To reduce our stockpiles and launchers, while ensuring our deterrent, the United States and Russia are completing negotiations on the farthest-reaching arms control treaty in nearly two decades. And at April's Nuclear Security Summit, we will bring 44 nations together here in Washington, D.C. behind a clear goal: securing all vulnerable nuclear materials around the world in four years, so that they never fall into the hands of terrorists.

Now, these diplomatic efforts have also strengthened our hand in dealing with those nations that insist on violating international agreements in pursuit of nuclear weapons. That's why North Korea now faces increased isolation, and stronger sanctions—sanctions that are being vigorously enforced. That's why the international community is more united.

That's the leadership that we are providing—engagement that advances the common security and prosperity of all people. We're working through the G20 to sustain a lasting global recovery. We're working with Muslim communities around the world to promote science and education and innovation. We have gone from a bystander to a leader in the fight against climate change. We're helping developing countries to feed themselves, and continuing the fight against HIV/AIDS. And we are launching a new initiative that will give us the capacity to respond faster and more effectively to bioterrorism or an infectious disease—a plan that will counter threats at home and strengthen public health abroad.

As we have for over 60 years, America takes these actions because our destiny is connected to those beyond our shores. But we also do it because it is right. That's why, as we meet here tonight, over 10,000 Americans are working with many nations to help the people of Haiti recover and rebuild. That's why we stand with the girl who yearns to go to school in Afghanistan; why we support the human rights of the women marching through the streets of Iran; why we advocate for the young man denied a job by corruption in Guinea. For America must always stand on the side of freedom and human dignity. Always.

Abroad, America's greatest source of strength has always been our ideals. The same is true at home. We find unity in our incredible diversity, drawing on the promise enshrined in our Constitution: the notion that we're all created equal; that no matter who you are or what you look like, if you abide by the law you should be protected by it; if you adhere to our common values you should be treated no different than anyone else.

We must continually renew this promise. My administration has a Civil Rights Division that is once again prosecuting civil rights violations and employment discrimination. We finally strengthened our laws to protect against crimes driven by hate. This year, I will work with Congress and our military to finally repeal the law that denies gay Americans the right to serve the country they love because of who they are. It's the right thing to do.

We're going to crack down on violations of equal pay laws—so that women get equal pay for an equal day's work. And we should continue the work of fixing our broken immigration system—to secure our borders and enforce our laws, and ensure that everyone who plays by the rules can contribute to our economy and enrich our nation.

In the end, it's our ideals, our values that built America—values that allowed us to forge a nation made up of immigrants from every corner of the globe; values that drive our citizens still. Every day, Americans meet their responsibilities to their families and their employers. Time and again, they lend a hand to their neighbors and give back to their country. They take pride in their labor, and are generous in spirit. These aren't Republican values or Democratic values that they're living by; business values or labor values. They're American values.

Unfortunately, too many of our citizens have lost faith that our biggest institutions—our corporations, our media, and, yes, our government—still reflect these same values. Each of these institutions are full of honorable men and women doing important work that helps our country prosper. But each time a CEO rewards himself for failure, or a banker puts the rest of us at risk for his own selfish gain, people's doubts grow. Each time lobbyists game the system or politicians tear each other down instead of lifting this country up, we lose faith. The more that TV pundits reduce serious debates to silly arguments, big issues into sound bites, our citizens turn away. No wonder there's so much cynicism out there. No wonder there's so much disappointment.

I campaigned on the promise of change—change we can believe in, the slogan went. And right now, I know there are many Americans who aren't sure if they still believe we can change—or that I can deliver it. But remember this—I never suggested that change would be easy, or that I could do it alone. Democracy in a nation of 300 million people can be noisy and messy and complicated. And when you try to do big things and make big changes, it stirs passions and controversy. That's just how it is.

Those of us in public office can respond to this reality by playing it safe and avoid telling hard truths and pointing fingers. We can do what's necessary to keep our poll numbers high, and get through the next election instead of doing what's best for the next generation. But I also know this: If people had made that decision 50 years ago, or 100 years ago, or 200 years ago, we wouldn't be here tonight. The only reason we are here is because generations of Americans were unafraid to do what was hard; to do what was needed even when success was uncertain; to do what it took to keep the dream of this nation alive for their children and their grandchildren.

Our administration has had some political setbacks this year, and some of them were deserved. But I wake up every day knowing that they are nothing compared to the setbacks that families all across this country have faced this year. And what keeps me going—what keeps me fighting—is that despite all these setbacks, that spirit of determination and optimism, that fundamental decency that has always been at the core of the American people, that lives on.

It lives on in the struggling small business owner who wrote to me of his company, "None of us," he said, "...are willing to consider, even slightly, that we might fail."

It lives on in the woman who said that even though she and her neighbors have felt the pain of recession, "We are strong. We are resilient. We are American."

It lives on in the 8-year-old boy in Louisiana, who just sent me his allowance and asked if I would give it to the people of Haiti.

And it lives on in all the Americans who've dropped everything to go someplace they've never been and pull people they've never known from the rubble, prompting chants of "U.S.A.! U.S.A.! U.S.A!" when another life was saved.

The spirit that has sustained this nation for more than two centuries lives on in you, its people.

We have finished a difficult year. We have come through a difficult decade. But a new year has come. A new decade stretches before us. We don't quit. I don't quit. Let's seize this moment—to start anew, to carry the dream forward, and to strengthen our union once more.

Thank you. God bless you. And God bless the United States of America.

议长女士、副总统拜登、美国国会议员、各位来宾、美国同胞：

我国宪法规定，总统应当不时地向国会提供有关国情的信息。220年来，我们的领导人一直履行这一职责。在繁荣与安宁的时期，他们这样做了。在战争和经济萧条中，在严重动乱和伟大斗争的时刻，他们也这样做了。

一种想法是具有诱惑力的，就是回顾这些时刻，以为我们的进步是不可避免的——以为美国总是注定要成功。但是，当北方联邦军在布尔朗战役中被击溃，当盟军第一次在奥马哈海滩登陆，胜利是有很大疑问的。

当黑色星期二市场崩溃，当血腥的星期日民权示威者被殴打，前途绝非是确定无疑的。这些时候考验了我们的信念与勇气和我们合众国的力量。尽管我们存在着种种分歧与不同意见、犹豫不决和恐惧，但美国胜利了，因为我们选择了团结一起，作为一个国家，作为一国人民向前迈进。

现在，我们再次接受考验。我们必须再次响应历史的召唤。

一年前我就职，当时两场战争正酣，还有一场严重的经济衰退，金融体系处于崩溃的边缘，政府债台高筑。来自各个政治派别的专家警告说，如果我们不采取行动，我们可能面临第二次经济萧条。因此，我们立即大刀阔斧地采取了行动。一年后，这场风暴的最严重阶段已经过去了，但破坏仍然存在。十个美国人当中仍有一个人无法找到工作，许多商家关门，住房价值下降，小城镇和农村社区受到的冲击尤其严重。而对于已经很贫穷的人们来说，生活变得困难得多。

经济衰退也加重了美国的家庭几十年来一直承担着的负担——更加努力地工作，工作时间也更长，但所得却更少，储蓄不足以退休或帮助上大学的子女。所以我知道民间目前存在的忧虑，这种担忧并不新鲜。这些问题是我竞选总统的理由，多年来在印第安纳州埃尔德哈特、伊利诺伊州盖尔斯堡，我目睹了这些困境。我在每天晚上读到的信件中听到他们的声音。最难以读下去的信件是孩子们写的，他们问为什么他们要离开自己的家，问他们的母亲或父亲何时可以重新上班。

对于这些美国人和许多其他人来说，已经发生的变革不够快。一些人感到沮丧，一些人感到愤怒。他们不明白，为什么似乎华尔街上的不良行为得到奖赏，而商业大街上的努力却没有，或者为何华盛顿一直无法或不愿解决我们的任何问题，他们对党派斗争、叫喊和卑鄙行为感到厌倦，他们知道我们承担不起这种负担，现在不行。

因此，我们面临着巨大的和棘手的挑战。美国人民所希望，也是他们所应看到的是我们大家，民主党人和共和党人消除分歧，克服我们的政治斗争所造成的令人麻木的重压。因为虽然把我们选到这里来的人民具有不同的背景、不同的故事、不同的信仰，但他们面临的忧虑是相同的。他们持有的愿望是共同的：一份能够付清账单的工作，有机会获得成功，最重要的是能够给子女以更好的生活。

大家知道他们还有哪些共同点吗？在逆境中，他们共有一种顽强的韧性。在我们历史上最困难的年份之一过后，他们仍忙于制造汽车和教育孩子，创办企业和回学校上学。他们担任少年棒球联盟的教练，帮助他们的邻居。一位妇女写信给我说："我们很紧张但也抱有希望，疲于应付但很受鼓舞。"

正是因为这种精神——这种伟大的尊严和巨大的力量，我从来都没有像今晚这样对美国的前途寄予厚望。尽管我们遇到困难，但我们的合众国是强大的。我们不放弃，我们不退出。我们不允许恐惧和分裂破坏我们的精神。这个新的十年，美国人民应当获得符合他们的道德标准和体现出他们的力量的政府。

今晚，我想谈谈我们如何能够共同兑现这一诺言。

事情得从我们的经济说起。

我们就职后最紧迫的任务是巩固银行的实力，正是这些银行导致了这场危机。这是不容易做到的。如果有一件事使民主党人和共和党人，以及这两者之间的每个人团结起来，那就是我们都厌恶银行救助。我讨厌它，我讨厌它，大家讨厌它。它的受欢迎程度与治疗牙疼时的根管疗法差不多。但是，我竞选总统时，我答应我不会只是做受欢迎的事情，我会做必要的事情。如果我们听任金融系统陷于崩溃，失业率可能会比今天高一倍。更多的企业肯定已经倒闭，更多人的住宅肯定已经失去。

因此，我支持了上届政府制订金融救援方案的努力。我们接管这一方案后，使之更加透明和更加负责。因此，目前市场稳定，我们已经收回了花在银行身上的绝大部分资金。绝大部分，但不是全部。为了收回其余部分，我已经提出对最大的几家银行征收一笔费用。现在我知道，华尔街对这个想法并不热衷。但是，如果这些公司能够再次负担得起支付高额奖金，他们就可以负担有限的收费，以偿还纳税人在他们需要时解救他们所花的钱。

现在，在我们使金融体系趋于稳定时，我们还采取措施，使我们的经济恢复增长，保住尽可能多的就业机会，帮助失业的美国人。这就是为什么我们向超过一千八百万的美国人提供或增加了失业救济；对通过《统一综合预算协调法案》获得医疗保险的家庭，使其费用降低了65%；并通过了25项不同的减税措施。

现在，让我再次重申：我们降低了税赋。我们降低了95%的劳动家庭的税赋，我们降低了小企业的税赋，我们降低了首次购房税，我们降低了照顾子女的父母的税赋，我们降低了要为上大学花钱的八百万美国人的税赋。

我认为我会为此得到一些掌声。

因此，千百万美国人有更多的钱可以用于购买汽油、食物和其他生活必需品，所有这些都有助于企业保留更多的工人。我们并没有把任何人的所得税提高分文，没有提高分文。

由于我们采取的措施，大约有二百万目前就业的美国人本来会失业。二十万人就业于建筑业和清洁能源产业，三十万人是教师和其他教育工作者，几十万人是警察、消防队员、惩教人员、急救人员。按照预期，到今年年底，我们将在这一总数基础上再增加一百五十万个就业岗位。

令这一切——从减税到增加就业成为可能的计划就是《经济复苏法案》。没错复苏法，也被称为《刺激法案》。左右两派的经济学家都说，这项法案帮助挽救了就业，避免了灾难。但是，你不必听信他们的话。

与凤凰城由于《复兴法案》而职工队伍将会扩大两倍的小企业谈一谈，与费城的窗户制造商谈一谈。他说，他曾经对《复兴法案》持怀疑态度，一直到由于该法案所创造的生意，使他不得不增加了两个班次的工作。与抚养两个孩子的单身教师谈一谈，学年的最后一周，她的校长对她说，由于《复兴法案》她不会被解雇了。

在全美各地都有这样的故事。两年的衰退过后，经济再次出现增长。养老金基金已经开始恢复部分的价值，工商企业正在开始恢复投资，一些企业正在缓慢地开始重新雇工。

但是，我意识到对于每一个成功事例来说，还有几个事例说的是男男女女一觉醒来，痛苦地不知道自己下一次将会从哪里领工资，一周又一周地发送简历，却没有听到任何答复。这就是为什么 2010 年我们的头号工作重点必须是就业，这也是为什么我今晚呼吁通过一项新的就业法案。

现在，美国创造就业机会的真正动力源泉将始终都是美国的企业。但是，政府能够创造企业拓展业务和雇佣更多工人所必需的条件。

我们应当从大多数新的就业岗位开始的地方开始——在小企业中，这些公司的创业之初，企业家抱着一种梦想碰运气，或者一名职工决定现在是自己当自己的老板的时候了。凭着纯粹的勇气和决心，这些公司经受住了这场经济衰退，现在准备实现增长。但是，当你与宾夕法尼亚州阿伦敦或者俄亥俄州伊利里亚等地的小企业主交谈时，你会发现尽管华尔街上的银行重新开始放贷，但他们主要是向比较大的公司放贷。对全国各地的小企业主甚至盈利的小区业主来说，融资依然困难。

因此，今晚我建议我们从华尔街已经偿还的钱里面拿出300亿美元，用于帮助社区银行为小企业提供它们持续经营所需的信贷。我还建议实行一项新的小企业税收优惠，这项优惠将提供给雇佣新职工或者提高工资的小企业，这些企业超过一百万家。在进行这项工作的同时，我们还要取消对小企业投资征收的所有资本利得税，并为所有大企业和所有小企业提供一项税收鼓励措施，促使其投资于开办新的工厂和采购新的设备。

其次，我们今天还可以让美国人在修建基础设施方面找到工作。从最初的铁路到州际高速公路系统，我们的国家一直是为了在竞争中获胜而进行建设的。没有任何理由只有欧洲或者中国应当拥有最快的列车，或者制造清洁能源产品的新工厂。

明天我将访问佛罗里达州的坦帕市。那里的工人很快就会破土动工，修筑《经济复苏法案》提供资助的一条新的高速铁路。全国各地都有类似的项目。这些项目将创造就业机会，帮助运输和传递我国的商品、劳务与信息。

我们应当让更多的美国人在修建清洁能源设施方面找到工作，并向提高自己的住宅的能源效率的美国人提供退税，因为这支撑着清洁能源领域中的就业机会。为了鼓励这些企业以及其他企业留在我国境内，现在要向把我们的就业岗位转移到海外的公司提供税收减免，把这种减免提供给在美国境内创造就业机会的公司。

现在，众议院已经通过了一项就业法案，其中包括了这些措施当中的一些。作为今年要办的头一件事，我敦促参议院也这样做。我知道他们会这样做的，他们会的。人们失去了工作，他们忍受着伤害，他们需要我们的帮助。我希望尽快地获得一项有关就业的提案。

但事情的真相是，这些举措不会弥补我们最近两年来所失去的700万个就业岗位。实现充分就业的唯一途径就是为经济的长期增长奠定新的基础，最终解决美国的家庭多年来所面临的问题。我们无法承受代价，迎接像最近十年来那样的一场新的所谓的经济“扩展”，一些人称之为“损失的十年”。在此期间，就业岗位的增加速度要比任何从前的经济扩展期间都缓慢，美国家庭的平均收入下降，医疗保健费用和学费达到了创纪录的高点，经济繁荣建立在一场住房建筑泡沫与金融投机基础上。

从我就职那天起我就被告知，应付我们的重大挑战过于雄心勃勃，这种努力会引起太大的争议。我一直被告知，我们的政治制度陷入僵局，因此我们应当暂时把问题搁置起来。对做出这种论断的人们，我有一个简单的问题：我们应当等待多久？美国应当把自己的前途搁置多久？

大家知道，华盛顿几十年来一直要求我们等待，尽管问题日益恶化。与此同时，中国并没有为重振经济而等待，德国没有等待，印度没有等待。这些国家都没有停滞不前。这些国家没有争当第二名，他们更加重视数学与科学。他们翻修了基础设施，他们在清洁能源方面进行了重大投资，因为他们想要获得这些就业机会。

好了，我不接受美国沦为第二名。

尽管工作可能会很棘手，辩论可能会令人不快和有争议，但现在是采取认真的态度，解决阻碍我们的经济增长的种种问题的时候了。

一个起步的地方就是实行重大的金融改革。我对惩罚银行不感兴趣，我感兴趣的是保护我们的经济。一个强有力的、健康的金融市场可以使企业获得信贷和创造新的就业机会。它引导家庭的储蓄成为提高收入的投资项目。但是，只有在我们对几乎使我们的整个经济陷于崩溃的那种鲁莽加以防范的情况下，这一目标才能达到。

我们需要确保消费者和中产阶级家庭掌握他们做出理财决策所需的信息。我们不能任凭金融机构，包括接受大家的存款的机构承担威胁到经济整体的风险。

众议院已经通过了包括许多这方面的变革在内的金融改革。游说分子正在千方百计地扼杀这项改革，但是我们不能让他们赢得这场战斗。如果最终提交给我的这项法案经受不住真正改革的考验，我将把它驳回，直到我们把工作做好。我们必须把工作做好。

其次，我们还需要鼓励美国的创新。去年，我们进行了基础研究拨款方面有史以来最大规模的投资，这项投资可能会带来世界上最廉价的太阳能电池，或者杀死癌细胞但却使健康细胞完好无损的疗法。在这种创新方面最成熟的领域非能源领域莫属。大家可以看到，去年在清洁能源方面投资所取得的成果将体现在给全国范围创造一千两百个就业岗位，从而帮助制造先进的蓄电池的一家北卡罗来纳公司，或者将使一千人在制造太阳能电池板方面找到工作的一家加利福尼亚企业之中。

但是，为了创造更多的这种清洁能源就业岗位，我们需要增加产量，提高效率，提供更多的鼓励措施。这意味着要在美国建设新一代安全、洁净的核电厂。这意味着要就开辟用于开采石油和天然气的新的近海海域问题做出棘手的决策。这意味着要继续在先进的生物燃料和清洁煤技术方面投资。是的，这还意味着要通过一项全面的能源和气候法案，包括最终会使清洁能源在美国成为有利可图的能源的鼓励措施。

我很感激众议院去年通过了这样一项法案。今年，我热切希望帮助参议院推进两党一致的这项努力。

我知道，在我们能否在经济困难下实施这种改革一直存在着争议。我知道，有一些人不同意在气候变化问题上的占压倒优势的科学证据。但这一点很重要——即使你怀疑这些证据，我们今后应当做的事情也是为提高能源效率和提供清洁能源提供鼓励措施，因为领导着清洁能源经济的国家将是领导全球经济的国家。美国必须成为这个国家。

第三，我们需要出口更多的商品。因为我们制造的和向别国出售的产品越多，我们在美国国内支撑的就业岗位也就越多。因此今晚，我们确定一个新的目标：我们将在今后五年内使出口翻一番。这一增长将会支持美国境内的二百万个就业岗位。为了帮助实现这一目标，我们即将启动一项全国范围的出口计划。这项计划将帮助农场主和小企业增加出口，并改革出口管制措施，使之与国家安全相符。

我们必须像竞争对手一样，大力谋求获得新的市场。如果在别国签订贸易协议的时候美国袖手旁观，我们就会失去在本国国内创造就业岗位的机会。但是，实现这些利益也意味着要加强这些协议，以便我们的贸易伙伴按照规则行事。这就是为什么，我们将继续影响签订一项开辟全球市场的多哈回合贸易协定。这也是为什么，我们将加强我们在亚洲的贸易关系以及同韩国、巴拿马和哥伦比亚等重要的伙伴国之间的贸易关系。

第四，我们需要在我国人民的技能和教育方面投资。今年，我们启动了一场全国性的竞争，以改善我们的学校，从而打破了左右两派之间的僵局。这里的想法很简单：我们不是奖励失败，而是只奖励成功。我们不是为维持现状拨款，而是只投资于改革——这种改革使得学生的学习成绩提高，激励学生们在数学与科学方面取得出类拔萃的成绩。使失败的、毁掉过多的年轻美国人前途的学校发生转变，这种情况从农村社区到市中心地带都有。在二十一世纪，最出色的消除贫困计划就是提供世界级的教育。在美国，孩子们能否成功不应取决于他们住在哪里，而应是他们的潜力。

当我们修订《小学和中学教育法》的时候，我们将与国会共同努力，以便把这些改革扩展到所有五十个州。尽管如此，在美国经济中，高中文凭不再能够保障获得一份好工作。这就是为什么，我敦促参议院像议众院一样，通过一项法案，重振我们的社区学院，因为这些学院为如此多的劳动家庭的孩子们提供了就业渠道。

为了使人们更加能够上得起大学，这项法案最终将取消对纳税人提供的使之到银行领取学生贷款的毫无保障的补贴。我们而是要把这笔钱拿来，向家庭提供 1 万美元的税收优惠，以便完成四年的大学学业和增加佩尔助学金。我们要再让一百万名学生在毕业时知道，他们只需支付自己收入的 10% 用于偿还学生贷款，他们的全部债务都将在二十年以后一笔勾销，而如果他们选择在政府就业，就会在十年后一笔勾销。因为在美国，没有人应当由于选择上大学而变得一贫如洗。顺便提一下，现在是高等院校认真考虑降低自己费用的时候了，因为他们也有责任帮助解决这一问题。

大学学费的要价问题仅仅是摆在中产阶级面前的负担之一。这就是为什么，我去年请求副总统拜登领导一个有关中产阶级家庭问题的专门委员会。这就是为什么，我们使有关儿童护理的税收优惠几乎翻一番，并向每个工人提供开设退休账户的机会，并增加对开始攒钱的人们的税收优惠，从而使人们更加容易进行储蓄，以便为退休生活做好准备。这就是为什么，我们正在努力提升家庭最大的一项投资，即住宅的价值。我们去年采取的巩固楼市的举措使千百万美国人得以获得新的贷款，并在抵押贷款偿还方面平均节省 1500 美元。今年，我们将加紧再融资，以使房主们能够获得具有更大偿还能力的抵押贷款。

恰恰是为了缓解中产阶级家庭的负担，我们才仍然需要实行医疗保险方面的改革。是的，我们就是如此。现在，我们要澄清一些事情。我之所以选择解决这一问题，并不是为了在立法方面稳操胜券。到目前为止应当很清楚的一点是，我之所以承担起解决医疗保健问题的职责，并不是因为这在政治上很有利。我承担起这一职责是因为我从一些美国人那里听到了一些故事，讲的是他们在申请医疗保险以前存在病情，而其生命取决于获得保险。我还听到一些被剥夺了保险的患者，只要得一次病就会穷困潦倒的故事，甚至具有保险的家庭也会因一场疾病破产的故事。

在进行了将近一个世纪的尝试之后——民主党与共和党的历届政府——我们比以往任何时候都更加接近于给如此多的美国人的生活带来更大的安全保障。我们所采取的策略将使每个美国人都获得保护，免遭保险业最恶劣的做法的侵害。它还会使小企业和没有保险的美国人获得机会，以便在竞争激烈的市场上选择自己支付得起的医疗保健计划。它还要求每项保险计划都为预防性医疗提供保险。

顺便提一下，我还希望向我们的第一夫人米歇尔奥巴马致谢。她今年即将创立一项全国性运动，以解决儿童肥胖病流行的问题，使儿童更加健康。

我们的做法将维护拥有保险的美国人接受治疗和保留医疗计划的权利。它将为数以百万计的家庭和公司减少费用和保险费。根据国会预算局——一个中立机构，两党都认为它是国会工作表现的官方记录者——的数字，我们的做法将使预算赤字在今后二十年里最多减少 1 万亿美元。

尽管如此，这仍是一个复杂的问题，对此辩论的时间越长，人们的怀疑就会越多。没有更加清楚地向美国人民解释，我要承担一部分责任。我知道，因为各种游说和讨价还价，这个过程让大多数美国人担心该计划最后还能给美国人带来什么。

但我还知道，这个问题并没有消失。到今晚我结束演讲的时候，将有更多美国人失去医疗保险，今年会有数以百万计的美国人失去医疗保险。我们的赤字会增加，保险费会上升。病人将得不到需要的医疗，小企业主将继续完全放弃医疗保险。我不会抛开这些美国人，在座的各位也不应抛弃这些美国人。

随着激烈情绪渐渐平息，我希望每个人重新考虑我们提出的计划。许多最了解我们体系的医生、护士和医疗问题专家都认为，这些措施将极大地改善现状，这是有原因的。但是不管哪个政党的什么人有更好的方案，能降低保险费、减少赤字、覆盖未投保者、加强老年人的医疗保险、并制止保险公司的不良做法，请告诉我。

不过，我要求国会做到下面这一点：不要回避改革。现在不能，因为我们已经接近完成这项工作。让我们想办法共同努力，为美国人完成这项工作。

虽然医疗改革可以削减赤字，但还不足以使我们摆脱我们陷入的严重的财政困境。这个难题使其他所有难题的解决更加困难，也受到很多政治因素的影响。

下面让我讨论一下政府开支，首先我要澄清事实。在上个十年开始时，美国有超过2000亿美元预算盈余。等到我就职的时候，我们每年的赤字超过1万亿美元，估计下一个十年的赤字将达到8万亿美元。主要原因是没有为两场战争、两次减税和昂贵的处方药计划支付费用。此外，这次衰退使我们的预算增加了3万亿美元的漏洞。这就是我来之前的情况。

如果是在平常时期就职，我最想做的就是削减赤字。但我们是在危机时期就职的，我们阻止第二次大萧条的行动又使我们的国债增加了1万亿美元。我完全相信这样做是正确的，但全国各地的家庭都在勒紧裤带，做出艰难的选择，联邦政府也应该这样。所以今晚，我将提出具体步骤来支付去年用以救助经济的1万亿美元。

从2011年开始，我们准备冻结政府开支三年。与我们的国家安全、老年医疗保险、医疗补助和社会保险相关的开支不会受影响。但是其他所有可自由决定的政府计划都会受到影响。像所有现金不够的家庭一样，我们将把预算控制在需要的范围内，放弃不需要的。如果不得不通过否决权实施这项制度，我会这样做。我们将继续逐条审查预算案，取消负担不起和没有用的计划，我们已经为明年节省了200亿美元。为帮助工薪家庭，我们将延长中产阶级税收优惠。但是在赤字达到最高点的时候，我们不会继续对石油公司、投资基金经理和年薪超过25万的人减税。我们承担不起。

现在，即便在支付了我任期内的开支以后，我们仍将面对在我就职时就已经存在的大量赤字。更重要的是，老年医疗保险、医疗补助和社会保险的费用将继续大幅上升。因此，我呼吁按照共和党人贾德格雷格和民主党人肯特康拉德的提议，设立一个由两党成员组成的财政委员会。这不可能是让我们假装已经解决了问题的华盛顿的花招之一。这个委员会必须在一定的期限之前提出一套具体的解决办法。

昨天，参议院阻挠了设立该委员会的议案。因此我将发布行政命令，使我们能继续向前推进，因为我不愿把这个问题留给下一代美国人。明天表决的时候，参议院应该恢复所得税预扣法，这是我们上世纪九十年代实现创纪录盈余的主要原因。

我知道，民主党的一些人会认为，在那么多人还在受苦的时候，我们不能解决赤字问题或冻结政府开支。我同意这一点，正因如此，我们将等到明年经济好转以后才实施冻结。但是要懂得这一点——如果我们不采取有目的的步骤控制债务，就可能损害我们的市场、增加借款成本并危害经济复苏——所有这些都会对就业机会的增加和家庭收入产生更坏的影响。

我估计一些右翼人士会有不同的观点，认为如果我们减少对人民的投资、延长对美国富人的减税措施、取消更多规定、保持医疗现状，我们的赤字就会消失。问题在于八年来我们都是这样做的，正是这种做法导致了这场危机，引起了这么多赤字。我们不能再这么做了。我们不应再继续充斥了华盛顿几十年的陈腐的战斗，现在是作出新尝试的时候了。让我们投资于我们的人民，不要留给他们一大堆债务。让我们承担起对投票支持我们的民众应该承担的责任。让我们尝试判断力。

为此，我们必须认识到我们面对的不只是赤字问题。我们面临的还有信任不足——多年来，对于华盛顿如何运转，深切而有害的怀疑不断增加。要重建信任我们必须在宾夕法尼亚大道的两端采取行动，结束院外活动集团成员的过多影响，公开政务，给予人民他们应该拥有的政府。

我来到华盛顿就是为了做到这一点。正因如此，政府有史以来第一次在网上公布白宫的参观者。正因如此，我们把院外活动集团成员排除在决策工作或各种联邦委员会之外。但我们不能就此止步。现在应该要求院外活动集团成员公开他们为了客户与政府或国会的所有接触，应该严格限制这些成员向联邦职务的候选人提供的捐款。

上周，最高法院废除了一项有百年历史的法律，为特殊利益集团包括外国公司不受限制地在我们的选举中花钱打开了闸门。我认为美国的选举不应由美国最强大的利益集团甚至是外国实体提供资金。它们应该由美国人民决定，这就是我敦促民主党人和共和党人通过一项议案来纠正这种错误的原因。

我还要求国会继续沿着“指定款项改革”的道路走下去。你们已经削减了部分开支，接受了一些有意义的改革。但是恢复公众的信任需要做更多，例如，一些议员要在网上公布部分指定款项要求。今晚，我呼吁国会设立单独的网站，在投票前公布所有指定款项要求，以便所有美国人都能看到他们的钱用在了哪里。

当然，如果我们不改变两党之间工作的方式，这些改革就无法实现。

我并不天真。我从未想过我当选的事实能带来和平、和谐，开创某种后党派时代。我知道，两党存在分歧，这种分歧是根深蒂固的。在一些问题上，理念上的分歧将使我们始终选择不同的道路。关于政府在我们生活中的作用、关于我们国家的优先事宜和我们的国家安全，这些分歧已经存在了两百多年。这是我们民主的本质。

但是让美国人民失望的是，如今在华盛顿似乎每天都是选举日。我们不能永久地置身于竞选运动中，唯一的目的就是让对手成为媒体最难堪的嘲弄的对象——抱着一种决出胜负的心态。任何一个政党都不应因为有能力就拖延或阻挠任何一项议案。合格公职人员的批准程序，不应被几名心怀不满的参议员为了自己偏爱的计划而当作要挟的条件。

在华盛顿人们也许认为，发表关于对方的任何评论，不管多么不正确，都只是游戏规则的一部分。但恰恰是这种政治状况使得两党都不能帮助美国人民，更糟糕的是它使我们民众产生更大分歧，并进一步加剧了民众对政府的不信任。所以，我不会停止改变我们的政治调子。我知道这是选举年。在上周以后，竞选热显然已经开始，比以往还早。但我们仍然需要治理国家。

我要提醒民主党人，我们仍然占据几十年来最大的多数，美国人民期待我们解决一些问题，而不是选择逃避。如果共和党领导层坚持说，做什么事情都需要在参议院得到60票，那么治理国家的责任也是你们的。否决一切从短期政治来看也许是好的，但这不是领导。我们来到这里是为了服务于人民，而不是满足自己的野心。所以，让我们向美国人民证明，我们可以共同努力。本周，我将在众议院共和党的会议上发表讲话。我希望开始与两党领导人举行月度会议。我知道你们不能等待。

纵观历史，最能让这个国家团结一致的莫过于安全问题。令人遗憾的是，在“9·11”事件以后出现的紧密团结已经逐渐消退。我们尽可以争论是谁的责任，但我不想纠缠于过去。我知道我们大家都热爱这个国家，我们都致力于保卫这个国家。所以，让我们停止互相嘲弄，不要在保护人民还是捍卫价值观之间作出错误的选择。让我们抛开恐惧和分歧，尽全力保卫我们的国家，开创更有希望的未来——为了美国也为了世界。

我们从去年就开始了这项工作。自从就职以来，我们重新开始关注威胁我们国家的恐怖分子。我们在国土安全方面投入了大量资金，瓦解了有可能夺走美国人生命的阴谋。我们正通过加强航班安全、加快情报工作的速度，来弥补圣诞未遂袭击事件暴露的不可接受的漏洞。我们已禁止酷刑，加强了与太平洋、南亚到阿拉伯半岛国家的伙伴关系。去年，成百上千名“基地”组织和分支机构成员包括许多高级领导人被抓获或消灭，比 2008 年多得多。

我们正向阿富汗增派兵力，训练阿富汗安全部队，使他们从 2011 年 7 月开始起带头作用，我们的军队可以开始回国。我们将奖励良好统治，打击腐败，支持所有阿富汗人——男性和女性的权益。我们的同盟和伙伴也加入了行动，他们已经各自加大承诺力度，并且明天将在伦敦召开会议重申我们的共同目标。今后还会有艰难的时刻，但我确信我们会成功。

我们还在抗击“基地”组织，同时我们正在负责地将伊拉克交还给他的人民。当我竞选总统时，我承诺我会结束这场战争，而这也是我身为总统正在做的。我们将会在今年 8 月底之前让所有的作战部队撤离伊拉克。我们将支持伊拉克政府举行选举，也将继续与伊拉克人民共同推动地区和平与繁荣。但不要怀疑：这场战争正在结束，我们的所有部队都要回家了。

今晚，我们所有穿着制服的军人，无论男女，无论他们身处伊拉克、阿富汗还是世界的其他地方都必须知道，我们尊敬、感谢并且全力支持他们。正如他们在战场上必须拥有足够的资源，我们有责任在他们回国后也给予他们支持。这就是为何我们加大了对退伍军人的投入，增长幅度是近几十年来最大的。这就是为何我们正在建设二十一世纪的退伍军人事务部。这就是为何米歇尔与吉尔拜登正在共同推动一项支持军人家庭的全国行动。

就在我们从事两场战争的同时，我们也面临着或许是对美国人民最大的威胁——核武器的威胁。我赞同约翰·F·肯尼迪和罗纳德·里根的远见，实施逆转这些武器扩散的战略，追求一个没有核武器的世界。为了削减我们核武器储备和发射装置，同时确保我们的威慑能力，美国和俄罗斯就一项近二十年来影响最深远的武器控制条约的谈判即将完成。在今年4月举行的核安全峰会上，我们将把44个国家聚集在一个清晰的目标下：在四年内确保全世界所有安全措施薄弱的核物质的安全，让它们永不落入恐怖分子之手。

这些外交努力还使我们能更有力地应对那些违反国际条约、执意发展核武器的国家。这就是为何朝鲜目前进一步受到孤立，并面临更严厉的制裁——制裁的执行力度很大。这就是为何国际社会更加团结。

这就是我们所贡献的领导力——通过各种接触推进所有民族的安全和繁荣。我们通过二十国集团保证全球复苏的持久性。我们与全球各地的穆斯林社会合作，推动科学、教育和创新。在抗击气候变化上，我们已从旁观者变为领导者。我们正在帮助发展中国家自给自足地养活人民，并继续从事艾滋病的防治。我们正在开展一项新的计划，使我们有能力更迅速、更有效地应对生物恐怖主义或传染性疾病。这一计划有助于应对国内威胁、加强全球公共卫生。

正如我们六十年来一直所做的，美国这么做是因为我们的命运与我们国家之外的人们是息息相关的，但我们这么做还因为这是对的。这就是为何，当我们今晚在这里聚首，有一万多美国人还在海地与许多国家一起帮助那里的人民恢复生产和重建。这就是为何，我们和阿富汗那个渴望读书的女孩站在一起，我们支持在街头游行示威要求人权的伊朗妇女，我们声援那个因国家腐败而找不到工作的几内亚年轻人。因为美国必须永远站在自由和个人尊严的一边。

在国际上，美国一直以来最大的力量源泉就是我们的理想。在国内也同样。我们在巨大的差异中发现统一，用写入我们宪法中的承诺：我们所有人生而平等，无论你是谁，你的外表如何，只要你遵守法律，你就应该受到法律的保护；只要你拥护我们的普世价值，你就应该得到与任何人相同的待遇。

我们必须不断完善这一承诺。我的政府有一个民权司，再度开始对违反民权和就业歧视提起公诉。我们终于加强了我们的法律，保护人们免受仇恨犯罪的侵害。今年，我将与国会和我们的军队共同废除一项法律，该法律由于同性恋者的身份而剥夺美国同性恋者效忠他们所热爱的国家的权利。

我们将严厉取缔违反同酬法的做法，使同样工作了一天的女性能获得同等的报酬。我们应该继续修复我们出故障的移民系统，以保护我们边境的安全、加强我们的法律、确保所有遵守规则的人能够对我们的经济作出贡献，令我们的国家更丰富多彩。

归根到底，是我们的理想、我们的价值标准筑起了美国。这些价值使我们得以打造一个由来自全世界各个角落的移民组成的国度，这些价值依然激励着我们的公民。每天，美国人承担着家庭和工作的责任。他们常常向他们的邻居伸出援手，回馈他们的国家。他们以劳动为荣，慷慨高尚。他们秉承的并非共和党或民主党的价值、商业价值或劳动价值，他们秉承的是美国价值。

不幸的是，我们的太多公民已经不再相信我们的大机构——我们的企业、我们的媒体，对，还有我们的政府——尽管这些机构依然还反映着这些价值。这些机构中不乏可敬的男性和女性工作者，他们从事的重要工作推动了国家的繁荣。但每当一名首席执行官事业失败了还要犒赏自己，或一位银行家为自己的私利而让人们陷入风险，人民的怀疑就会增加。每当说客们玩弄制度，或政客们只顾着相互诋毁，而不去振兴国家，我们就会失去信念。电视评论员越来越多地将严肃的辩论降格为愚蠢的争吵，或对重大问题一语带过，我们的公民也越来越多地转过身去。无怪乎社会上有那么多人愤世嫉俗，无怪乎有那么多的失望。

我竞选时的承诺是变革，口号是我们相信变革。但如今我知道，很多美国人不再确定他们是否依然相信我们能改变，或至少我能带来改变。但请记住这点——我从来没有说过变革会很容易，或者我可以独自完成。在一个拥有三亿人口的国家，民主可能变得喧嚣、混乱和复杂。当你试图做大事或带来大的变革，就会激起强烈的情绪和纷争。事情就是这样。

我们身为官员面对这样的情况可以明哲保身，避免道出令人难以接受的事实。我们可以做些必要的事，保持较高的民调支持率以顺利通过下一次选举，而不去做那些造福下一代的事。但我也知道这一点：如果五十年前或一百年前或二百年前的人们做了这样的决定，我们今晚就不可能在这里。我们能够在这里的唯一原因就是世世代代的美国人无所畏惧地承担起艰难的重任，不畏失败地去做必须做的事，让这个国家的梦想世代传承、恒久不灭。

这一年来，我们的政府经历过一些政治挫折，其中有些是应得的。但我每天醒来，都会想到他们与全国上下无数家庭这一年来所遭遇的困难相比微不足道。而支撑我继续前行、支撑我继续奋斗的是，尽管经历种种挫折，那种坚定和乐观的精神，那种与生俱来的尊严，它一直以来都是美国人最核心的精神，始终存在。

它存在于那位小企业主写给我的信中。他说："我们没有人愿意考虑，甚至只是闪过这个念头，我们可能失败。"

它存在于那位女性的话中。她说，即使她和她的邻居们感受到衰退带来的痛苦，但"我们很坚强，我们有恢复力，我们是美国人"。

它存在于那位八岁的路易斯安那小男孩身上。他刚刚把自己的零花钱寄给我，问我能不能交给海地人民。

它还存在于所有义无反顾地前往从未去过的地方、将素昧平生的人拉出废墟的美国人，他们在又一个生命获救时高呼"美国！美国！美国"！

这种两百多年来一直支撑和鼓舞着这个国家的精神存在于你们，这个国家的人民身上。

我们结束了艰难的一年，我们走过了艰难的十年。但新的一年业已来到，新的十年也已开始。我们不放弃，我不放弃。让我们把握这一刻，重新开始，让梦想延续，让我们再次团结得更紧密。

谢谢。上帝保佑你们。上帝保佑美利坚合众国。

2011 国情咨文——2011 年 1 月 25 日美国众议院

Mr. Speaker, Mr. Vice President, Members of Congress, distinguished guests, and fellow Americans:

Tonight I want to begin by congratulating the men and women of the 112th Congress, as well as your new Speaker, John Boehner. And as we mark this occasion, we are also mindful of the empty chair in this Chamber, and pray for the health of our colleague—and our friend—Gabby Giffords.

It's no secret that those of us here tonight have had our differences over the last two years. The debates have been contentious; we have fought fiercely for our beliefs. And that's a good thing. That's what a robust democracy demands. That's what helps set us apart as a nation.

But there's a reason the tragedy in Tucson gave us pause. Amid all the noise and passions and rancor of our public debate, Tucson reminded us that no matter who we are or where we come from, each of us is a part of something greater—something more consequential than party or political preference.

We are part of the American family. We believe that in a country where every race and faith and point of view can be found, we are still bound together as one people; that we share common hopes and a common creed; that the dreams of a little girl in Tucson are not so different than those of our own children, and that they all deserve the chance to be fulfilled. That, too, is what sets us apart as a nation.

Now, by itself, this simple recognition won't usher in a new era of cooperation. What comes of this moment is up to us. What comes of this moment will be determined not by whether we can sit together tonight, but whether we can work together tomorrow. I believe we can. I believe we must. That's what the people who sent us here expect of us. With their votes, they've determined that governing will now be a shared responsibility between parties. New laws will only pass with support from Democrats and Republicans. We will move forward together, or not at all—for the challenges we face are bigger than party, and bigger than politics.

At stake right now is not who wins the next election—after all, we just had an election. At stake is whether new jobs and industries take root in this country, or somewhere else. It's whether the hard work and industry of our people is rewarded. It's whether we sustain the leadership that has made America not just a place on a map, but a light to the world.

We are poised for progress. Two years after the worst recession most of us have ever known, the stock market has come roaring back. Corporate profits are up. The economy is growing again. But we have never measured progress by these yardsticks alone. We measure progress by the success of our people. By the jobs they can find and the quality of life those jobs offer. By the prospects of a small business owner who dreams of turning a good idea into a thriving enterprise. By the opportunities for a better life that we pass on to our children. That's the project the American people want us to work on. Together.

We did that in December. Thanks to the tax cuts we passed, Americans' paychecks are a little bigger today. Every business can write off the full cost of the new investments they make this year. These steps, taken by Democrats and Republicans, will grow the economy and add to the more than one million private sector jobs created last year. But we have more work to do. The steps we've taken over the last two years may have broken the back of this recession—but to win the future, we'll need to take on challenges that have been decades in the making.

Many people watching tonight can probably remember a time when finding a good job meant showing up at a nearby factory or a business downtown. You didn't always need a degree, and your competition was pretty much limited to your neighbors. If you worked hard, chances are you'd have a job for life, with a decent paycheck, good benefits, and the occasional promotion. Maybe you'd even have the pride of seeing your kids work at the same company.

That world has changed. And for many, the change has been painful. I've seen it in the shuttered windows of once booming factories, and the vacant storefronts of once busy Main Streets. I've heard it in the frustrations of Americans who've seen their paychecks dwindle or their jobs disappear—proud men and women who feel like the rules have been changed in the middle of the game. They're right. The rules have changed. In a single generation, revolutions in technology have transformed the way we live, work and do business. Steel mills that once needed 1,000 workers can now do the same work with 100. Today, just about any company can set up shop, hire workers, and sell their products wherever there's an internet connection.

Meanwhile, nations like China and India realized that with some changes of their own, they could compete in this new world. And so they started educating their children earlier and longer, with greater emphasis on math and science. They're investing in research and new technologies. Just recently, China became home to the world's largest private solar research facility, and the world's fastest computer.

So yes, the world has changed. The competition for jobs is real. But this shouldn't discourage us. It should challenge us. Remember—for all the hits we've taken these last few years, for all the naysayers predicting our decline, America still has the largest, most prosperous economy in the world. No workers are more productive than ours. No country has more successful companies, or grants more patents to inventors and entrepreneurs. We are home to the world's best colleges and universities, where more students come to study than any other place on Earth.

What's more, we are the first nation to be founded for the sake of an idea—the idea that each of us deserves the chance to shape our own destiny. That is why centuries of pioneers and immigrants have risked everything to come here. It's why our students don't just memorize equations, but answer questions like "What do you think of that idea? What would you change about the world? What do you want to be when you grow up?"

The future is ours to win. But to get there, we can't just stand still. As Robert Kennedy told us, "The future is not a gift. It is an achievement." Sustaining the American Dream has never been about standing pat. It has required each generation to sacrifice, and struggle, and meet the demands of a new age. Now it's our turn. We know what it takes to compete for the jobs and industries of our time. We need to out-innovate, out-educate, and out-build the rest of the world. We have to make America the best place on Earth to do business. We need to take responsibility for our deficit, and reform our government. That's how our people will prosper. That's how we'll win the future. And tonight, I'd like to talk about how we get there.

The first step in winning the future is encouraging American innovation.

None of us can predict with certainty what the next big industry will be, or where the new jobs will come from. Thirty years ago, we couldn't know that something called the Internet would lead to an economic revolution. What we can do—what America does better than anyone—is spark the creativity and imagination of our people. We are the nation that put cars in driveways and computers in offices; the nation of Edison and the Wright brothers; of Google and Facebook. In America, innovation doesn't just change our lives. It's how we make a living. Our free enterprise system is what drives innovation. But because it's not always profitable for companies to invest in basic research, throughout history our government has provided cutting-edge scientists and inventors with the support that they need. That's what planted the seeds for the Internet. That's what helped make possible things like computer chips and GPS. Just think of all the good jobs —from manufacturing to retail—that have come from those breakthroughs.

Half a century ago, when the Soviets beat us into space with the launch of a satellite called Sputnik? We had no idea how we'd beat them to the moon. The science wasn't there yet. NASA didn't even exist. But after investing in better research and education, we didn't just surpass the Soviets; we unleashed a wave of innovation that created new industries and millions of new jobs.

This is our generation's Sputnik moment. Two years ago, I said that we needed to reach a level of research and development we haven't seen since the height of the Space Race. In a few weeks, I will be sending a budget to Congress that helps us meet that goal. We'll invest in biomedical research, information technology, and especially clean energy technology—an investment that will strengthen our security, protect our planet, and create countless new jobs for our people.

Already, we are seeing the promise of renewable energy. Robert and Gary Allen are brothers who run a small Michigan roofing company. After September 11th, they volunteered their best roofers to help repair the Pentagon. But half of their factory went unused, and the recession hit them hard. Today, with the help of a government loan, that empty space is being used to manufacture solar shingles that are being sold all across the country. In Robert's words, "We reinvented ourselves."

That's what Americans have done for over two hundred years: reinvented ourselves. And to spur on more success stories like the Allen Brothers, we've begun to reinvent our energy policy. We're not just handing out money. We're issuing a challenge. We're telling America's scientists and engineers that if they assemble teams of the best minds in their fields, and focus on the hardest problems in clean energy, we'll fund the Apollo Projects of our time.

At the California Institute of Technology, they're developing a way to turn sunlight and water into fuel for our cars. At Oak Ridge National Laboratory, they're using supercomputers to get a lot more power out of our nuclear facilities. With more research and incentives, we can break our dependence on oil with biofuels, and become the first country to have 1 million electric vehicles on the road by 2015.

We need to get behind this innovation. And to help pay for it, I'm asking Congress to eliminate the billions in taxpayer dollars we currently give to oil companies. I don't know if you've noticed, but they're doing just fine on their own. So instead of subsidizing yesterday's energy, let's invest in tomorrow's.

Now, clean energy breakthroughs will only translate into clean energy jobs if businesses know there will be a market for what they're selling. So tonight, I challenge you to join me in setting a new goal: by 2035, 80% of America's electricity will come from clean energy sources. Some folks want wind and solar. Others want nuclear, clean coal, and natural gas. To meet this goal, we will need them all—and I urge Democrats and Republicans to work together to make it happen.

Maintaining our leadership in research and technology is crucial to America's success. But if we want to win the future—if we want innovation to produce jobs in America and not overseas—then we also have to win the race to educate our kids. Think about it. Over the next ten years, nearly half of all new jobs will require education that goes beyond a high school degree. And yet, as many as a quarter of our students aren't even finishing high school. The quality of our math and science education lags behind many other nations. America has fallen to 9th in the proportion of young people with a college degree. And so the question is whether all of us—as citizens, and as parents—are willing to do what's necessary to give every child a chance to succeed.

That responsibility begins not in our classrooms, but in our homes and communities. It's family that first instills the love of learning in a child. Only parents can make sure the TV is turned off and homework gets done. We need to teach our kids that it's not just the winner of the Super Bowl who deserves to be celebrated, but the winner of the science fair; that success is not a function of fame or PR, but of hard work and discipline.

Our schools share this responsibility. When a child walks into a classroom, it should be a place of high expectations and high performance. But too many schools don't meet this test. That's why instead of just pouring money into a system that's not working; we launched a competition called Race to the Top. To all fifty states, we said, "If you show us the most innovative plans to improve teacher quality and student achievement, we'll show you the money." Race to the Top is the most meaningful reform of our public schools in a generation. For less than one percent of what we spend on education each year, it has led over 40 states to raise their standards for teaching and learning. These standards were developed, not by Washington, but by Republican and Democratic governors throughout the country. And Race to the Top should be the approach we follow this year as we replace *No Child Left Behind* with a law that is more flexible and focused on what's best for our kids.

You see, we know what's possible for our children when reform isn't just a top-down mandate, but the work of local teachers and principals; school boards and communities. Take a school like Bruce Randolph in Denver. Three years ago, it was rated one of the worst schools in Colorado; located on turf between two rival gangs. But last May, 97% of the seniors received their diploma. Most will be the first in their family to go to college. And after the first year of the school's transformation, the principal who made it possible wiped away tears when a student said "Thank you, Mrs. Waters, for showing that we are smart and we can make it."

Let's also remember that after parents, the biggest impact on a child's success comes from the man or woman at the front of the classroom. In South Korea, teachers are known as "nation builders." Here in America, it's time we treated the people who educate our children with the same level of respect. We want to reward good teachers and stop making excuses for bad ones. And over the next ten years, with so many Baby Boomers retiring from our classrooms, we want to prepare 100,000 new teachers in the fields of science, technology, engineering, and math. In fact, to every young person listening tonight who's contemplating their career choice: If you want to make a difference in the life of our nation; if you want to make a difference in the life of a child—become a teacher. Your country needs you.

Of course, the education race doesn't end with a high school diploma. To compete, higher education must be within reach of every American. That's why we've ended the unwarranted taxpayer subsidies that went to banks, and used the savings to make college affordable for millions of students. And this year, I ask Congress to go further, and make permanent our tuition tax credit—worth $10,000 for four years of college.

Because people need to be able to train for new jobs and careers in today's fast-changing economy, we are also revitalizing America's community colleges. Last month, I saw the promise of these schools at Forsyth Tech in North Carolina. Many of the students there used to work in the surrounding factories that have since left town. One mother of two, a woman named Kathy Proctor, had worked in the furniture industry since she was 18 years old. And she told me she's earning her degree in biotechnology now, at 55 years old, not just because the furniture jobs are gone, but because she wants to inspire her children to pursue their dreams too. As Kathy said, "I hope it tells them to never give up."

If we take these steps—if we raise expectations for every child, and give them the best possible chance at an education, from the day they're born until the last job they take—we will reach the goal I set two years ago: by the end of the decade, America will once again have the highest proportion of college graduates in the world.

One last point about education. Today, there are hundreds of thousands of students excelling in our schools who are not American citizens. Some are the children of undocumented workers, who had nothing to do with the actions of their parents. They grew up as Americans and pledge allegiance to our flag, and yet live every day with the threat of deportation. Others come here from abroad to study in our colleges and universities. But as soon as they obtain advanced degrees, we send them back home to compete against us. It makes no sense. Now, I strongly believe that we should take on, once and for all, the issue of illegal immigration. I am prepared to work with Republicans and Democrats to protect our borders, enforce our laws and address the millions of undocumented workers who are now living in the shadows. I know that debate will be difficult and take time. But tonight, let's agree to make that effort. And let's stop expelling talented, responsible young people who can staff our research labs, start new businesses, and further enrich this nation.

The third step in winning the future is rebuilding America. To attract new businesses to our shores, we need the fastest, most reliable ways to move people, goods, and information—from high-speed rail to high-speed internet.

Our infrastructure used to be the best—but our lead has slipped. South Korean homes now have greater internet access than we do. Countries in Europe and Russia invest more in their roads and railways than we do. China is building faster trains and newer airports. Meanwhile, when our own engineers graded our nation's infrastructure, they gave us a "D."

We have to do better. America is the nation that built the transcontinental railroad, brought electricity to rural communities, and constructed the interstate highway system. The jobs created by these projects didn't just come from laying down tracks or pavement. They came from businesses that opened near a town's new train station or the new off-ramp.

Over the last two years, we have begun rebuilding for the 21st century, a project that has meant thousands of good jobs for the hard-hit construction industry. Tonight, I'm proposing that we redouble these efforts.

We will put more Americans to work repairing crumbling roads and bridges. We will make sure this is fully paid for, attract private investment, and pick projects based on what's best for the economy, not politicians.

Within 25 years, our goal is to give 80% of Americans access to high-speed rail, which could allow you go places in half the time it takes to travel by car. For some trips, it will be faster than flying—without the pat-down. As we speak, routes in California and the Midwest are already underway.

Within the next five years, we will make it possible for business to deploy the next generation of high-speed wireless coverage to 98% of all Americans. This isn't just about a faster internet and fewer dropped calls. It's about connecting every part of America to the digital age. It's about a rural community in Iowa or Alabama where farmers and small business owners will be able to sell their products all over the world. It's about a firefighter who can download the design of a burning building onto a handheld device; a student who can take classes with a digital textbook; or a patient who can have face-to-face video chats with her doctor.

All these investments—in innovation, education, and infrastructure—will make America a better place to do business and create jobs. But to help our companies compete, we also have to knock down barriers that stand in the way of their success.

Over the years, a parade of lobbyists has rigged the tax code to benefit particular companies and industries. Those with accountants or lawyers to work the system can end up paying no taxes at all. But all the rest are hit with one of the highest corporate tax rates in the world. It makes no sense, and it has to change.

So tonight, I'm asking Democrats and Republicans to simplify the system. Get rid of the loopholes. Level the playing field. And use the savings to lower the corporate tax rate for the first time in 25 years—without adding to our deficit.

To help businesses sell more products abroad, we set a goal of doubling our exports by 2014—because the more we export, the more jobs we create at home. Already, our exports are up. Recently, we signed agreements with India and China that will support more than 250,000 jobs in the United States. And last month, we finalized a trade agreement with South Korea that will support at least 70,000 American jobs. This agreement has unprecedented support from business and labor; Democrats and Republicans, and I ask this Congress to pass it as soon as possible.

Before I took office, I made it clear that we would enforce our trade agreements, and that I would only sign deals that keep faith with American workers, and promote American jobs. That's what we did with Korea, and that's what I intend to do as we pursue agreements with Panama and Colombia, and continue our Asia Pacific and global trade talks.

To reduce barriers to growth and investment, I've ordered a review of government regulations. When we find rules that put an unnecessary burden on businesses, we will fix them. But I will not hesitate to create or enforce commonsense safeguards to protect the American people. That's what we've done in this country for more than a century. It's why our food is safe to eat, our water is safe to drink, and our air is safe to breathe. It's why we have speed limits and child labor laws. It's why last year, we put in place consumer protections against hidden fees and penalties by credit card companies, and new rules to prevent another financial crisis. And it's why we passed reform that finally prevents the health insurance industry from exploiting patients.

Now, I've heard rumors that a few of you have some concerns about the new health care law. So let me be the first to say that anything can be improved. If you have ideas about how to improve this law by making care better or more affordable, I am eager to work with you. We can start right now by correcting a flaw in the legislation that has placed an unnecessary bookkeeping burden on small businesses. What I'm not willing to do is go back to the days when insurance companies could deny someone coverage because of a pre-existing condition. I'm not willing to tell James Howard, a brain cancer patient from Texas, that his treatment might not be covered. I'm not willing to tell Jim Houser, a small business owner from Oregon, that he has to go back to paying $5,000 more to cover his employees. As we speak, this law is making prescription drugs cheaper for seniors and giving uninsured students a chance to stay on their parents' coverage. So instead of re-fighting the battles of the last two years, let's fix what needs fixing and move forward.

Now, the final step—a critical step—in winning the future is to make sure we aren't buried under a mountain of debt.

We are living with a legacy of deficit-spending that began almost a decade ago. And in the wake of the financial crisis, some of that was necessary to keep credit flowing, save jobs, and put money in people's pockets. But now that the worst of the recession is over, we have to confront the fact that our government spends more than it takes in. That is not sustainable. Every day, families sacrifice to live within their means. They deserve a government that does the same. So tonight, I am proposing that starting this year, we freeze annual domestic spending for the next five years. This would reduce the deficit by more than $400 billion over the next decade, and will bring discretionary spending to the lowest share of our economy since Dwight Eisenhower was president.

This freeze will require painful cuts. Already, we have frozen the salaries of hardworking federal employees for the next two years. I've proposed cuts to things I care deeply about, like community action programs. The Secretary of Defense has also agreed to cut tens of billions of dollars in spending that he and his generals believe our military can do without. I recognize that some in this Chamber have already proposed deeper cuts, and I'm willing to eliminate whatever we can honestly afford to do without. But let's make sure that we're not doing it on the backs of our most vulnerable citizens. And let's make sure what we're cutting is really excess weight. Cutting the deficit by gutting our investments in innovation and education is like lightening an overloaded airplane by removing its engine. It may feel like you're flying high at first, but it won't take long before you'll feel the impact.

Now, most of the cuts and savings I've proposed only address annual domestic spending, which represents a little more than 12% of our budget. To make further progress, we have to stop pretending that cutting this kind of spending alone will be enough. It won't. The bipartisan Fiscal Commission I created last year made this crystal clear. I don't agree with all their proposals, but they made important progress. And their conclusion is that the only way to tackle our deficit is to cut excessive spending wherever we find it—in domestic spending, defense spending, health care spending, and spending through tax breaks and loopholes.

This means further reducing health care costs, including programs like

Medicare and Medicaid, which are the single biggest contributor to our long-term deficit. Health insurance reform will slow these rising costs, which is part of why nonpartisan economists have said that repealing the health care law would add a quarter of a trillion dollars to our deficit. Still, I'm willing to look at other ideas to bring down costs, including one that Republicans suggested last year: medical malpractice reform to rein in frivolous lawsuits.

To put us on solid ground, we should also find a bipartisan solution to strengthen Social Security for future generations. And we must do it without putting at risk current retirees, the most vulnerable, or people with disabilities; without slashing benefits for future generations; and without subjecting Americans' guaranteed retirement income to the whims of the stock market.

And if we truly care about our deficit, we simply cannot afford a permanent extension of the tax cuts for the wealthiest 2% of Americans. Before we take money away from our schools, or scholarships away from our students, we should ask millionaires to give up their tax break. It's not a matter of punishing their success. It's about promoting America's success.

In fact, the best thing we could do on taxes for all Americans is to simplify the individual tax code. This will be a tough job, but members of both parties have expressed interest in doing this, and I am prepared to join them.

So now is the time to act. Now is the time for both sides and both houses of Congress—Democrats and Republicans—to forge a principled compromise that gets the job done. If we make the hard choices now to rein in our deficits, we can make the investments we need to win the future. Let me take this one step further. We shouldn't just give our people a government that's more affordable. We should give them a government that's more competent and efficient. We cannot win the future with a government of the past. We live and do business in the information age, but the last major reorganization of the government happened in the age of black and white TV. There are twelve different agencies that deal with exports. There are at least five different entities that deal with housing policy. Then there's my favorite example: the Interior Department is in charge of salmon while they're in fresh water, but the Commerce Department handles them in when they're in saltwater. And I hear it gets even more complicated once they're smoked.

Now, we have made great strides over the last two years in using technology and getting rid of waste. Veterans can now download their electronic medical records with a click of the mouse. We're selling acres of federal office space that hasn't been used in years, and we will cut through red tape to get rid of more. But we need to think bigger. In the coming months, my administration will develop a proposal to merge, consolidate, and reorganize the federal government in a way that best serves the goal of a more competitive America. I will submit that proposal to Congress for a vote—and we will push to get it passed.

In the coming year, we will also work to rebuild people's faith in the institution of government. Because you deserve to know exactly how and where your tax dollars are being spent, you will be able to go to a website and get that information for the very first time in history. Because you deserve to know when your elected officials are meeting with lobbyists, I ask Congress to do what the White House has already done: put that information online. And because the American people deserve to know that special interests aren't larding up legislation with pet projects, both parties in Congress should know this: if a bill comes to my desk with earmarks inside, I will veto it.

A 21st century government that's open and competent. A government that lives within its means. An economy that's driven by new skills and ideas. Our success in this new and changing world will require reform, responsibility, and innovation. It will also require us to approach that world with a new level of engagement in our foreign affairs.

Just as jobs and businesses can now race across borders, so can new threats and new challenges. No single wall separates East and West; no one rival superpower is aligned against us. And so we must defeat determined enemies wherever they are, and build coalitions that cut across lines of region and race and religion. America's moral example must always shine for all who yearn for freedom, justice, and dignity. And because we have begun this work, tonight we can say that American leadership has been renewed and America's standing has been restored.

Look to Iraq, where nearly 100,000 of our brave men and women have left with their heads held high; where American combat patrols have ended; violence has come down; and a new government has been formed. This year, our civilians will forge a lasting partnership with the Iraqi people, while we finish the job of bringing our troops out of Iraq. America's commitment has been kept; the Iraq War is coming to an end.

Of course, as we speak, al Qaeda and their affiliates continue to plan attacks against us. Thanks to our intelligence and law enforcement professionals, we are disrupting plots and securing our cities and skies. And as extremists try to inspire acts of violence within our borders, we are responding with the strength of our communities, with respect for the rule of law, and with the conviction that American Muslims are a part of our American family.

We have also taken the fight to al Qaeda and their allies abroad. In Afghanistan, our troops have taken Taliban strongholds and trained Afghan Security Forces. Our purpose is clear—by preventing the Taliban from reestablishing a stranglehold over the Afghan people, we will deny al Qaeda the safe-haven that served as a launching pad for 9/11. Thanks to our heroic troops and civilians, fewer Afghans are under the control of the insurgency. There will be tough fighting ahead, and the Afghan government will need to deliver better governance. But we are strengthening the capacity of the Afghan people and building an enduring partnership with them. This year, we will work with nearly 50 countries to begin a transition to an Afghan lead. And this July, we will begin to bring our troops home.

In Pakistan, al Qaeda's leadership is under more pressure than at any point since 2001. Their leaders and operatives are being removed from the battlefield. Their safe-havens are shrinking. And we have sent a message from the Afghan border to the Arabian Peninsula to all parts of the globe: we will not relent, we will not waver, and we will defeat you.

American leadership can also be seen in the effort to secure the worst weapons of war. Because Republicans and Democrats approved the New *START Treaty*, far fewer nuclear weapons and launchers will be deployed. Because we rallied the world, nuclear materials are being locked down on every continent so they never fall into the hands of terrorists.

Because of a diplomatic effort to insist that Iran meet its obligations, the Iranian government now faces tougher and tighter sanctions than ever before. And on the Korean peninsula, we stand with our ally South Korea, and insist that North Korea keeps its commitment to abandon nuclear weapons.

This is just a part of how we are shaping a world that favors peace and prosperity. With our European allies, we revitalized NATO, and increased our cooperation on everything from counter-terrorism to missile defense. We have reset our relationship with Russia, strengthened Asian alliances, and built new partnerships with nations like India. This March, I will travel to Brazil, Chile, and El Salvador to forge new alliances for progress in the Americas. Around the globe, we are standing with those who take responsibility—helping farmers grow more food; supporting doctors who care for the sick; and combating the corruption that can rot a society and rob people of opportunity.

Recent events have shown us that what sets us apart must not just be our power—it must be the purpose behind it. In South Sudan—with our assistance—the people were finally able to vote for independence after years of war. Thousands lined up before dawn. People danced in the streets. One man who lost four of his brothers at war summed up the scene around him: "This was a battlefield for most of my life. Now we want to be free."

We saw that same desire to be free in Tunisia, where the will of the people proved more powerful than the writ of a dictator. And tonight, let us be clear: the United States of America stands with the people of Tunisia, and supports the democratic aspirations of all people.

We must never forget that the things we've struggled for, and fought for, live in the hearts of people everywhere. And we must always remember that the Americans who have borne the greatest burden in this struggle are the men and women who serve our country. Tonight, let us speak with one voice in reaffirming that our nation is united in support of our troops and their families. Let us serve them as well as they have served us—by giving them the equipment they need; by providing them with the care and benefits they have earned; and by enlisting our veterans in the great task of building our own nation.

Our troops come from every corner of this country—they are black, white, Latino, Asian and Native American. They are Christian and Hindu, Jewish and Muslim. And, yes, we know that some of them are gay. Starting this year, no American will be forbidden from serving the country they love because of who they love. And with that change, I call on all of our college campuses to open their doors to our military recruiters and the ROTC. It is time to leave behind the divisive battles of the past. It is time to move forward as one nation.

We should have no illusions about the work ahead of us. Reforming our schools; changing the way we use energy; reducing our deficit—none of this is easy. All of it will take time. And it will be harder because we will argue about everything. The cost. The details. The letter of every law. Of course, some countries don't have this problem. If the central government wants a railroad, they get a railroad—no matter how many homes are bulldozed. If they don't want a bad story in the newspaper, it doesn't get written. And yet, as contentious and frustrating and messy as our democracy can sometimes be, I know there isn't a person here who would trade places with any other nation on Earth.

We may have differences in policy, but we all believe in the rights enshrined in our Constitution. We may have different opinions, but we believe in the same promise that says this is a place where you can make it if you try. We may have different backgrounds, but we believe in the same dream that says this is a country where anything's possible. No matter who you are. No matter where you come from.

That dream is why I can stand here before you tonight. That dream is why a working class kid from Scranton can stand behind me. That dream is why someone who began by sweeping the floors of his father's Cincinnati bar can preside as Speaker of the House in the greatest nation on Earth.

That dream—that American Dream—is what drove the Allen Brothers to reinvent their roofing company for a new era. It's what drove those students at Forsyth Tech to learn a new skill and work towards the future. And that dream is the story of a small business owner named Brandon Fisher.

Brandon started a company in Berlin, Pennsylvania that specializes in a new kind of drilling technology. One day last summer, he saw the news that halfway across the world, 33 men were trapped in a Chilean mine, and no one knew how to save them. But Brandon thought his company could help. And so he designed a rescue that would come to be known as Plan B. His employees worked around the clock to manufacture the necessary drilling equipment. And Brandon left for Chile. Along with others, he began drilling a 2,000 foot hole into the ground, working three or four days at a time with no sleep. Thirty-seven days later, Plan B succeeded, and the miners were rescued. But because he didn't want all of the attention, Brandon wasn't there when the miners emerged. He had already gone home, back to work on his next project. Later, one of his employees said of the rescue, "We proved that Center Rock is a little company, but we do big things."

We do big things.

From the earliest days of our founding, America has been the story of ordinary people who dare to dream. That's how we win the future.

We are a nation that says, "I might not have a lot of money, but I have this great idea for a new company. I might not come from a family of college graduates, but I will be the first to get my degree. I might not know those people in trouble, but I think I can help them, and I need to try. I'm not sure how we'll reach that better place beyond the horizon, but I know we'll get there. I know we will."

We do big things.

The idea of America endures. Our destiny remains our choice. And tonight, more than two centuries later, it is because of our people that our future is hopeful, our journey goes forward, and the state of our union is strong.

Thank you, God Bless You, and may God Bless the United States of America.

众议院议长先生、副总统先生、各位国会议员、尊敬的客人们、同胞们:

今晚我想首先向美国第112届国会的男女议员、你们的新议长约翰·博纳表示祝贺。在我们庆祝这一时刻时，我们仍然很清楚一位国会议员的座位是空着的，让我们为我们的同事、我们的朋友加布里埃尔·吉福兹的健康祈祷。

我们这些今晚出席这一活动的人在过去两年曾存在分歧，这不是秘密。辩论是非常激烈的，我们为我们各自的观点进行了激烈的斗争。这是一件好事，这是强有力的民主所要求的。这种争论帮助美国成为区别于其他国家的民主国家。

但图森市的悲剧给了我们一个停止争论的理由，我们进行的公共辩论引发了噪音、情绪、怨恨。图森的悲剧提醒我们，不管我们是谁、来自何方，我们中的每一个人都是一个更伟大事务的一部分，它比政党或者政治倾向更具必然性。

我们是美国大家庭的组成部分。我们相信在这个各种种族、信仰、观点并存的国家，我们仍是一个团结在一起的民族。我们拥有共同的希望和信条，图森小女孩的梦想与我们自己孩子的梦想没有什么差别，这些梦想都应有获得实现的机会。这也是使我们作为一个国家产生分歧的原因。

现在，简单地认识到这一点本身将不会开启一个合作的新时代。这一时刻所能产生的成果取决于我们。这一时刻所产生的成果将不会由我们是否今晚坐在一起而决定，它将被我们明天是否合作所决定。我认为我们能够实现合作，我认为我们必须这样。这是那些把我们送到这里的人们所期望的。他们通过他们的选票决定，执政将是两党共同的责任，新的法案只有在获得民主党和共和党议员的支持下才能通过。在面对比党派或者政治更大的挑战面前，我们将一起前行，或者原地不动。

现在的利害不是谁将赢得下次选举，毕竟，我们刚刚举行完一次选举。现在的利害是新的就业机会和新的行业是否会在美国生根或者在其他地方。这事关我们人民的辛劳工作和行业是否能得到回报。这事关我们是否能继续保持领导能力，这种领导能力使美国不只局限于地图上的某一个地方，美国因为这种领导能力而成为世界的灯光。

我们做好了前进的准备。在我们大多数人经历最为糟糕的经济衰退两年后，股市已再次大幅上升，公司赢利在增加，经济在再次增长。但我们从不只以这些标准来衡量进展，我们以我们人民的成功来评估进展。通过他们所能找到的工作和这些工作所提供的生活质量，通过小企业主把好点子的梦想转变成兴旺发达的企业的前景，通过我们给我们孩子更好生活的机遇。这是一个美国人民想让我们从事的事业，美国人民想让我们共同致力于这项事业。

我们去年 12 月做了这方面的工作。由于我们通过的减税法案，美国人今天收到的支票金额要比过去多。所有的企业都可以把它今年所作投资的全部开支注销。这些由民主党人和共和党人合作采取的措施将使经济增长，增加就业岗位，私人行业去年已创造一百多万个就业岗位。但我们有更多的工作要做。我们在过去两年所采取的措施可能已克服了经济衰退的主要困难，但是为了赢得未来，我们必须直接应对那些在过去数十年来一直积累起来的挑战。

许多观看今晚演讲的人可能还记得那个找到好工作意味着在附近工厂或者市中心商业区就业的时候，你并不总是需要获得一个学位，你的竞争基本只限于你的邻居。如果你努力工作，你可能会终身拥有这个职位，这个工作会给你带来体面的收入，好的福利，有时还会升职。你可能还会拥有看到你的孩子在同一公司工作的自豪感。

世界已发生了变革。对于许多人来说，变革是痛苦的。在曾经一度业务繁忙的工厂面临关闭时，我透过百叶窗看到了这种痛苦；在一度繁忙的商业街道空空如也的店门前，我看到了这种痛苦；在那些看到收入不断缩水或者失业美国人的绝望言论中，我听到了这种痛苦。这就好像在比赛进行到一半时，表现出色而又颇感自豪的运动员发现规则突然改变了。他们是正确的，规则发生了变化。仅仅用了一代人的时间，技术革命已改变了我们的工作、生活和做生意的方式。一度需要一千名工人的钢铁厂现在用一百名工人就可以完成同样的工作。今天，任何一家公司都可以设立商店、雇佣员工、把产品销售给有互联网连接的所有地方。

与此同时，中国和印度等国已意识到，他们在做出一些变革后将能够在新世界里与其他国家进行竞争。所以，他们开始对他们的孩子进行更早和更长时间的教育，更加重视数学和科学。他们投资于研发和新技术。就在不久之前，中国已拥有世界上最大的私营太阳能研究设施，世界上运行速度最快的计算机。

所以，是的，世界发生了变革。就业岗位的竞争是真实存在的，但这不应当使我们灰心，它应当成为激励我们的动力。请记住，尽管我们在过去几年遭受到了巨大打击，尽管所有的悲观者预言美国在衰落，但美国仍是世界上最大、最繁荣的经济体。我们工人的劳动生产率是最高的，我们的公司是最成功的，我们的投资者和企业家所拥有的专利数是最多的。我们拥有世界上最好的院校和大学，来美国就读的学生超过任何其他国家。

更为重要的是，我们是首个以思想立国的国家，这个思想是我们中的每个人都应当有机会来塑造自己的命运。这就是为什么先驱们和移民们数个世纪以来不惜冒着失去一切的风险来到美国的原因。这就是我们的学生不只是记住方程式，而是会提出“你认为这个想法如何？你想如何改变世界？当你长大后你想成为什么样的人”等问题。

我们将赢得未来，但为了实现这一点，我们不能原地踏步。正如罗伯特·肯尼迪所说的那样“未来不是一个礼物，它是一个成就”。维持美国梦从来不是墨守成规。它需要每一代人作出牺牲、斗争，满足新时代的要求。现在轮到我们这一代人了。我们知道在我们的时代为工作和行业进行竞争需要什么。我们需要在创新、教育和建设方面超越其他国家。我们要使美国成为商业环境最好的国家。我们需要对我们的赤字负责任，对我们的政府进行改革。这就是我们的人民实现繁荣的方法。这就是我们如何赢得未来的方法。今晚，我想谈谈我们如何做到这些。

赢得未来的首个步骤是鼓励美国人创新。

我们所有人都无法肯定地预言下一个主要行业将是什么行业或者新的就业岗位来自哪里。三十年前，我们不知道一个被称作互联网的东西会引发经济革命。我们所能做的是争取在激发美国人民的创造性和想象力这些方面比其他国家的人做得更好。我们是一个将车开到车道上、把计算机放在办公室的国家，是一个拥有爱迪生、莱特兄弟的国家，是一个拥有谷歌和脸谱的国家。在美国，创新不只改变我们的生活，更重要的是这是我们赖以谋生的方法。我们的自由企业制度驱动着创新，但是由于公司投资基础研究并不总是有利可图，在历史上，我们的政府向一流的科学家和发明家提供了他们所需要的支持。这些支持种下了互联网的种子，这些支持帮助制造出计算机芯片和全球定位仪这样的东西。想想所有的好工作，从制造业到零售业都来自于这些突破。

半个世纪之前，当苏联人发射一颗名为“伴侣号”的人造卫星从而在太空竞赛领域击败我们时，我们不知道我们如何在登月方面击败他们。那方面的科学当时还不存在，美国宇航局当时甚至都还未组建。但在更好的研究和教育方面投资后，我们不仅超过了苏联人，我们还推动了一系列的创新，这些创新创造了新的行业和数百万个新就业岗位。

这是我们那一代人创造的“伴侣号”走在世界前沿的时刻。我在两年前说过，我们需要将研发拓展到自太空竞赛高峰后再也没有出现过的新层次上。我将在未来几周内向国会提交一份预算案，它将帮助我们实现这一目标。我们将投资于生物医药研究、信息技术，尤其是清洁能源技术，这一投资将会强化我们的安全、保护我们的地球、为我们的人民创造无数新就业岗位。

我们已看到了可再生能源的潜力。罗伯特·阿伦和加里·阿伦是一对在密歇根州经营屋顶公司的兄弟。他们在“9·11”恐怖袭击事件后志愿派出他们最好的装修屋顶员工来帮助维修五角大楼，但是他们工厂的半个厂区没有开工，经济衰退重创了他们的工厂。今天，在政府贷款的帮助下，空闲的厂房被用于制造销往全球各地的太阳能电池板。用罗伯特的话说：“我们再造了自己。”

这就是美国人在过去两百多年里一直在做的事情，再造自我。为了推动更多像阿伦兄弟这样的成功故事，我们已开始再造我们的能源政策。我们将不只提供款项，我们还将提供挑战。我们将告诉美国的科学家和工程师，如果他们组建他们领域最好的科学家小组，致力解决清洁能源最困难问题，我们将向我们时代的“阿波罗项目”提供资金支持。

在加州理工学院，科学家正在寻找一种将太阳光和水转换成汽车燃料的方法。在橡树岭国家实验室，科学家们正在通过超级计算机以使从我们的核设施获得更多能量。在进行更多的研究和激励措施后，我们可以用生物燃料来打破我们对石油的依赖，成为在 2015 年前首个拥有一百万电动汽车上路的国家。

我们需要找到创新背后的要素。为了向创新提供经费支持，我将请求国会取消向石油公司所提供的数十亿美元税款补贴。我不知道你是否注意到这一情况，石油公司自身运营得很不错。所以，与其向昨天的能源业提供补贴，我们不如投资于未来的能源。

现在，清洁能源领域的技术突破只有在业界知道有销售市场的情况下才会转变成清洁能源业的工作岗位。所以，今晚，我想让你们和我一起来制订一个新目标：争取在 2035 年之前使美国 85% 的电力供应量来自清洁能源。一些人想要风力和太阳能，其他人想要核电、清洁煤炭和天然气。为了实现这一目标，我们将需要所有这些清洁能源。我呼吁民主党人和共和党人通过合作来实现这一目标。

保持我们在研究和技术领域的领导地位对于美国的成功至关重要。如果我们想拥抱未来，如果我们想让创新在美国而不是海外创造就业岗位，那么我们必须赢得教育我们孩子的竞赛。思考一下吧，在未来十年，近半数新就业岗位将需要拥有高中以上的教育程度。虽然如此，美国仍有近四分之一的学生甚至未完成中学教育。我们教育和科学的教育质量落后于许多国家，美国年轻人拥有大学学位比例的排行已降至世界第九位。所以问题是我们所有的人，作为公民，作为父母，是否愿意做那些必要的事情以便让每个孩子都有成功的机会?

这一责任不仅是在我们的教室内开始的，也是在我们的家庭和社区里开始的。是家庭首先培养了孩子爱好学习的习惯，只有父母在确保关掉电视的情况下，孩子的家庭作业才会完成。我们需要教育我们的孩子，不仅是超级碗比赛的获胜者值得庆祝，那些科学大赛的赢家也应当值得庆祝。成功不是名气或者公共关系所带来的，它是由辛劳的工作和自律造就的。

我们的学校也有责任。当一名儿童步入教室，它就应当是一个被寄予厚望和拥有很高教学能力的地方，但是太多的学校未能达到这一标准。这就是为什么我们没有向教育系统注入大笔资金原因，我们启动了一个名为“冲顶赛跑”的竞争。我们对所有五十个州说：“如果你们能够向我们展示提高教师质量和学生成就的最具创新力的方案，我们将向你们提供款项。”“冲顶赛跑”是我们公共学校在十年内所进行的最有意义的改革。它只使用了不到我们每年教育开支的 1% 的经费，但它已使四十个州提高了教学和学习标准。这些标准不是由华盛顿所决定的，它是由美国各个州的共和党和民主党州长们所决定的。“冲顶赛跑”应当成为我们今年所采取的方法。我们今年将用一个更为灵活、专注于用给我们的孩子带来最大益处的法律来取代《不让一个儿童落后法》。

你们应该知道，当改革不仅仅是从上到下的指示时，我们的孩子所能够取得的成绩有多大。改革措施将由当地的教师和校长、校董事会和社区来决定。以丹佛的布鲁斯·兰多夫学校为例，它在三年前被评为科罗拉多州最差的学校之一，它位于两个敌对黑帮争夺的地盘内。但在去年五月，该校 97% 的高三学生获得了毕业证，大多数人将是他们家庭中上大学的第一人。在学校实现转变后的第一年，一位学生的话使这一切成为现实的校长流下了眼泪。这个学生说：“感谢你，威特斯女士，感谢你向我们表明，我们是聪明的，我们能够成功。”

让我们也记住，除了父母之外，对一个孩子成功的最大影响来自于站在教室前的男女教师们。在韩国，教师们被称作“国家建造者”。在美国，现是我们该以同样程度的尊重对待那些教育我们孩子的人的时候了。我们应当奖励好教师，停止为糟糕的教师找借口。在未来十年，由于非常多的婴儿潮，一代教师将退休，我们将需要准备十万名科学、技术、工程和数学学科教师。事实上，对于今晚收听讲演的、正在考虑职业选择的年轻人，如果你想让我们国家前途有所不同，如果你想让一个孩子的生命有所不同，成为一位教师吧。你的国家需要你。

当然，教育竞赛不会止步于高中毕业证，为了竞争必须让每位美国人都有接受高等教育的机会。这就是我们为什么结束向银行提供没有充分根据的税款补贴，用节省下来的钱来使数百万学生能有能力上大学。我今年将请求国会采取进一步措施，使我们的学费税收抵免永久化，对一个人四年的大学来说，这笔钱相当于 1 万美元。

由于人们需要在今天快速变化的经济领域里接受新工作和职业的培训，我们也将重新使美国的社区学院恢复活力。我上个月看到了北卡罗来纳州福费斯社区技术学院的潜力，学院的许多学生曾在现在已搬离城镇的附近工厂就业。凯西·普罗克托是一位两个孩子的母亲，她十八岁就开始在家具业工作。她告诉我，现年55岁的她正在攻读生物技术学位，不只是因为家具业的工作没有了，而是因为她想鼓励她的孩子也追求他们的梦想。凯西说：“我希望这将能教会他们永不放弃。”

如果我们采取这些措施，如果我们提高对每个孩子的期望值，给他们在教育方面最好的机遇，从他们出生至他们最后的就业岗位，我们将实现我在两年前确定的目标：在这个十年结束的时候，美国将再度成为拥有大学生比例最高的国家。

有关教育的最后一点。今天，我们的学校里有数百万学业优秀的非美国公民。一些人是非法工人的孩子，他们与他们父母的行为没有任何关系。他们是以美国人的身份长大的，宣誓效忠美国，但却每天生活在将被驱逐的威胁之下。其他人来自海外，在我们的院校和大学里学习，但他们一旦获得学位，我们就把他们送回国和我们进行竞争。这没有道理。现在，我强烈地认为，我们应当立即解决非法移民的问题。我做好了与共和党人和民主党人合作以保护我们边境的准备，执行我们的法律，解决数百万生活在阴影之下的非法移民问题。我知道，这方面的辩论将是艰难的，将需要时间。但是今晚，让我们就开始作出努力达成共识。停止驱逐那些有才能、负责任的年轻人，他们可以在我们的实验室工作、创业、给美国带来新的财富。

赢得未来的第三步是重建美国。为了吸引新的行业来到美国，我们需要运送人员、商品、信息最快捷、最可靠的方法，从高速铁路至高速互联网等基础设施。

我们的基础设施曾经是世界上最棒的，但现在我们的领先优势已经下滑。韩国家庭的互联网接入比例已超过了美国。欧洲国家和俄罗斯在公路和铁路的投资额超过了美国。中国正在建造更快的火车和新机场。与此同时，当我们自己的工程师给我们的基础设施打分时，他们给我们打了一个“D”。

我们必须做得更好，美国是一个建设了州际铁路，将电力输往乡村社区，建设了州际高速公路的国家。这些项目创造的工作不只来自于铺设铁轨或者路面，工作机会也来自在镇里新建火车站或者新外匝道附近开设的行业。

在未来两年，我们已开始为二十一世纪进行重建。这个项目已为遭到沉重打击的建筑业带来了数千个好工作。今晚，我提议我们加倍这方面的努力。

我们将让更多的美国人从事修理年久失修的道路和桥梁工作。我们将确保这方面的工作有充分的经费保证，吸引私人投资，根据项目对经济而不是对政治家的最佳益处来选择项目。

在未来二十五年内，我们的目标是使 80% 的美国人能够拥有高速铁路，这将使你乘高速铁路出行的时间比开车出行的时间减少一半。对于一些旅程来说，它将比乘飞机出行更快，而且没有严格的安检措施。在我们讲话之时，加州和中西部地区的高铁线路已在建设之中。

在未来五年内，我们将使业界向 98% 的美国人提供下一代高速无线网络连接成为可能。这并不只是更快的互联网和更少的漏接电话。这使美国的各个地区都进入数字化时代。这事关衣阿华州或者阿拉巴马州乡村社区的农民和小企业主能够向全世界出售他们的产品，这事关消防队员能够用手持装置来下载着火建筑物的设计图。这事关一名学生可以用数字教科书上课或者一位病人能够与她的医生进行面对面的视频聊天。

所有这些投资，在创新、教育、基础设施方面的投资将为美国带来更好的商业环境并且创造就业。但是为了帮助我们的公司竞争，我们还必须打破那些阻碍他们成功的障碍物。

多年以来，众多的游说人士利用税法来为某些公司和行业谋利，那些在这一系统中就业的会计师或者律师最终什么税都不交，而所有其他人则要承受世界上最高的公司税率。这毫无道理，这需要改变。

所以，今晚我请求民主党和共和党人简化税率，根除漏洞，实现公平竞争。用这些节省下来的钱来降低公司税率，这将是二十五年来的第一次，而且是在不增加我们赤字的情况下。

为了帮助商业界向海外出售更多的产品，我们确定了在 2014 年将出口额翻一倍的目标，因为我们出口的越多，在国内创造的就业岗位就会越多。我们的出口额已经开始上升。我们最近与印度和中国签署了协议，这些协议将为美国二十五万多个就业岗位提供支持。我们上个月与韩国完成了贸易协议的最后文本，它将支持至少七万个美国就业岗位。这一协议获得来自行业和劳工组织、民主党人和共和党人前所未有的支持。我请求国会尽早通过这一协议。

在我就职之前，我明确表示我们将执行我们的贸易协议。我将只会签署那些对美国工人有信心、增加美国就业岗位的协议。我们与韩国签署协议时就是这样做的，我想在与巴拿马和哥伦比亚寻求签署类似协议时也会这样做，在继续与我们的亚太和全球贸易会谈时持同样立场。

为了降低增长和投资的障碍，我已下令对政府规则进行重新评估。当我们发现那些给行业带来不必要负担的规则时，我们将会修改这些规则。我将毫不迟疑地设立或者强制执行常识性的保护性规则，以保护美国人民。我们在过去一个多世纪一直是这样做的。这就是为什么我们的食物、水、空气是安全的。这就是我们为什么去年对信用卡公司隐藏资费和惩罚规定采取消费者保护措施，为了避免新的金融危机采取新规则的原因。这就是我们为什么最终通过改革法案以防止医保行业剥削病人的原因。

现在，我听说了有关你们中的一些人对新的医保法律有一些担心的传闻。所以让我来首先说，所有的事情都有改善的可能。如果你有使医疗护理更加高质量或者更便宜的想法，我很愿意与你合作。我们现在可以着手开始解决法案中给小企业带来不必要记账负担的缺陷，但我不愿意去做的事情是重返保险公司以先决条件为由来否决一些人获得医疗保险的时代。我不愿意告诉来自得州的脑癌患者詹姆斯·霍华德，医保公司可能不会支付他的治疗费用。我不愿意告诉俄勒冈州的小企业主吉姆·豪斯，他还得多支付 5000 美元来使他的雇员获得医保。就在我们讲话时，这一法案正使给老年人所开的处方药更为便宜，使没有医疗保险的学生有继续享受他们父母医保的机会。所以，与其重开过去两年在这方面的斗争，不如让我们纠正需要纠正的地方向前走。

现在，赢得未来的最后一步，也是最关键的一步，是确保我们不会葬身于如山的债务之中。

几乎从十年前开始，赤字财政就一直与我们形影相随。在金融危机爆发后，这在一定程度上对于保持银行流动性、保护就业以及增加人民收入来说是必要的。但现在经济衰退的最糟时刻已经结束，我们必须直面政府财政入不敷出的现实。这是不可持续的。每天美国的家庭在节衣缩食以保证营收平衡，他们的政府也应如此。所以，今晚我建议从今年开始冻结未来五年部分年度国内项目支出。这将使美国财政赤字在未来十年减少 4000 多亿美元，进而使政府可自由支配的开支所占经济的比例降低到艾森豪威尔总统时期以来的最低水平。

冻结需要进行痛苦的削减。我们已经冻结了未来两年辛劳工作的联邦雇员的工资水平。我也建议削减我一直非常关注的一些项目的支出，比如社区行动项目。国防部长也已同意削减他与他的将军们认为对我们军事影响不大的数百亿美元的军费支出。我承认在座各位中有些人已提出了进一步削减开支的提案，我愿意删除任何的确可节省的开支。不过我们必须确保不加重最脆弱的民众的负担，而且我们还要确保所削减开支属真正超重部分。通过减少对改革和教育的投资来实现赤字削减，就相当于拆除发动机以实现超载飞机减重的目的。这样做或许可能让你一开始觉得飞得很高，但没过多久，你就会感受到冲击。

现在，我提出的大部分削减和节省提案只包括在年度国内支出中，而这种开支仅占我国预算的12%多一点。为了取得进一步进展，我们必须停止仅削减此类开支就已足够的臆测，这还不够。去年我组建的两党联立财政委员会已经明确了这一点。我并不认同他们的全部提案，但他们的确取得了重大进步。他们的结论是解决我国赤字问题的唯一办法是削减我们能够发现的所有过度消费，包括国内项目开支、国防开支、医疗开支等。

这就意味着进一步降低卫生保健开支，包括像医疗保险和医疗补贴这样我国长期赤字最大单一来源项目。医疗保险改革将减缓这些开支的上升，这就是无党派经济学家认为废止卫生保健法会使我国赤字增加2500亿美元的部分原因。我很愿意看到其他降低开支的想法，包括去年共和党的一项提案：进行医疗事故改革，降低草率的医疗诉讼发生率。

为了构建坚实的基础，我们还应制定两党解决方案，强化后代社会保障。在这一点上，我们不应危及当前退休人员，最易受到伤害的人群，或残疾人，不应有损后代利益，不应使美国退休收入保障受制于充满不确定性的股市。

如果我们真的关心我们的赤字，我们就不能允许永久延长有关2%最富裕美国人的减税法案。在削减学校资金或学生的奖学金之前，我们应该让那些百万富翁们放弃他们的减税优惠。这不是惩罚他们所取得的成功。而是要促进美国的成功。

实际上，在税收方面，我们能为所有美国人做得最好的事莫过于简化个人税码。这将会是一项艰巨的工作，不过两党成员已经表示有意从事这项工作，而且我也准备加入他们。

所以，现在是时候采取行动了。现在是时候两党及国会两院在原则上做出让步，共同从事这项工作了。如果我们现在做出这一艰难决定，从而严加控制我们的赤字，那么我们便能够进行赢得未来所需的投资。更进一步地说，我们的政府不能负担得更多。我们应该给人民一个更强有力、更高效的政府。过去的政府无法赢得未来。我们生活和工作在信息时代，但上一次政府大规模重组却还是在黑白电视机的时代。涉及出口的有十二个机构。涉及住房政策的则至少有五个实体。我常举的一个例子是大马哈鱼在淡水中时由内政部负责，而在咸水中时则由商业部负责。而我听说一旦被熏烤之后情况就更复杂。

现在，我们已经在过去的两年里，在利用技术以及消灭浪费方面实现了突飞猛进。退伍军人现在点一下鼠标，就能下载他们的电子病历。我们正在出售几英亩数年都未曾使用的联邦办公地点，而且我们将去除繁文缛节以便摆脱更多负担。不过，我们需要考虑更多。未来的几个月里，我的政府将会提出一项建议，以最有助于实现打造更具竞争力美国的目标的方法，合并、巩固并整顿联邦政府。我将会把这一建议提交给国会进行投票，我们将会推动这一建议的通过。

未来一年里，我们将继续努力重建人民对政府机构的信任。因为你们应当确切知道你们所缴的税花在哪里，花了多少，你们也将能够在第一时间登录网站获得这些信息。因为你们应当知道自己选出的官员何时会见游说团体，我已要求国会按照白宫已经在做的将这些信息公布上网。而且因为美国人民应当知道，特殊利益不能穿插在小项目的立法中，国会中的两党议员应该知道这一点：如果呈现在我案头的法案中存在“特殊专款”（注：一般是指国会议员各自根据其选区或者集团需要插入预算报告中的“相关项目专款”），我将会予以否决。

一个具备公开和竞争力的二十一世纪政府，一个量入为出的政府。一个由新技术与理念驱动的经济体系。要在这个不断变化的新世界中取得成功，我们需改革、责任和创新。这还需要我们在外交事务中通过新方法接触世界。

正如就业和商贸现在可以跨越国界一样，新威胁和新挑战也是如此。隔在东西方之间的不是一堵墙，与我们为敌的也不是某个超级大国。所以，我们必须战胜敌人，无论他们在哪里，并建立跨越地区、种族和宗教界线的联盟。美国的道德榜样必需始终照耀着渴望自由、正义和尊严的所有人。因此我们已经开始了这项工作，所以今晚我们能够说美国领导阶层已经复兴，美国的地位已经恢复。

看看伊拉克，我们有近十万勇敢的男女士兵已经昂首挺胸撤离伊拉克，美国的战斗任务也已经结束。在那里，暴力现象已经开始下降，新政府已经组建。今年，我们的民众将与伊拉克人民建立持久伙伴关系，与此同时，我们从伊拉克撤军的工作也将结束。美国遵守了承诺，伊拉克战争即将结束。

当然，诚如我们所言，基地组织及其附属组织仍在计划攻击我们。感谢我们的情报和执法人员，我们正在挫败他们阴谋，保护我们的城市和天空。对于极端分子激发我们国内暴力行动的企图，我们正以社区力量、对法规的尊重，以及对美国穆斯林是我们美国大家庭一份子的坚定信仰作出回应。

我们也同基地组织及其海外盟友展开了战斗。在阿富汗，我们的军队已经占据了塔利班的根据地，并且训练了阿富汗安全部队。我们的目标很明显：通过阻止塔利班再次压榨阿富汗人民，我们将会阻止基地组织获得充当“9·11”起点的避风港。经过英勇的军队及平民的奋战，只剩下少数阿富汗人仍处于塔利班这一叛乱组织的控制之下。摆在前面的将会是激烈的战斗，而且阿富汗政府需要进行更好的管制。不过，我们正在增强阿富汗人民的力量，并与他们构建持久的伙伴关系。今年，我们将会同近五十个国家一起，开始向由阿富汗主导的状态过渡。今年 7 月，我们将开始撤军。

在巴基斯坦，基地组织领导阶层承受着比 2001 年以来任何时候都要大的压力。他们的首领和骨干正在被清除出战场，他们的避风港正在收缩。而且，我们已经从阿富汗边界向阿拉伯半岛以及全球各地的恐怖分子发出警告：我们不会留情，我们不会动摇，我们将击败你们。

美国领导人也在努力确保最厉害战争武器的安全。因为共和党和民主党通过了新《削减战略武器条约》，可部署的武器和发射器会更少。因为我们要重振世界，要在各大洲限制核材料，以免落入恐怖分子手中。

因为美国也在通过外交努力坚持要求伊朗履行其义务，所以伊朗政府现在面临着比以往更加严厉的制裁。在朝鲜半岛上，我们与盟国韩国站在一起，坚持朝鲜践行其放弃核武器的诺言。

这仅是我们重塑世界、维护世界和平和繁荣所作出努力的一部分。我们与欧洲同盟一道，在努力恢复北约的活力，增加从反恐到导弹防御等各方面的合作。我们已经重新设定了与俄罗斯的关系，强化亚洲同盟，并与印度等国家建立了新的伙伴关系。今年三月，我将访问巴西、智利和萨尔瓦多，打造美洲新的进步同盟。在全球，我们与那些负责任的国家一道，帮助农民生产更多的粮食，支持医治伤患的医生，并与败坏社会风气和掠夺人民财富的腐败行为作斗争。

最近的事件告诉我们，使我们与众不同的不仅是我们的力量，也必然还有其后的目的。在我们的帮助下，南苏丹人民在经历了多年的战争后，最终能够投票选择自己的独立。他们在黎明前排起了数千人的长队，人民在大街上欢舞。一名在战争中失去了四名兄弟的男子在描述他身边的景象时这样说道，“这曾是我生命大多时间中的战场，现在我们希望自由”。

我们在突尼斯看到了同样的要求自由的愿望，在那里，事实证明人民的意志比独裁者的敕令更有力量。今晚，我们要明确宣示：美利坚合众国人民与突尼斯人民站在一起，并支持全体人民的民主愿望。

我们绝对不能忘记我们为之努力、为之奋斗、所有人都铭记心中的事情。我们必须永远记住，在这场斗争中负担最为沉重的美国人正是那些报效我们祖国的男男女女。今晚，让我们共同重申，我们的国家会团结一致地支持我们的军队及其家人。让我们为他们服务，就像他们为我们服务那样，给予他们需要的装备，为他们提供应得的保健和福利，并在建设祖国的伟大任务中，为退伍军人提供支持。

我们的军人来自这个国家的每一个角落。他们是黑人、白人、拉丁裔、亚裔和印第安人。他们是基督教教徒、印度教教徒、犹太教教徒和穆斯林。的确，我们知道其中有一些人是同性恋。从今年开始，美国人都不会因为他们的爱人而被禁止报效其所爱的国家。接下来，我呼吁所有大学校园向我们的军方征兵人员和后备军官训练队敞开大门。现在，是时候和过去的分裂斗争说再见了。我们应该作为一个民族向前迈进。

我们不应该对摆在我们面前的工作心存任何幻想。改革学校、改变能源使用方式、减少赤字，这一切都并非易事，这需要时间。我们会围绕一切事情展开争论，这会使难度变得更高，成本、细节、每一个法律条文。当然，有些国家不存在这个问题，如果中央政府说要建一条铁路，他们就会建成一条铁路，无论这需要拆除多少个家庭的房屋；如果他们不希望一件坏事见报，就没人会去写报道。可是，尽管我们的民主有时可能引起争议、令人沮丧乃至像一团乱麻，但我知道在场的各位没有一个人会愿意与地球上任何其他国家的人交换位置。

我们在政策上可能有分歧，但对于我们的宪法所赋予的权利我们都深信不疑；我们可能有不同的见解，但我们都坚持一个共同的信念：在这个国家里，只要你努力尝试，你就有可能成功；我们可能来自不同的背景，但我们抱有同一个梦想：在这个国家里，任何想法都可能成为现实，无论你是谁，也无论你来自何方。

正是这个梦想使我今晚能够站在这里、站在你们面前。正是这个梦想使一名来自斯克兰顿的劳工子弟能够端坐在我身后。正是这个梦想使一个最初曾在他父亲于辛辛那提开设的酒吧里扫地的人后来能够在这个地球上最伟大的国家里当上众议院议长。

这个梦想——美国梦驱使着艾伦兄弟为了一个新时代而彻底改造了他们的屋顶工程公司。这个梦想驱使着那些在佛塞斯技术社区学院求学的学生们学习新技术，为了未来努力奋斗。这个梦想也驱使一个名为布兰登·费舍尔的小企业主有了自己的故事。

布兰登在宾夕法尼亚州的柏林市开设了一家公司，专攻新型钻探技术。去年夏季的一天，他看到新闻，智利矿井中有三十三人被困，无人知道如何营救。但布兰登认为他的公司可以帮忙，他设计了一套营救方案称为 B 计划。他的员工二十四小时工作，生产所需的钻探设备。然后布兰登前往智利。他同其他人一起钻了一个 2000 英尺的洞，连续不眠不休工作了三四天。三十七天后 B 计划成功，矿工获救。但布兰登不想引起注意，矿工升井后，他并没有在那里，他已经回家开始致力于下一个项目了。后来，他的一名雇员在谈到这次救援行动时说：“森特·罗克是一家小公司，但我们做的却是大事情。”

我们做的是大事情。

自建国之初起，美国一直在讲述敢于追求远大理想的普通人的故事。未来我们也将因此而成功。

我们是一个会这样说话的民族："我或许没有巨款，但是我有成立一家新公司的高见。我或许没有出生在一个拥有大学学历的家庭，但我将会成为这个家庭里第一个获得大学学历的人。我或许并不认识那些处于困境中的人们，但我认为我能够帮助他们，而且我需要试一试。虽然我不确定我们将如何超越地平线到达更好的地方，但我知道我们将会到达那里。我知道我们能够做到。"

我们做的是大事情。

美国的理念经久不衰。我们的命运依然取决于我们的选择。今晚，在两个多世纪之后，正因为有了我们的人民，我们的未来才充满希望，我们的征程才一路向前，我们的国家才强大繁盛。

谢谢大家。愿上帝保佑你们，愿上帝保佑美利坚合众国。

2012 国情咨文——2012 年 1 月 24 日美国众议院

Mr. Speaker, Mr. Vice President, members of Congress, distinguished guests, and fellow Americans:

Last month, I went to Andrews Air Force Base and welcomed home some of our last troops to serve in Iraq. Together, we offered a final, proud salute to the colors under which more than a million of our fellow citizens fought—and several thousand gave their lives.

We gather tonight knowing that this generation of heroes has made the United States safer and more respected around the world. For the first time in nine years, there are no Americans fighting in Iraq. For the first time in two decades, Osama bin Laden is not a threat to this country. Most of al Qaeda's top lieutenants have been defeated. The Taliban's momentum has been broken, and some troops in Afghanistan have begun to come home.

These achievements are a testament to the courage, selflessness and teamwork of America's Armed Forces. At a time when too many of our institutions have let us down, they exceed all expectations. They're not consumed with personal ambition. They don't obsess over their differences. They focus on the mission at hand. They work together.

Imagine what we could accomplish if we followed their example. Think about the America within our reach: A country that leads the world in educating its people. An America that attracts a new generation of high-tech manufacturing and high-paying jobs. A future where we're in control of our own energy, and our security and prosperity aren't so tied to unstable parts of the world. An economy built to last, where hard work pays off, and responsibility is rewarded.

We can do this. I know we can, because we've done it before. At the end of World War II, when another generation of heroes returned home from combat, they built the strongest economy and middle class the world has ever known. My grandfather, a veteran of Patton's Army, got the chance to go to college on the *GI Bill*. My grandmother, who worked on a bomber assembly line, was part of a workforce that turned out the best products on Earth. The two of them shared the optimism of a nation that had triumphed over a depression and fascism. They understood they were part of something larger; that they were contributing to a story of success that every American had a chance to share—the basic American promise that if you worked hard, you could do well enough to raise a family, own a home, send your kids to college, and put a little away for retirement.

The defining issue of our time is how to keep that promise alive. No challenge is more urgent. No debate is more important. We can either settle for a country where a shrinking number of people do really well while a growing number of Americans barely get by, or we can restore an economy where everyone gets a fair shot, and everyone does their fair share, and everyone plays by the same set of rules. What's at stake aren't Democratic values or Republican values, but American values. And we have to reclaim them.

Let's remember how we got here. Long before the recession, jobs and manufacturing began leaving our shores. Technology made businesses more efficient, but also made some jobs obsolete. Folks at the top saw their incomes rise like never before, but most hardworking Americans struggled with costs that were growing, paychecks that weren't, and personal debt that kept piling up.

In 2008, the house of cards collapsed. We learned that mortgages had been sold to people who couldn't afford or understand them. Banks had made huge bets and bonuses with other people's money. Regulators had looked the other way, or didn't have the authority to stop the bad behavior. It was wrong. It was irresponsible. And it plunged our economy into a crisis that put millions out of work, saddled us with more debt, and left innocent, hardworking Americans holding the bag. In the six months before I took office, we lost nearly 4 million jobs. And we lost another 4 million before our policies were in full effect.

Those are the facts. But so are these: In the last 22 months, businesses have created more than 3 million jobs. Last year, they created the most jobs since 2005. American manufacturers are hiring again, creating jobs for the first time since the late 1990s. Together, we've agreed to cut the deficit by more than $2 trillion. And we've put in place new rules to hold Wall Street accountable, so a crisis like this never happens again.

The state of our Union is getting stronger. And we've come too far to turn back now. As long as I'm President, I will work with anyone in this chamber to build on this momentum. But I intend to fight obstruction with action, and I will oppose any effort to return to the very same policies that brought on this economic crisis in the first place. No, we will not go back to an economy weakened by outsourcing, bad debt, and phony financial profits.

Tonight, I want to speak about how we move forward, and lay out a blueprint for an economy that's built to last—an economy built on American manufacturing, American energy, skills for American workers, and a renewal of American values.

Now, this blueprint begins with American manufacturing.

On the day I took office, our auto industry was on the verge of collapse. Some even said we should let it die. With a million jobs at stake, I refused to let that happen. In exchange for help, we demanded responsibility. We got workers and automakers to settle their differences. We got the industry to retool and restructure. Today, General Motors is back on top as the world's number-one automaker. Chrysler has grown faster in the U.S. than any major car company. Ford is investing billions in U.S. plants and factories. And together, the entire industry added nearly 160,000 jobs. We bet on American workers. We bet on American ingenuity. And tonight, the American auto industry is back.

What's happening in Detroit can happen in other industries. It can happen in Cleveland and Pittsburgh and Raleigh. We can't bring every job back that's left our shore. But right now, it's getting more expensive to do business in places like China. Meanwhile, America is more productive. A few weeks ago, the CEO of Master Lock told me that it now makes business sense for him to bring jobs back home. Today, for the first time in 15 years, Master Lock's unionized plant in Milwaukee is running at full capacity.

So we have a huge opportunity, at this moment, to bring manufacturing back. But we have to seize it. Tonight, my message to business leaders is simple: Ask yourselves what you can do to bring jobs back to your country, and your country will do everything we can to help you succeed.

We should start with our tax code. Right now, companies get tax breaks for moving jobs and profits overseas. Meanwhile, companies that choose to stay in America get hit with one of the highest tax rates in the world. It makes no sense, and everyone knows it. So let's change it.

First, if you're a business that wants to outsource jobs, you shouldn't get a tax deduction for doing it. That money should be used to cover moving expenses for companies like Master Lock that decide to bring jobs home. Second, no American company should be able to avoid paying its fair share of taxes by moving jobs and profits overseas. From now on, every multinational company should have to pay a basic minimum tax. And every penny should go towards lowering taxes for companies that choose to stay here and hire here in America. Third, if you're an American manufacturer, you should get a bigger tax cut. If you're a high-tech manufacturer, we should double the tax deduction you get for making your products here. And if you want to relocate in a community that was hit hard when a factory left town, you should get help financing a new plant, equipment, or training for new workers.

So my message is simple. It is time to stop rewarding businesses that ship jobs overseas, and start rewarding companies that create jobs right here in America. Send me these tax reforms, and I will sign them right away.

We're also making it easier for American businesses to sell products all over the world. Two years ago, I set a goal of doubling U.S. exports over five years. With the bipartisan trade agreements we signed into law, we're on track to meet that goal ahead of schedule. And soon, there will be millions of new customers for American goods in Panama, Colombia, and South Korea. Soon, there will be new cars on the streets of Seoul imported from Detroit, and Toledo, and Chicago.

I will go anywhere in the world to open new markets for American products. And I will not stand by when our competitors don't play by the rules. We've brought trade cases against China at nearly twice the rate as the last administration—and it's made a difference. Over a thousand Americans are working today because we stopped a surge in Chinese tires. But we need to do more. It's not right when another country lets our movies, music, and software be pirated. It's not fair when foreign manufacturers have a leg up on ours only because they're heavily subsidized.

Tonight, I'm announcing the creation of a Trade Enforcement Unit that will be charged with investigating unfair trading practices in countries like China. There will be more inspections to prevent counterfeit or unsafe goods from crossing our borders. And this Congress should make sure that no foreign company has an advantage over American manufacturing when it comes to accessing financing or new markets like Russia. Our workers are the most productive on Earth, and if the playing field is level, I promise you—America will always win.

I also hear from many business leaders who want to hire in the United States but can't find workers with the right skills. Growing industries in science and technology have twice as many openings as we have workers who can do the job. Think about that—openings at a time when millions of Americans are looking for work. It's inexcusable. And we know how to fix it.

Jackie Bray is a single mom from North Carolina who was laid off from her job as a mechanic. Then Siemens opened a gas turbine factory in Charlotte, and formed a partnership with Central Piedmont Community College. The company helped the college design courses in laser and robotics training. It paid Jackie's tuition, then hired her to help operate their plant.

I want every American looking for work to have the same opportunity as Jackie did. Join me in a national commitment to train 2 million Americans with skills that will lead directly to a job. My administration has already lined up more companies that want to help. Model partnerships between businesses like Siemens and community colleges in places like Charlotte, and Orlando, and Louisville are up and running. Now you need to give more community colleges the resources they need to become community career centers—places that teach people skills that businesses are looking for right now, from data management to high-tech manufacturing.

And I want to cut through the maze of confusing training programs, so that from now on, people like Jackie have one program, one website, and one place to go for all the information and help that they need. It is time to turn our unemployment system into a reemployment system that puts people to work. These reforms will help people get jobs that are open today.

But to prepare for the jobs of tomorrow, our commitment to skills and education has to start earlier. For less than 1 percent of what our nation spends on education each year, we've convinced nearly every state in the country to raise their standards for teaching and learning—the first time that's happened in a generation. But challenges remain. And we know how to solve them.

At a time when other countries are doubling down on education, tight budgets have forced states to lay off thousands of teachers. We know a good teacher can increase the lifetime income of a classroom by over $250,000. A great teacher can offer an escape from poverty to the child who dreams beyond his circumstance. Every person in this chamber can point to a teacher who changed the trajectory of their lives. Most teachers work tirelessly, with modest pay, sometimes digging into their own pocket for school supplies—just to make a difference.

Teachers matter. So instead of bashing them, or defending the status quo, let's offer schools a deal. Give them the resources to keep good teachers on the job, and reward the best ones. And in return, grant schools flexibility: to teach with creativity and passion; to stop teaching to the test; and to replace teachers who just aren't helping kids learn. That's a bargain worth making.

We also know that when students don't walk away from their education, more of them walk the stage to get their diploma. When students are not allowed to drop out, they do better. So tonight, I am proposing that every state—every state—requires that all students stay in high school until they graduate or turn 18.

When kids do graduate, the most daunting challenge can be the cost of college. At a time when Americans owe more in tuition debt than credit card debt, this Congress needs to stop the interest rates on student loans from doubling in July. Extend the tuition tax credit we started that saves millions of middle-class families thousands of dollars, and give more young people the chance to earn their way through college by doubling the number of work-study jobs in the next five years.

Of course, it's not enough for us to increase student aid. We can't just keep subsidizing skyrocketing tuition; we'll run out of money. States also need to do their part, by making higher education a higher priority in their budgets. And colleges and universities have to do their part by working to keep costs down.

Recently, I spoke with a group of college presidents who've done just that. Some schools redesign courses to help students finish more quickly. Some use better technology. The point is, it's possible. So let me put colleges and universities on notice: If you can't stop tuition from going up, the funding you get from taxpayers will go down. Higher education can't be a luxury—it is an economic imperative that every family in America should be able to afford.

Let's also remember that hundreds of thousands of talented, hardworking students in this country face another challenge: the fact that they aren't yet American citizens. Many were brought here as small children, are American through and through, yet they live every day with the threat of deportation. Others came more recently, to study business and science and engineering, but as soon as they get their degree, we send them home to invent new products and create new jobs somewhere else.

That doesn't make sense.

I believe as strongly as ever that we should take on illegal immigration. That's why my administration has put more boots on the border than ever before. That's why there are fewer illegal crossings than when I took office. The opponents of action are out of excuses. We should be working on comprehensive immigration reform right now.

But if election-year politics keeps Congress from acting on a comprehensive plan, let's at least agree to stop expelling responsible young people who want to staff our labs, start new businesses, defend this country. Send me a law that gives them the chance to earn their citizenship. I will sign it right away.

You see, an economy built to last is one where we encourage the talent and ingenuity of every person in this country. That means women should earn equal pay for equal work. It means we should support everyone who's willing to work, and every risk-taker and entrepreneur who aspires to become the next Steve Jobs.

After all, innovation is what America has always been about. Most new jobs are created in start-ups and small businesses. So let's pass an agenda that helps them succeed. Tear down regulations that prevent aspiring entrepreneurs from getting the financing to grow. Expand tax relief to small businesses that are raising wages and creating good jobs. Both parties agree on these ideas. So put them in a bill, and get it on my desk this year.

Innovation also demands basic research. Today, the discoveries taking place in our federally financed labs and universities could lead to new treatments that kill cancer cells but leave healthy ones untouched. New lightweight vests for cops and soldiers that can stop any bullet. Don't gut these investments in our budget. Don't let other countries win the race for the future. Support the same kind of research and innovation that led to the computer chip and the Internet; to new American jobs and new American industries.

And nowhere is the promise of innovation greater than in American-made energy. Over the last three years, we've opened millions of new acres for oil and gas exploration, and tonight, I'm directing my administration to open more than 75 percent of our potential offshore oil and gas resources. Right now—right now—American oil production is the highest that it's been in eight years. That's right—eight years. Not only that—last year, we relied less on foreign oil than in any of the past 16 years. But with only 2 percent of the world's oil reserves, oil isn't enough. This country needs an all-out, all-of-the-above strategy that develops every available source of American energy. A strategy that's cleaner, cheaper, and full of new jobs.

We have a supply of natural gas that can last America nearly 100 years. And my administration will take every possible action to safely develop this energy. Experts believe this will support more than 600,000 jobs by the end of the decade. And I'm requiring all companies that drill for gas on public lands to disclose the chemicals they use. Because America will develop this resource without putting the health and safety of our citizens at risk.

The development of natural gas will create jobs and power trucks and factories that are cleaner and cheaper, proving that we don't have to choose between our environment and our economy. And by the way, it was public research dollars, over the course of 30 years, that helped develop the technologies to extract all this natural gas out of shale rock—reminding us that government support is critical in helping businesses get new energy ideas off the ground.

Now, what's true for natural gas is just as true for clean energy. In three years, our partnership with the private sector has already positioned America to be the world's leading manufacturer of high-tech batteries. Because of federal investments, renewable energy use has nearly doubled, and thousands of Americans have jobs because of it.

When Bryan Ritterby was laid off from his job making furniture, he said he worried that at 55, no one would give him a second chance. But he found work at Energetx, a wind turbine manufacturer in Michigan. Before the recession, the factory only made luxury yachts. Today, it's hiring workers like Bryan, who said, "I'm proud to be working in the industry of the future."

Our experience with shale gas, our experience with natural gas, shows us that the payoffs on these public investments don't always come right away. Some technologies don't pan out; some companies fail. But I will not walk away from the promise of clean energy. I will not walk away from workers like Bryan. I will not cede the wind or solar or battery industry to China or Germany because we refuse to make the same commitment here.

We've subsidized oil companies for a century. That's long enough. It's time to end the taxpayer giveaways to an industry that rarely has been more profitable, and double-down on a clean energy industry that never has been more promising. Pass clean energy tax credits. Create these jobs.

We can also spur energy innovation with new incentives. The differences in this chamber may be too deep right now to pass a comprehensive plan to fight climate change. But there's no reason why Congress shouldn't at least set a clean energy standard that creates a market for innovation. So far, you haven't acted. Well, tonight, I will. I'm directing my administration to allow the development of clean energy on enough public land to power 3 million homes. And I'm proud to announce that the Department of Defense, working with us, the world's largest consumer of energy, will make one of the largest commitments to clean energy in history—with the Navy purchasing enough capacity to power a quarter of a million homes a year.

Of course, the easiest way to save money is to waste less energy. So here's a proposal: Help manufacturers eliminate energy waste in their factories and give businesses incentives to upgrade their buildings. Their energy bills will be $100 billion lower over the next decade, and America will have less pollution, more manufacturing, more jobs for construction workers who need them. Send me a bill that creates these jobs.

Building this new energy future should be just one part of a broader agenda to repair America's infrastructure. So much of America needs to be rebuilt. We've got crumbling roads and bridges; a power grid that wastes too much energy; an incomplete high-speed broadband network that prevents a small business owner in rural America from selling her products all over the world.

During the Great Depression, America built the Hoover Dam and the Golden Gate Bridge. After World War II, we connected our states with a system of highways. Democratic and Republican administrations invested in great projects that benefited everybody, from the workers who built them to the businesses that still use them today.

In the next few weeks, I will sign an executive order clearing away the red tape that slows down too many construction projects. But you need to fund these projects. Take the money we're no longer spending at war, use half of it to pay down our debt, and use the rest to do some nation-building right here at home.

There's never been a better time to build, especially since the construction industry was one of the hardest hit when the housing bubble burst. Of course, construction workers weren't the only ones who were hurt. So were millions of innocent Americans who've seen their home values decline. And while government can't fix the problem on its own, responsible homeowners shouldn't have to sit and wait for the housing market to hit bottom to get some relief.

And that's why I'm sending this Congress a plan that gives every responsible homeowner the chance to save about $3,000 a year on their mortgage, by refinancing at historically low rates. No more red tape. No more runaround from the banks. A small fee on the largest financial institutions will ensure that it won't add to the deficit and will give those banks that were rescued by taxpayers a chance to repay a deficit of trust.

Let's never forget: Millions of Americans who work hard and play by the rules every day deserve a government and a financial system that do the same. It's time to apply the same rules from top to bottom. No bailouts, no handouts, and no copouts. An America built to last insists on responsibility from everybody.

We've all paid the price for lenders who sold mortgages to people who couldn't afford them, and buyers who knew they couldn't afford them. That's why we need smart regulations to prevent irresponsible behavior. Rules to prevent financial fraud or toxic dumping or faulty medical devices—these don't destroy the free market. They make the free market work better.

There's no question that some regulations are outdated, unnecessary, or too costly. In fact, I've approved fewer regulations in the first three years of my presidency than my Republican predecessor did in his. I've ordered every federal agency to eliminate rules that don't make sense. We've already announced over 500 reforms, and just a fraction of them will save business and citizens more than $10 billion over the next five years.

We got rid of one rule from 40 years ago that could have forced some dairy farmers to spend $10,000 a year proving that they could contain a spill, because milk was somehow classified as an oil. With a rule like that, I guess it was worth crying over spilled milk. Now, I'm confident a farmer can contain a milk spill without a federal agency looking over his shoulder. Absolutely.

But I will not back down from making sure an oil company can contain the kind of oil spill we saw in the Gulf two years ago. I will not back down from protecting our kids from mercury poisoning, or making sure that our food is safe and our water is clean. I will not go back to the days when health insurance companies had unchecked power to cancel your policy, deny your coverage, or charge women differently than men.

And I will not go back to the days when Wall Street was allowed to play by its own set of rules. The new rules we passed restore what should be any financial system's core purpose: Getting funding to entrepreneurs with the best ideas, and getting loans to responsible families who want to buy a home, or start a business, or send their kids to college.

So if you are a big bank or financial institution, you're no longer allowed to make risky bets with your customers' deposits. You're required to write out a "living will" that details exactly how you'll pay the bills if you fail—because the rest of us are not bailing you out ever again. And if you're a mortgage lender or a payday lender or a credit card company, the days of signing people up for products they can't afford with confusing forms and deceptive practices—those days are over. Today, American consumers finally have a watchdog in Richard Cordray with one job: To look out for them.

We'll also establish a Financial Crimes Unit of highly trained investigators to crack down on large-scale fraud and protect people's investments. Some financial firms violate major anti-fraud laws because there's no real penalty for being a repeat offender. That's bad for consumers, and it's bad for the vast majority of bankers and financial service professionals who do the right thing. So pass legislation that makes the penalties for fraud count.

And tonight, I'm asking my Attorney General to create a special unit of federal prosecutors and leading state attorney general to expand our investigations into the abusive lending and packaging of risky mortgages that led to the housing crisis. This new unit will hold accountable those who broke the law, speed assistance to homeowners, and help turn the page on an era of recklessness that hurt so many Americans.

Now, a return to the American values of fair play and shared responsibility will help protect our people and our economy. But it should also guide us as we look to pay down our debt and invest in our future.

Right now, our most immediate priority is stopping a tax hike on 160 million working Americans while the recovery is still fragile. People cannot afford losing $40 out of each paycheck this year. There are plenty of ways to get this done. So let's agree right here, right now: No side issues. No drama. Pass the payroll tax cut without delay. Let's get it done.

When it comes to the deficit, we've already agreed to more than $2 trillion in cuts and savings. But we need to do more, and that means making choices. Right now, we're poised to spend nearly $1 trillion more on what was supposed to be a temporary tax break for the wealthiest 2 percent of Americans. Right now, because of loopholes and shelters in the tax code, a quarter of all millionaires pay lower tax rates than millions of middle-class households. Right now, Warren Buffett pays a lower tax rate than his secretary. Do we want to keep these tax cuts for the wealthiest Americans? Or do we want to keep our investments in everything else—like education and medical research; a strong military and care for our veterans? Because if we're serious about paying down our debt, we can't do both.

The American people know what the right choice is. So do I. As I told the Speaker this summer, I'm prepared to make more reforms that rein in the long-term costs of Medicare and Medicaid, and strengthen Social Security, so long as those programs remain a guarantee of security for seniors.

But in return, we need to change our tax code so that people like me, and an awful lot of members of Congress, pay our fair share of taxes. Tax reform should follow the Buffett Rule. If you make more than $1 million a year, you should not pay less than 30 percent in taxes. And my Republican friend Tom Coburn is right: Washington should stop subsidizing millionaires. In fact, if you're earning a million dollars a year, you shouldn't get special tax subsidies or deductions. On the other hand, if you make under $250,000 a year, like 98 percent of American families, your taxes shouldn't go up. You're the ones struggling with rising costs and stagnant wages. You're the ones who need relief. Now, you can call this class warfare all you want. But asking a billionaire to pay at least as much as his secretary in taxes? Most Americans would call that common sense.

We don't begrudge financial success in this country. We admire it. When Americans talk about folks like me paying my fair share of taxes, it's not because they envy the rich. It's because they understand that when I get a tax break I don't need and the country can't afford, it either adds to the deficit, or somebody else has to make up the difference—like a senior on a fixed income, or a student trying to get through school, or a family trying to make ends meet. That's not right. Americans know that's not right. They know that this generation's success is only possible because past generations felt a responsibility to each other, and to the future of their country, and they know our way of life will only endure if we feel that same sense of shared responsibility. That's how we'll reduce our deficit. That's an America built to last.

Now, I recognize that people watching tonight have differing views about taxes and debt, energy and health care. But no matter what party they belong to, I bet most Americans are thinking the same thing right about now: Nothing will get done in Washington this year, or next year, or maybe even the year after that, because Washington is broken. Can you blame them for feeling a little cynical?

The greatest blow to our confidence in our economy last year didn't come from events beyond our control. It came from a debate in Washington over whether the United States would pay its bills or not. Who benefited from that fiasco?

I've talked tonight about the deficit of trust between Main Street and Wall Street. But the divide between this city and the rest of the country is at least as bad—and it seems to get worse every year.

Some of this has to do with the corrosive influence of money in politics. So together, let's take some steps to fix that. Send me a bill that bans insider trading by members of Congress; I will sign it tomorrow. Let's limit any elected official from owning stocks in industries they impact. Let's make sure people who bundle campaign contributions for Congress can't lobby Congress, and vice versa—an idea that has bipartisan support, at least outside of Washington.

Some of what's broken has to do with the way Congress does its business these days. A simple majority is no longer enough to get anything—even routine business—passed through the Senate. Neither party has been blameless in these tactics. Now both parties should put an end to it. For starters, I ask the Senate to pass a simple rule that all judicial and public service nominations receive a simple up or down vote within 90 days.

The executive branch also needs to change. Too often, it's inefficient, outdated and remote. That's why I've asked this Congress to grant me the authority to consolidate the federal bureaucracy, so that our government is leaner, quicker, and more responsive to the needs of the American people.

Finally, none of this can happen unless we also lower the temperature in this town. We need to end the notion that the two parties must be locked in a perpetual campaign of mutual destruction; that politics is about clinging to rigid ideologies instead of building consensus around common-sense ideas.

I'm a Democrat. But I believe what Republican Abraham Lincoln believed: That government should do for people only what they cannot do better by themselves, and no more. That's why my education reform offers more competition, and more control for schools and states. That's why we're getting rid of regulations that don't work. That's why our health care law relies on a reformed private market, not a government program.

On the other hand, even my Republican friends who complain the most about government spending have supported federally financed roads, and clean energy projects, and federal offices for the folks back home.

The point is, we should all want a smarter, more effective government. And while we may not be able to bridge our biggest philosophical differences this year, we can make real progress. With or without this Congress, I will keep taking actions that help the economy grow. But I can do a whole lot more with your help. Because when we act together, there's nothing the United States of America can't achieve. That's the lesson we've learned from our actions abroad over the last few years.

Ending the Iraq war has allowed us to strike decisive blows against our enemies. From Pakistan to Yemen, the al Qaeda operatives who remain are scrambling, knowing that they can't escape the reach of the United States of America.

From this position of strength, we've begun to wind down the war in Afghanistan. Ten thousand of our troops have come home. Twenty-three thousand more will leave by the end of this summer. This transition to Afghan lead will continue, and we will build an enduring partnership with Afghanistan, so that it is never again a source of attacks against America.

As the tide of war recedes, a wave of change has washed across the Middle East and North Africa, from Tunis to Cairo; from Sana'a to Tripoli. A year ago, Qaddafi was one of the world's longest-serving dictators—a murderer with American blood on his hands. Today, he is gone. And in Syria, I have no doubt that the Assad regime will soon discover that the forces of change cannot be reversed, and that human dignity cannot be denied.

How this incredible transformation will end remains uncertain. But we have a huge stake in the outcome. And while it's ultimately up to the people of the region to decide their fate, we will advocate for those values that have served our own country so well. We will stand against violence and intimidation. We will stand for the rights and dignity of all human beings—men and women; Christians, Muslims and Jews. We will support policies that lead to strong and stable democracies and open markets, because tyranny is no match for liberty.

And we will safeguard America's own security against those who threaten our citizens, our friends, and our interests. Look at Iran. Through the power of our diplomacy, a world that was once divided about how to deal with Iran's nuclear program now stands as one. The regime is more isolated than ever before; its leaders are faced with crippling sanctions, and as long as they shirk their responsibilities, this pressure will not relent. Let there be no doubt: America is determined to prevent Iran from getting a nuclear weapon, and I will take no options off the table to achieve that goal. But a peaceful resolution of this issue is still possible, and far better, and if Iran changes course and meets its obligations, it can rejoin the community of nations.

The renewal of American leadership can be felt across the globe. Our oldest alliances in Europe and Asia are stronger than ever. Our ties to the Americas are deeper. Our ironclad commitment—and I mean ironclad—to Israel's security has meant the closest military cooperation between our two countries in history.

We've made it clear that America is a Pacific power, and a new beginning in Burma has lit a new hope. From the coalitions we've built to secure nuclear materials, to the missions we've led against hunger and disease; from the blows we've dealt to our enemies, to the enduring power of our moral example, America is back.

Anyone who tells you otherwise, anyone who tells you that America is in decline or that our influence has waned, doesn't know what they're talking about.

That's not the message we get from leaders around the world who are eager to work with us. That's not how people feel from Tokyo to Berlin, from Cape Town to Rio, where opinions of America are higher than they've been in years. Yes, the world is changing. No, we can't control every event. But America remains the one indispensable nation in world affairs and as long as I'm President, I intend to keep it that way.

That's why, working with our military leaders, I've proposed a new defense strategy that ensures we maintain the finest military in the world, while saving nearly half a trillion dollars in our budget. To stay one step ahead of our adversaries, I've already sent this Congress legislation that will secure our country from the growing dangers of cyber-threats.

Above all, our freedom endures because of the men and women in uniform who defend it. As they come home, we must serve them as well as they've served us. That includes giving them the care and the benefits they have earned—which is why we've increased annual VA spending every year I've been President. And it means enlisting our veterans in the work of rebuilding our nation.

With the bipartisan support of this Congress, we're providing new tax credits to companies that hire vets. Michelle and Jill Biden have worked with American businesses to secure a pledge of 135,000 jobs for veterans and their families. And tonight, I'm proposing a Veterans Jobs Corps that will help our communities hire veterans as cops and firefighters, so that America is as strong as those who defend her.

Which brings me back to where I began. Those of us who've been sent here to serve can learn a thing or two from the service of our troops. When you put on that uniform, it doesn't matter if you're black or white; Asian, Latino, Native American; conservative, liberal; rich, poor; gay, straight. When you're marching into battle, you look out for the person next to you, or the mission fails. When you're in the thick of the fight, you rise or fall as one unit, serving one nation, leaving no one behind.

One of my proudest possessions is the flag that the SEAL Team took with them on the mission to get bin Laden. On it are each of their names. Some may be

Democrats. Some may be Republicans. But that doesn't matter. Just like it didn't matter that day in the Situation Room, when I sat next to Bob Gates—a man who was George Bush's defense secretary and Hillary Clinton—a woman who ran against me for president.

All that mattered that day was the mission. No one thought about politics. No one thought about themselves. One of the young men involved in the raid later told me that he didn't deserve credit for the mission. It only succeeded, he said, because every single member of that unit did their job—the pilot who landed the helicopter that spun out of control; the translator who kept others from entering the compound; the troops who separated the women and children from the fight; the SEALs who charged up the stairs. More than that, the mission only succeeded because every member of that unit trusted each other—because you can't charge up those stairs, into darkness and danger, unless you know that there's somebody behind you, watching your back.

So it is with America. Each time I look at that flag, I'm reminded that our destiny is stitched together like those 50 stars and those 13 stripes. No one built this country on their own. This nation is great because we built it together. This nation is great because we worked as a team. This nation is great because we get each other's backs. And if we hold fast to that truth, in this moment of trial, there is no challenge too great; no mission too hard. As long as we are joined in common purpose, as long as we maintain our common resolve, our journey moves forward, and our future is hopeful, and the state of our Union will always be strong.

Thank you, God bless you, and God bless the United States of America.

众议院议长先生、副总统先生、各位国会议员、贵宾们和美国同胞们：

上个月，我前往安德鲁斯空军基地，欢迎在伊拉克服役的最后一批军人回国。我们一起最后骄傲地向国旗敬礼。一百多万美国同胞曾为之作战，其中数千人献出了自己的生命。

我们今晚聚集在此，深知这一代的英雄使美国更安全，在全世界更受尊敬。现在不再有美国人在伊拉克作战，这是九年来的第一次。乌萨马·拉登不再对美国构成威胁，这是二十年来的第一次。“基地”的大多数头目都已溃散，塔利班的气焰已经破灭。驻阿富汗的一些部队已经开始撤回国内。

这些成就见证了美国军队的英勇无畏、无私和团队精神。在我们的许多机构都令人失望之时，他们的作为超出了所有人的期望。他们不沉溺于个人的欲望，他们不计较相互间的分歧，他们全神贯注于肩负的使命，他们为此同心协力。

可以想象，如果我们以他们为榜样，我们能完成什么样的业绩。想一想我们可以为美国实现的目标：人民接受的教育领先全世界；吸引新一代高科技制造业和高薪工作；实现我们的未来，由我们自己掌握能源，我们的安全和繁荣不再依赖世界上某些不稳定地区；经济长盛不衰，辛勤工作总有回报，尽职尽责受到奖励。

我们可以做到这一点。我知道我们可以，因为我们曾这样做过。二战结束时，上一代英雄离开战场返回家园，建成全世界迄今为止最强大的经济体和中产阶级。我祖父，巴顿麾下的老兵，有机会借助《退伍军人法》上大学。我祖母，在一个轰炸机装配线上工作，作为劳动大军的一员生产全世界第一流产品。他们两个人都发扬了战胜大萧条和法西斯主义国家拥有的乐观向上的精神。他们了解自己是一个伟大事业的组成部分，他们为每一个美国人都有机会踏上的成功之路做出贡献——在美国可以实现最普遍的希望：你如果辛勤工作就足以养活家庭，拥有住房，送孩子上大学，还可以为退休存点钱。

我们这个时代的关键问题是如何让这样的希望生生不息。没有任何挑战比这更为迫切，没有任何争论比这更重要。我们可以满足于这样一个国家，其中越来越少的人富甲一方，而越来越多的美国人却勉强度日；或者我们可以重建我国经济，让人人都得到公平的机会，人人都尽自己的一份力量，人人都遵守同样的规则。利害攸关的问题不是民主党的价值观或共和党的价值观，而是美国的价值观。我们必须重新树立这些价值观。

让我们谨记我们是如何走到这一步的。在经济衰退爆发前，就业岗位和制造业早已开始离开我们的海岸。技术使各行各业更有效率，但一些工作岗位也因此陈旧过时。位于最高层的同胞们看到他们的收入前所未有地增长，但大多数勤奋工作的美国人开支上升，工资水平停滞，债务不断增加，为此生活十分艰难。

2008年，纸牌搭建的房子坍塌了。我们知道，抵押贷款批给了没有能力支付或对此一知半解的人。银行拿着别人的钱投下巨大的赌注，得到了丰厚的报酬。监管人员视若无睹，或没有权力阻止不良行为。这是不对的，这是不负责任的。这使我们的经济陷入危机，数百万人失业，我们背上了更多的债务，让无辜、勤劳的美国人代人受过。在我上任前的六个月中，我们失去了近四百万个就业岗位。在我们的政策全面落实之前，我们又失去四百万个就业岗位。

这些都是事实，但是以下这些也是事实。在过去二十二个月内，各行各业创造了三百多万个就业岗位。去年，这些行业创造了2005年以来的大多数就业岗位。美国制造商重新开始雇人，自二十世纪九十年代末期以来首次创造了工作机会。我们共同努力，已同意将赤字至少降低两万亿美元，并且制定了让华尔街承担责任的新规则，防止类似的危机再度发生。

我们合众国的国情日益强盛。我们已取得长足的进展，绝不能走回头路。只要我还担任总统之职，就将与在座的每一位一起再接再厉。但是，我将采取行动打破障碍，并将反对恢复原有政策的任何要求，因为当初正是这些政策引发了这场经济危机。不，我们不能重蹈覆辙，听任外包、坏账和虚假的金融利润削弱我国经济。

今晚，我希望谈一谈今后如何取得进展，并为建设长盛不衰的经济制定蓝图——以美国制造业、美国能源、美国劳工的技能以及继续发扬美国价值观为出发点的经济。

这份蓝图以美国制造业为开端。

在我就职之日，我国的汽车产业正濒临崩溃。有些人甚至说我们应该任其消亡。但这事关上百万个就业岗位，我拒绝让这种情况发生。作为提供帮助的交换条件，我们要求他们负起责任。我们让工人和汽车制造商解决他们的分歧。我们让汽车产业更新设备，重新改组。今天，通用汽车重新坐上世界头号汽车制造商的宝座。克莱斯勒在美国的增长速度比其他任何大型汽车公司都快。福特正在美国的车间和厂房挹注数十亿美元的资金。整个汽车产业总计增加了将近十六万个就业岗位。我们坚信美国的劳动者，我们坚信美国的创新能力。今晚，美国汽车产业已经东山再起。

在底特律发生的事情也可以在其他行业发生。它可以在克里夫兰、匹兹堡和罗利发生。我们不可能把所有流失到海外的工作都找回来，但是现在，在诸如中国等地从事经营的成本越来越高。与此同时，美国的生产效率也越来越高。几周前，玛斯特锁公司的首席执行长告诉我，在他看来把就业岗位带回美国现在是明智的经营之道。今天，玛斯特锁公司坐落在密尔沃基实行工会制的工厂已全面投产，这是十五年来的第一次。

因此，我们面前有一个把制造业迁回来的大好机会，可是我们必须抓住机会。今晚，我对企业领导人要说的话很简单：问一问你们自己怎样才能把工作机会带回美国，你们的国家就会尽一切努力助你们成功。

我们应该从我国的税法入手。目前，公司把工作和利润移到海外会获得税收优惠。与此同时，选择留在美国的公司却要承受在全球最高之列的税率。这样做没有道理，人人都知道这一点。因此我们必须着手改革。

首先，如果你是想要外包的企业，你就不应当因此获得减税。这笔钱应当用来贴补像玛斯特锁等决定把工作迁回美国的公司的搬迁费用。其次，任何美国公司都不能通过把工作和利润移到海外而逃避公平纳税。从现在起，每个跨国公司都应当支付基本的最低税金。每一分钱都应当用来为选择留在美国并雇用美国人力的公司减税。第三，如果你是美国制造商，你就应当获得幅度更大的减税。如果你是高科技制造商，我们应当为你在美国本地制造产品而加倍减税。如果你想迁入一个因为工厂迁出而受到重创的社区，你在为新工厂、设备或者新员工培训融资时应当得到帮助。

我要说的很简单。现在应当停止奖励将工作迁到海外的企业，而应当开始奖励在美国国内创造就业岗位的企业。把这些税法改革方案交给我，我会立刻签署。

我们还使美国工商企业更容易在全世界各地销售产品。两年前，我提出美国出口在五年内翻一番的目标。随着两党一致的各项贸易协定经我们签署成为法律，我们正朝着这个目标稳步迈进并可超前实现。不久以后，美国产品将在巴拿马、哥伦比亚和韩国获得数以百万计的新顾客。不久以后，来自底特律、托利多和芝加哥的新进口汽车将在首尔街头出现。

我将前往全世界任何地方为美国产品打开新市场。当我们的竞争对手不按规则行事的时候，我不会坐视不顾。我们对中国提起贸易诉讼的案例数量是上一届政府的近两倍，而且已经看到成效。由于我们制止了中国轮胎的倾销，一千多名美国人在今天得以有工作。可是我们需要再接再厉。当另一个国家听任我们的影片、音乐和软件被盗版，这是不对的。当外国制造商只因受到大量补贴而取得高于我们的优势，这是不公平的。

今晚，我宣布创建一个“贸易执法单位”，负责调查中国等国的不公平贸易作法。我们将加强检验，防止假冒或者不安全的商品跨越边境进入我国。本届国会应做到勿使外国公司在取得融资或者进入俄罗斯等新市场方面取得高于美国制造商的优势。我们的工人是全世界生产效率最高的，如果有一个公平的竞争环境，我敢保证美国将永远立于不败之地。

我也听到许多企业领导人说，他们想要在美国雇用人手，但却找不到拥有他们所需技能的人员。不断发展的科学和技术产业需要招聘的人员数量是能够胜任这类工作的人员的两倍。思考一下这个现象，这些在数百万美国人找工作的时候依然空缺的岗位。没有任何借口可言，而我们也知道如何补救。

杰基·布雷是北卡罗莱纳的一位单身母亲，当过机械师，但被裁员。当时西门子公司在夏洛特开办了一家天然气汽轮机厂，并与中部皮埃蒙特社区学院结成了伙伴关系。西门子公司帮助该学院设计激光和机器人技术培训方面的课程。公司为杰基付了培训费用，然后雇用她来工厂工作。

我要让每一位正在找工作的美国人都得到杰基那样的机会。请与我一道努力在全国各地培训两百万美国人，让他们掌握能够直接解决就业的技能。我的政府已经汇集起更多的乐意帮忙的企业。像西门子这样的企业与夏洛特、奥兰多和路易斯维尔等地的社区学院之间的样板伙伴关系正在建立并发挥效力。现在必须把资源给予更多的社区学院，让它们成为社区职业培训中心，教会人们目前企业所急需的从数据管理到高科技生产等各项技能。

我要精简令人眼花缭乱的种种培训项目，从现在起，让杰基这样的民众可以只上一个培训项目、一个网站、一个地方就能获得他们所需的一切信息和帮助。现在是把我们的失业救助系统变成让人们重新走上工作岗位的再就业系统的时候了。这些改革将帮助人们获得目前依然空缺的就业岗位。

但是，要为未来谋职做好准备，我们加强技能培训和提高教育质量的努力就必须开始得更早。我们仅用了我国年度教育经费的不到百分之一，就说服了国内几乎每一个州提高其教学和学习标准，这是几十年来的第一次。我们仍然面临诸多难题，但我们知道应当如何解决这些难题。

在一个其他国家正在加倍投资于教育的时候，拮据的预算已迫使各州解雇数以千计的教师。我们知道，一名好教师能够使一个班的学生一生增加 25 万美元的收入，一名好教师能够让一个梦想冲出困境的孩子获得摆脱贫困的机会。在这个大厅中的每一个人都能说出一位改变了他们的生活轨迹的教师。大多数教师诲人不倦，他们收入不高，有时还得自己掏钱购买教学用品，只是为了尽自己的一份力。

教师的作用重大。因此，不要责怪他们或者为现状辩护，而是让我们给学校提一个协议，为学校提供保留好教师所需要的资源，奖励优秀教师。作为交换，让学校享有灵活性，创造性地、富于激情地进行教学，不再实行应试教育，并且取代对孩子的学习没有帮助的教师。这是一个值得做的交换。

我们还知道，如果学生不中途退学，更多人会走上领取毕业证书的讲台。如果不允许学生辍学，他们会取得更好的成绩。因此，今晚我提议，每一个州——每一个州——要求学生留在高中就读，直到毕业或十八岁。

在孩子们毕业时，最严峻的挑战可能是大学费用。此时此刻，美国人的学费债务超过了信用卡债务，国会必须阻止学生贷款利息在 7 月份成倍上涨。把我们开始的为数百万中产家庭节省成千上万美元学费的减税优惠延长下去，并通过在未来五年加倍提供半工半读机会，让更多的年轻人有机会自己挣钱念完大学。

当然，仅仅增加学生援助是不够的。我们无法一再补贴不断猛涨的学费，我们会耗光资金。各州也需要尽一份力，把高等教育作为其预算的一项重要内容。各高等院校必须尽量努力降低费用。

最近，我与一批已经这样做的大学校长进行了交谈。一些学校重新设计课程，帮助学生更快完成学业。有些采用了更好的技术手段。这就是说，这是可以办到的。所以，让我告知高等院校：如果你们不能停止学费上涨，那么你们从纳税人那里得到的资金就将减少。高等教育不能是奢侈品，它是经济之必需，美国每一个家庭都应能支付得起。

我们还要记住，在这个国家几十万才华横溢、勤奋好学的学生面临着另一个挑战：他们尚不是美国公民。他们许多人是小时候被带到这里，是地地道道的美国人，然而却每天面临被遣返的威胁。还有一些人最近才来这里攻读商学、科学和工程学，但他们一拿到学位，我们便送他们回国，到其他地方去发明新产品，创造新就业机会。

这毫无道理可言。

我极其坚定地相信，我们应着手解决非法移民问题。正因为如此，我的政府已经向边界派遣了人数比以往任何时候都多的边防人员。也正因为如此，现在非法越境事件比我上任时减少。反对这项行动的人再也找不到借口，我们现在应当立即努力制定全面的移民改革方案。

但是，如果选举年的政局使国会不情愿就一项全面方案采取行动，那么让我们至少同意停止遣返那些有责任感的年轻人，他们希望去我们的实验室、创业和捍卫这个国家。向我提交一项法案，让他们有机会通过奋斗取得公民身份，我将立刻签署。

要知道，长盛不衰的经济要求我们激发这个国家每个人的聪明才智和创造力。这意味着对妇女应当实行同工同酬。这意味着应当支持每一个愿意工作的人，每一个敢于承担风险的人，每一个有志成为下一个史蒂夫•乔布斯的实业家。

毕竟，创新是美国的根本。大多数新的就业岗位是由初创企业和小型企业创造的。因此让我们通过一项有助于他们成功的议程。打破妨碍有抱负的企业家进行发展融资的条条框框，将减税优惠扩大到那些增加工资和创造良好就业岗位的小型企业。两党都同意这些设想。因此，请把它们变成法案，今年放在我的办公桌上。

创新还要求从事基础研究。今天，在我们联邦政府资助的实验室和大学获得的各种发现有可能带来新的治疗方法，杀死癌细胞而不损坏健康细胞。新型的警察和士兵使用的轻便防弹背心可以挡住任何子弹。请不要在预算中除掉这些投资，请不要让其他国家在未来的竞赛中占上风。请支持研究与创新，正是它们带来了电脑芯片和因特网、带来了美国的新就业岗位和新兴行业。

谈到创新的前途，没有任何一个领域能比美国能源产业更有希望。近三年来，我们进行了数百万英亩的石油和天然气勘探。今晚，我指示我的政府开发我国 75% 以上的潜在近海石油和天然气资源。目前——目前——美国的石油产量达到八年来最高水平。是的，八年。不仅如此，去年，我们对外国石油的依赖比以往十六年中的任何一年都少。但是，鉴于我们仅有世界 2% 的石油储备量，石油是不够的。这个国家需要有一个全方位的综合战略，开发美国能源的各项潜能，这项战略意味着更清洁、更便宜并充满新的就业岗位。

我们拥有将近满足美国一百年需要的天然气资源，本届政府将采取一切可能的措施安全地开发这种能源。专家认为，这将在十年内带来六十多万个就业岗位。我要求在公有土地上钻探天然气的所有公司将他们使用的化学物质成分公诸于众。这是因为美国在开发这种资源时不会把我国公民的健康与安全置于危险境地。

开发天然气将创造就业岗位，为货车和工厂提供更清洁和更便宜的能源，从而证明我们不必在环境与经济两者之间只取其一。顺便提一下，是过去三十年间政府拨出的研究资金帮助开发了从页岩中提炼天然气的技术。这一点提醒我们：政府的支持对帮助企业把新能源设想转化为现实至关重要。

天然气的道理同样适用于清洁能源。三年来，我们与民间行业建立的伙伴关系已经使美国在世界高科技电池生产中处于领先位置。由于联邦政府的投资，可再生能源的使用几乎翻了一番，并给成千上万美国人带来就业机会。

布赖恩・里特比从家具制造业下岗时，曾担心已经五十五岁的他不再会有另一次机会。但他在密歇根州一家叫做“活力”的风力涡轮机制造厂找到了工作。在经济衰退前，这家工厂只建造豪华游艇。今天，它在招聘像布赖恩这样的工人。布赖恩说：“我为在这个未来行业工作感到自豪。”

我们在页岩气，我们在天然气方面的经验告诉我们，这些公共投资不一定带来立竿见影的回报。某些技术未取得成果，有些企业倒闭，但我不会背弃对清洁能源作出的承诺。我不会背弃像布赖恩这样的工人。我不会因为我们拒绝在这里作出同样的承诺而把风力或太阳能或电池工业让给中国或德国。

我们对石油公司的补贴已经长达一个世纪，时间足矣。现在应该是停止向这个利润鲜逊于任何人的产业提供纳税人馈赠，转向为前途从未如此光明的清洁能源加倍投资的时候了。请批准清洁能源减税优惠，请创造这些就业机会。

我们也能够通过新的鼓励项目来刺激能源创新。目前国会的分歧或许太深，难以为解决气候变化问题通过一项全面的方案。然而那是没有理由的，国会至少应制定一项清洁能源标准，为发明革新开辟市场。迄今你们尚未采取行动，今晚我将采取行动。我将指示本届政府批准在公共土地上开发足以供三百万家庭用电需要的清洁能源。我很自豪地宣布，国防部与我们一道为这个世界最大的能源消费国，作出有史以来对清洁能源最大的承诺之一——海军将购买足以每年为二十五万家庭提供电力的供电量。

当然，节省资金的最简便方式是节约能源。因此，我在此提议：帮助厂家杜绝工厂的能源浪费，为公司提供改造建筑的奖励计划。这样一来，未来十年的能源费用将会减少 1000 亿美元，使美国的污染降低，制造业扩大，给建筑业带来工人所需的更多就业岗位。请提交给我一项创造这类就业岗位的法案。

开创新能源的前景，应该只是修整美国基础设施的更宏大计划中的一项内容。美国有许多领域需要重建。我们的道路和桥梁失修，供电网浪费能源过多，高速宽带网络不健全，致使美国乡村地区的小企业难以将产品行销全球。

在大萧条时期，美国修建了胡佛水坝和金门大桥。二次大战后，我们修建了连接各州的高速公路。民主党和共和党政府均为大型项目作出投资，造福了所有人——从当年的建设者到今天仍在使用它们的公司企业。

在今后几周内，我将签署一项行政令，以排除使许多建筑项目停滞不前的官僚障碍。但是，你们需要为这些项目出资。利用我们不再为战争开支的经费，以其中二分之一支付我们的债务，用另一半来进行我们的国内建设。

现在是从事基建的最佳时机，特别是由于建筑业是在房地产泡沫破裂时遭受最大重创的行业之一。当然，受到冲击的不仅是建筑工人。数百万无辜的美国人也受到冲击，他们的房屋价值下跌。虽然政府无法单独解决这一问题，但不应让负责任的房主等到房地产市场跌入谷底才可获得救助。

因此，我将向本届国会提交一项方案，为每位负责任的房主提供机会，通过有史以来最低的利息进行重新贷款，使他们可在房贷上每年节省 3,000 美元。不再有官僚挡道，不再有银行拖延。对规模最大的金融机构收取一小笔费用，可确保不导致赤字递增，并使那些被纳税人救助的银行有机会偿还它们的信用赤字。

让我们永远不要忘记：每天都勤奋工作、遵纪守法的千百万美国人理当拥有一个以同样方式行事的政府和金融体系。现在应该从上到下实行同一个规则：不再允许纾困、施舍和逃避责任。美国的长盛不衰要求每一个人都承担责任。

由于贷款人向无力偿还抵押贷款的申请人贷款，由于购买方明知负担不起仍勉为其难，我们所有的人已经为此付出了代价。正是因为这个原因，我们需要采取有效的监管制止不负责任的行为。防止金融欺诈的规定，禁止倾倒有毒物品或生产劣质医疗设备的条例——这些都不会损害自由市场，反而会促使自由市场更好地运作。

毫无疑问，有些规章已经过时，并非必须而且代价过高。事实上，我在总统任期内的头三年批准的规章比我的共和党籍前任在同期内所颁行的规章要少。我已指令每个联邦机构取消不合理的规章。我们已经宣布实行五百多项改革，仅其中的一小部分便能在今后五年为企业和公民节省 100 多亿美元。

我们取消了四十多年前制定的一项规定，这项规定导致一些奶牛场可能每年要花 1 万美元来证明他们能够控制泄漏——因为牛奶不知何故被归为油类。有了这样的规定，我想即使洒了牛奶也值得大哭一场。而我确信一名牧民有能力处理牛奶泄漏，不需要一个联邦机构插手。这是毫无疑问的。

但我不会放松对石油公司防止漏油的要求，确保不再发生我们两年前在墨西哥湾看到的漏油事故。我不会放松为保护我们的孩子们免受汞中毒危害提出的要求，不会放松我们为保证食品安全和清洁用水提出的要求。我不会回到过去允许医疗保险公司任意取消保单，拒绝承保，对女性收取与男性不同保费的日子。

我也不会回到允许华尔街自行其是的日子。我们已经批准的新规则重新确立了任何一个金融体制都应遵循的核心宗旨：向提出最佳创意的创业者提供资金，向希望买房子、开公司或送子女上大学的负责任的家庭提供贷款。

因此，如果你是一家大银行或金融机构，你就不能再用客户的存款从事冒险的交易。你必须开出一份详细说明你一旦倒闭将如何偿清款项的“预嘱”——因为我们其他的人不愿再为你们纾困。如果你是一家抵押贷款机构或薪金预支行或信用卡公司，利用难懂的表格和欺诈手段导致人们签购他们负担不起的金融产品——这样的日子已经一去不复返。今天，美国消费者终于有了由理查德·科德雷负责的监管机构，承担保护他们的专门职能。

我们还将建立一个金融犯罪调查组，由训练有素的调查人员组成，打击大规模欺诈活动并保护民众的投资。某些金融公司违反重要的反欺诈法规，因为屡屡违犯者并没有受到实质性惩治。这损害了消费者，也损害了绝大多数遵纪守法的银行及金融服务业专业人员。因此，通过惩治欺诈的立法意义重大。

今晚，我要求司法部长成立由联邦检察官和具有主导地位的各州司法部长组成的特别工作组，对导致房产危机的违章借贷与包装风险房贷展开更大规模调查。这个工作组将追究违法责任，加快为房主提供帮助，加速结束这个伤害到如此之多美国人的无节制时期。

再次倡导公平合理和共同责任的美国价值观将有利于保护我们的人民和我们的经济，而它也应对我们努力摆脱债务负担和对未来投资具有指导作用。

眼下，我们最直接的当务之急是，在经济复苏仍然脆弱的情况下，避免给一亿六千万美国工薪阶层加税。人们今年无法承受从每次工资中减少 40 美元。可以有许多途径达到上述目标。为此，让我们在此地此时一致同意：不要附加议题，不要造势，毫无耽搁地批准削减工资税。让我们完成这项工作。

在赤字问题上，我们已就削减和节省 2 万亿以上美元开支达成协议。但我们还需进一步努力，而这意味着作出选择。目前，我们要额外花费将近 1 万亿美元来支持一项本应是临时性的为美国 2% 最富有的人减税的项目。如今，由于税法的缺陷和保护规定，四分之一的百万富翁享有比数百万中产阶层家庭要低的税率。今天，沃伦·巴菲特的税率比他的秘书的税率还低。我们希望保留这些给美国富人的减税措施吗？还是说我们希望把投资用于其他方面，如教育和医学研究，加强军力和照料退伍军人？因为如果我们真想摆脱债务，就不可能两者兼得。

美国人民知道什么是正确的选择。我也知道。正如去年夏天我对众议院议长所说，我有准备作出进一步改革，控制医疗照顾和医疗补助开销，巩固社会安全福利，只要这些项目继续能为老年人提供保障。

但与此相应，我们需要修改税法，让像我这样以及像国会中许多人一样的人，缴纳我们应该承担的税收。税务改革应该遵循巴菲特规则，即如果你年收入超过 1 亿美元，你的税率就不应低于 30%。我的共和党朋友汤姆·科伯恩说的对：华盛顿应该停止补贴百万富翁。实际上，如果你的年收入超过 1 亿美元，你就不应享有纳税补贴和减免。而另一方面，如果你的收入不到 25 万美元一年，98% 的家庭都是这样，那么你们的税率就不应增加。你们面对着价格上涨而工资不动的艰难，你们是需要得到减税的人。谁要称这是阶级对抗，请自便。但要求百万富翁至少同他的秘书一样纳税应该被称作什么？大多数美国人会称这是常理。

在这个国家，我们并不妒忌财务上的成功，我们对此表示赞赏。当人们谈论像我这样的人付出我应付的那一部分税金时，那不是因为他们妒忌我的富有，那是因为他们理解，我如果获得一个我并不需要同时国家又无力负担的税务减免时，只会增加赤字或让旁人去承担这个差额，例如一个靠固定收入维生的老年人，或一个正奋力完成学业的学生，或一个勉力维持日常开销的家庭。那是不对的，美国人也都知道，那是不对的。他们知道，正因为以前的几代人认识到他们彼此肩负的责任，对国家未来肩负的责任，这一代人才有可能获得成功；他们知道，只有当我们也具有共同的责任感，我们的生活方式才有可能持续下去。这就是我们今后降低赤字的途径。这样美国才能长盛不衰。

我承认今晚正在收看我的讲话的人们对税务和债务、能源和医疗保健等事项有不同的看法，但是不论他们属于哪一个党派，我可以断定此时此刻大多数美国人都在思考同一件事：今年，明年甚至后年，华盛顿将一事无成，因为华盛顿四分五裂。他们感觉有点悲观你能责怪他们吗？

去年对我们经济的信心最大的打击不是来自我们不能控制的事件，而是来自华盛顿关于美国能否弥补开支的讨论。谁能从这样的不利局面中得利？

我今晚谈到民众和华尔街之间的信任危机。但这个城市和这个国家其余地方之间的分歧至少同样严重——而且似乎年复一年逐渐恶化。

有些问题与金钱政治的腐蚀性有关。为此让我们一起采取一些步骤解决这个问题。请给我提交一项禁止国会议员进行内幕交易的法案，我明天就签署。让我们限制任何民选官员在他们可以产生影响的行业拥有股票。让我们确保为国会竞选集中筹款的人不得游说国会，反之亦然。这个想法至少在华盛顿之外得到两党的支持。

某些方面出现的失常现象与国会近来工作的方式有关。简单多数不再足以在参议院通过任何法案，甚至包括日常事务。对于这种种策略，任何一党都不能回避自己的责任。现在，两党都应该加以制止。首先，我要求参议院通过一个简单的规则，对所有司法和公共服务部门的提名必须在九十天内给予赞成或否定的简单表决。

行政部门也需要改变。这个部门往往效率不高、陈旧过时、脱离实际。这就是为什么我要求本届国会给予我整合联邦官僚体制的权力，使我们的政府更精简、反应更快、更能适应美国人民的需要。

最后，我们也需要降低这个城市积聚的高温，否则将一事无成。我们应该抛弃一些观念，例如两党必然会党同伐异，相互摧毁；政治意味着坚持僵化的意识形态，无法按照事理常情建立共识等。

我是民主党人，但是我相信共和党亚伯拉罕·林肯的信念：政府只应该为人民做他们自己无法做得更好的事情，仅此而已。正是因为这个原因，我的教育改革要求各学校和各州有更多的竞争、更多的自主。正是因为这个原因，我们正在取消不起作用的监管条例。正是因为这个原因，我们的医疗保健法律依靠改革后的民营市场，不再依靠政府项目。

另外一方面，我的某些共和党朋友，即使对政府支出最强烈地表示不满，也支持联邦拨款用于建造道路，实施清洁能源项目和为国内服务的联邦机构。

问题在于，我们都希望有一个更明智、更有效的政府。尽管我们可能无法在今年弥合我们之间观念上最大的分歧，我们仍然可以取得实际进展。无论本届国会是否参与，我都会采取行动促进经济增长。但如果得到你们的帮助，我可以做更多的事情。因为如果我们共同努力，美利坚合众国就没有达不到的目标。这是我们在过去几年的海外行动中取得的经验。

结束伊拉克战争让我们能够给我们的敌人以致命的打击。从巴基斯坦到也门，残余的“基地”组织成员仓皇失措，知道自己无法逃脱美利坚合众国的恢恢天网。

从这个实力地位出发，我们已经开始逐步紧缩在阿富汗的战事。我军有一万人已经回国，还有两万三千多人到今年夏天将会撤离。这个让阿富汗发挥主导作用的过渡将继续，我们将与阿富汗建立持久的伙伴关系，让它永远不可能再成为攻击美国的一个发源地。

随着战争浪潮的消退，一股变革的潮流席卷整个中东和北非，从突尼斯到开罗，从萨那到的黎波里。一年前，卡扎菲还是世界上当权时间最长的独裁者之一，是双手沾满了美国人鲜血的凶手。今天，他已不复存在。在叙利亚，我毫不怀疑阿萨德政权很快就会发现，变革的力量无法逆转，人类尊严不容抹杀。

这场令人震撼的变革结果如何仍无法确定。但我们与其最终结果利害攸关。本地区人民的命运归根结底由他们自己决定，但我们将倡导那些使我们自己的国家受益匪浅的价值观。我们将反对暴力和恐吓。我们将捍卫全人类的权利和尊严——男性和女性；基督徒、穆斯林和犹太人。我们将支持有助于建设强大稳定的民主和开放市场的政策，因为自由必将战胜暴政。

我们将维护美国自身的安全，防范那些威胁我国公民、我国盟友和我国利益的人。看看伊朗，我国外交的有力作用让一个曾对如何应对伊朗的核计划存在分歧的世界现在团结一致。该政权比以往任何时候都更加孤立，该国领导人面临着严厉制裁。只要他们还在逃避自己的责任，这样的施压就不会放松。毫无疑问：美国决心阻止伊朗获得核武器，为实现这一目标，我将不排除任何方案。但和平解决这个问题仍然是可能的，而且益处大得多。伊朗如果改弦易辙并履行其义务，就可以重新加入国际社会。

美国领导地位的重振在全球各地都有所体现。我们在欧洲和亚洲历史最悠久的同盟比以往任何时候都更强大。我们与美洲的关系更加深厚。我们对以色列的安全作出的牢不可破的承诺，我是说牢不可破，意味着我们两国在历史上最密切的军事合作。

我们已经很清楚地表明，美国是一个太平洋大国，缅甸的新开端点燃了新的希望。从我们建立的保障核材料安全的联盟，到我们领导的消除饥饿和疾病的使命；从我们对敌人的打击，到我们作为道义典范的持久力量——美国回来了。

如果有人另有别论，如果有人说美国正在衰落或我们的影响力已经减弱，都是不知所云。

这不是我们从渴望与我们合作的世界各国领导人那里得到的信息。这也不是从东京到柏林，从开普敦到里约等地人民的感觉，这些地方对美国的看法比数年来的任何时候都好。是的，世界正在改变；不错，我们不能控制每一事件，但美国仍然是世界事务中不可或缺的国家——只要我仍担任总统之职就将保持已成的盛业。

那就是为什么我与我们的军事将领一起提出新的国防战略，确保我们维持全世界最优异的军力，同时为我们的预算节省将近5000亿美元。为了抢占制敌的先机，我已经将此提案送交国会，以保障我国避免日益严重的网络威胁。

说到底，由于我国男女军人捍卫自由，我们才得以维系自由。随着他们班师回国，我们必须为他们服务，就像他们为我们服务一样。这包括给予他们应得的照顾和福利，那就是为什么自我担任总统以来，我们为退伍军人的年度开支年年增长。它意味着召唤我们的退役军人重建我们的国家。

由于获得本届国会两党一致的支持，我们正在为聘用退役军人的公司提供新的税务抵免。米歇尔和吉尔·拜登已与美国企业合作，承诺为退役军人及其家人提供十三万五千份工作。今晚，我提议组成一个退伍军人就业团，帮助我们的社区聘用退役军人担任警察和消防员，使美国及其保卫者同样强盛。

这就带回我一开始的主题。我们被派到此地服务的人可以从我们军队的服务学到几件事。当你穿上军服时，无论你是黑人或白人；亚裔、拉美裔、美国原住民；保守派、自由派；富人、穷人；还是同性恋、异性恋都不重要。当你走上战场，你会照顾身边的袍泽，否则任务将会失败。当你处在枪林弹雨之中，你们会全体共进退，效忠同一个国家，不会抛下任何一个人。

我保存的最令人自豪的物品之一，是海豹突击队在执行捉拿本·拉登使命时携带的一面旗帜，上面有每一位勇士的姓名。他们中有些可能是民主党人，有些可能是共和党人，但这并没有任何关系。就像那天在情况室一样，我坐在鲍勃·盖茨旁边，他是乔治·布什政府的国防部长；当时还有希拉里·克林顿，她曾是我竞选总统时的对手。

那一天最重要的是完成使命。谁也没有想到政治，谁也没有想到自己。参加突袭行动的一位年轻人后来对我说，他没有资格为这项使命获得嘉奖。他说，这次使命获得成功是因为参加行动的每一位成员都尽了自己的一份力量——将盘旋失控的直升机降落在地面上的驾驶员；阻止其他人进入大院的翻译；将妇女和儿童与作战区隔离的军人；冲上楼道的海豹突击队。不仅如此，这次使命获得成功也是因为参加行动的成员相互信任——因为除非你知道有人在你身后做掩护，否则你不可能冲上楼道，在黑夜中履险如夷。

这就是美国精神。每当看到这面旗帜，我都体会到我们的命运如同旗帜上紧密相连的五十颗星和十三道红白相间的条纹。建成这个国家并非个人之功。这个国家之所以伟大，是因为我们共襄盛举；这个国家之所以伟大，是因为我们同心协力；这个国家之所以伟大，是因为我们相互扶持。如果我们坚持这个真理，那么在这艰难的时刻，就没有我们不能战胜的挑战，就没有我们不能完成的使命。只要我们为了同一个目标休戚与共，只要我们坚持我们的共同意志，我们在征途上将一往无前，我们的未来会充满希望，我们的国家将永远强盛。

谢谢大家。愿上帝保佑你们，愿上帝保佑美利坚合众国。